LEADERSHIP IN CHILD AND FAMILY PRACTICE

This edited collection situates the wellbeing ⸺ e children as the focus of leadership. It provides a guide to theories and practice of leadership for those who want to make a difference to the lives of these children and their families.

Drawing on the experience of a highly successful postgraduate program in Child and Family Practice Leadership, the book explores the changing context of Child and Family Practice and the role of leadership, in addition to the knowledge and skills required for effective practice. Contributors draw upon their own practice experiences and insights into the most effective ways to support the work of practitioners to achieve the best outcomes for children and families. The content comprises a mixture of theoretical consideration, discussion of original research and interviews with child and family practitioners.

Bringing together contributions from leading specialists and professionals in the field, this book will be essential reading for individual practitioners, organisations and policymakers looking to assist the development of leadership within the child and family practice sector. It will also be of interest to those working in child protection and related workforces.

Margarita Frederico is Professor and Graduate Research Coordinator in Social Work and Social Policy at La Trobe University, Australia, and Principal Research Consultant Berry Street Take Two Program. She has taught and researched in social work, child protection, child and family welfare and leadership for many years. Her research is applied and translational, and her focus is on contributing to the development of knowledge to make a difference to the lives of vulnerable children and their families.

Maureen Long is a qualified social worker and family therapist who worked in the child and family practice sector as a practitioner and manager for more than 25 years in both the community and public sectors. For the past 11 years, she has taught in the Social Work program at La Trobe University, Australia, where she is a senior lecturer and discipline course coordinator.

Nadine Cameron has been involved in social work, social policy and sociological research and teaching for nearly 20 years. She also co-wrote the groundbreaking book *Social Work and the Body*.

'This is an excellent resource that pushes us to consider where current systems fail and how to cultivate leadership that will transform child and family services. It is an essential read for those committed to reshaping models of workforce development to improve child outcomes.'

– Todd I. Herrenkohl, PhD, Marion Elizabeth Blue Professor of Child and Family, University of Michigan School of Social Work, USA

'This is an excellent book covering some difficult issues of central importance to both social work and related disciplines. It tackles the question of how high professional practice standards can be achieved and maintained, how practice knowledge, organisational knowledge and research knowledge can be brought to practitioners and used by them. It is one of the few books to focus on this complex matter. It places professional and organisational leadership at the centre of this dynamic and shows how education needs to be integrated into the goals and content of practice. Note: it is very clearly written and engages the reader quickly.'

– Professor Emeritus Thea Brown, Department of Social Work, Monash University, Australia

LEADERSHIP IN CHILD AND FAMILY PRACTICE

Edited by Margarita Frederico, Maureen Long and Nadine Cameron

Routledge
Taylor & Francis Group

LONDON AND NEW YORK

First published 2018
by Routledge
2 Park Square, Milton Park, Abingdon, Oxon OX14 4RN

and by Routledge
711 Third Avenue, New York, NY 10017

Routledge is an imprint of the Taylor & Francis Group, an informa business

© 2018 selection and editorial matter, Margarita Frederico, Maureen Long and Nadine Cameron; individual chapters, the contributors

British Library Cataloguing in Publication Data
A catalogue record for this book is available from the British Library

Library of Congress Cataloging in Publication Data
A catalog record for this book has been requested

ISBN: 978-0-415-79382-7 (hbk)
ISBN: 978-0-415-79383-4 (pbk)
ISBN: 978-1-315-21086-5 (ebk)

Typeset in Bembo
by Taylor & Francis Books

Printed and bound in Great Britain by
TJ International Ltd, Padstow, Cornwall

To child and family practitioners who each day walk alongside vulnerable children and their families to assist them to be safe and achieve their potential; to the children and families confronting major difficulties in their lives; and to leaders in Child and Family Practice who strive to create caring, knowledge-informed organisations which promote best practice and facilitate positive differences for children and families.

CONTENTS

ILLUSTRATIONS

Figures

Tables

Boxes

CONTRIBUTORS

Adjunct Professor Muriel Bamblett, AM, is a Yorta Yorta and Dja Dja Wurrung woman who has made an outstanding contribution to Aboriginal welfare, particularly in the area of child and family services. Since 1999 she has been CEO of the Victorian Aboriginal Child Care Agency (VACCA). She is Adjunct Professor at La Trobe University. Muriel was chairperson of the Secretariat of National Aboriginal and Islander Child Care (SNAICC) for ten years. Muriel is active on many committees, including the Victorian Children's Council; the Aboriginal Treaty Working Group; the Indigenous Family Violence Partnership Forum and the Aboriginal Justice Forum. Muriel has received many awards honouring her leadership in Indigenous welfare and affairs, including: the Centenary of Federation Medal; the Robin Clark Memorial Award for Inspirational Leadership in the Field of Child and Family Welfare; and the Women's Electoral Lobby Inaugural Vida Goldstein Award; and was a finalist for a Human Rights Medal with the Australian Human Rights Commission. She is also a Member of the Order of Australia. In 2017 she was inducted into the Victorian Aboriginal Honour Roll and awarded an honorary degree of Doctor of Letters in Social Work by the University of Sydney.

Carlina Black has worked in the area of child welfare for over 15 years, specifically in the areas of research, evaluation and policy of therapeutic services for children who have experienced abuse and neglect, and in outcomes and evidence-informed research and Indigenous child welfare. Carlina currently works in an evaluation, policy and advocacy role with the Royal Commission into Institutional Responses to Child Sexual Abuse Support Service at the Victorian Aboriginal Child Care Agency (VACCA). She is also a PhD candidate at La Trobe University, researching the role of cultural connection in healing for Aboriginal children in out of home care, and was awarded the Berry Street Take Two Robin Clark postgraduate scholarship.

Dr Cindy Blackstock is a member of the Gitksan First Nation. Cindy is the Executive Director of the First Nations Child and Family Caring Society and a Professor at McGill University School of Social Work. Her work focuses on educating and engaging children, and the public at large, to ensure culturally based equity for First Nations children in Canada. She is best known for a landmark human rights case in 2016 finding the Canadian Government's provision of inequitable services to First Nations children to be racially discriminatory and contrary to Canadian law. She has written extensively on First Nations theory, child welfare and the inequity in First Nations children's services, and currently serves as a Commissioner for the Pan American Health Organization Commission on Health Equity and Inequity. Cindy is a fearless and effective human rights advocate and activist, and has received many awards and honours recognising this. Cindy completed her PhD at Toronto University and has been awarded ten honorary doctorates.

Dr Nadine Cameron is a researcher and teacher across various institutions in Australia. She has been involved in social work, social policy and sociological research and teaching for nearly 20 years. She co-wrote the groundbreaking book *Social Work and the Body* (Palgrave Macmillan, 2007).

Professor Margarita Frederico is Graduate Research Coordinator in Social Work and Social Policy at La Trobe University, and Principal Research Consultant of Australia's Berry Street Take Two program. She teaches and researches in child protection and child and family welfare and leadership. She was awarded life membership of the Australian Association of Social Workers and of Berry Street. She is also a Director of Jesuit Social Services and Odyssey House Victoria.

Professor Cathy Humphreys is Professor of Social Work at the University of Melbourne. She is an international expert in domestic violence and child welfare. Previous positions include the Alfred Felton Chair of Child and Family Welfare at the University of Melbourne.

Adjunct Associate Professor Annette L. Jackson is Regional Director Gippsland Berry Street, where she was formerly Director of the Take Two program, and an Adjunct Associate Professor at La Trobe University. Annette has extensive experience as a practitioner, supervisor, trainer and senior manager in child protection and child welfare services.

Dr Maureen Long is Discipline Head of Social Work and Social Policy and a senior lecturer at La Trobe University. She has many years' experience in direct practice in the area of child and family welfare.

Dr Lynne McPherson is a Senior Lecturer in the Department of Social Work at Southern Cross University, Australia. She was previously at La Trobe University, and prior to that held senior management positions within Child Protection,

Department of Human Services, Victoria. She is the joint author with Noel Macnamara of *Supervising Child Protection Practice: What Works? An Evidence Informed Approach* (2017).

Dr Robyn Miller is a social worker and family therapist with over 30 years' experience in the community sector, local government and child protection. Robyn has practised in the public and private sectors as a therapist, clinical supervisor, consultant and lecturer, and was a member of the Victorian Child Death Review Committee for ten years. Robyn is currently the CEO of MacKillop Family Services, one of the largest providers of specialist services to vulnerable and disadvantaged children, young people and their families in Victoria, New South Wales and Western Australia.

Connie Salamone has worked in the human services field for over 30 years, mostly in child and family services. Connie has served on the board of North Careforce, and was the Principal Child Protection Advisor to Protecting Children in the Pacific Project. Connie has held a range of senior positions within the Department of Human Services, and is currently Executive Director of Strategy and Services at the Victorian Aboriginal Child Care Agency. Connie has represented VACCA on many statewide committees and governance structures, and has contributed to a range of publications. In 2012 she was awarded the Robin Clark Memorial Award for Inspirational Leadership in the Field of Child and Family Welfare.

Dr Menka Tsantefski is a Senior Lecturer in the Department of Human Services at Griffith University, Queensland. She has expertise in working with substance-affected parents and their children, as well as in Child and Family Practice. She worked for several years in direct practice in the areas of substance abuse, children and families.

Bruce D. Perry, MD, PhD, is Senior Fellow of The ChildTrauma Academy, Houston, Texas, and Adjunct Professor in the Department of Psychiatry and Behavioral Sciences at the Feinberg School of Medicine at Northwestern University in Chicago. He is internationally renowned in relation to the neurobiology of child trauma. His books include: *The Boy Who Was Raised As a Dog* and *Born for Love: Why Empathy is Essential and Endangered* (both with Maia Szalavitz); *Brief, Reflections on Childhood, Trauma and Society*; and *A Child's Loss: Helping Children Exposed to Traumatic Death* (with Jana Rosenfelt).

Sarah Waters is the Senior Consultant, Clinical Practice Development with Berry Street Take Two. She is an accredited mental health social worker with experience in direct practice, supervision, project management and training.

FOREWORD

I lead one of the services that participated in and benefited from the training for Child and Family Practice leadership that is covered so effectively in the contents of this book. The Berry Street Take Two program has just completed its fourteenth year of operation. It is an intensive therapeutic service for children in the state child protection system. Shared international knowledge and understanding of the impact of child trauma has grown rapidly since the inception of our program, and we are increasingly able to apply sophisticated diagnostics and targeted evidence-informed treatments for children impacted by abuse or neglect. This technical knowledge and skill-building is vital to good service provision, but it is not sufficient.

There are many reasons to be very grateful for the addition of this book to the resource set of those of us who care for abused and neglected children who find themselves in state-supported systems of child protection and care. The most important premise of this book is the emphasis it provides on service organisation and leadership. Whatever role we may play within a system of child protection and care – be it the role of protector, case manager, carer, therapist or other contributing professional – the technical aspects of our work can only be effective if delivered within a context that is child-centred and has a congruence of purpose in provision of safety and support. At a client level this is usually reflected in the care teams that are assembled in service of child safety, care and healing. Ideally, many significant adults – including family members, carers, protective workers and other professionals – are organised together to collaborate in the care of a child. Ideally, we hope the adults who participate in care teams are well cared for themselves, so they can bring undivided interest and energy to their care team tasks. Ideally, the child who is the subject of the care team is able to participate in care design and care planning. At a practice level, we call a successful mix of expert knowledge and the voice of the child 'shared decision making'. As I read this text, the successful mix looks a lot like the 'live knowledge' applied to leadership development.

Care teams don't arise spontaneously, and neither do the service organisations that support all their contributing adults. If organisations are to deploy carers and workers who can be child-centred, child-allied and skilled in working with a child and with other caring adults to clear purposes, those workers need to be well equipped and supported in such deployment. I can attest to the practice described in this book in achieving this capacity-building because I still continually bear witness to effective collaboration between children, volunteers and workers in meetings at varied levels, from care team meetings to consultations about systems policy and funding.

This book is effective because its principles parallel the best features of collaborative practice. At a high level, this book is the product of a genuine collaboration across universities and government and non-government agencies. This high-level collaboration reflects the ways agencies and institutions in our industry, in which workers employed to a wide variety of purposes, from professional services and support services to applied research and continuing practice development and training, are required to work together day by day to create and maintain service systems. At a frontline level it parallels the best principles of good care and good care team collaboration. Evidence-based knowledge must be shared to ensure the purposes of intervention are well founded, and the varied ways such knowledge could be applied to any specific case must be respectfully negotiated. This is a responsibility of leadership.

Most importantly, this book doesn't resile from the frailties and vulnerabilities of all of us who seek to contribute to child protection and care. It is not easy to learn of the varieties and vulgarities of child maltreatment, or to sit with the pain experienced by those who have been impacted by abuse and neglect. Every worker knows you can hear too many disturbing stories, and you can meet discouragement in too many varied and unexpected ways. The children caught in these distressing circumstances need support, care and hopefulness, and those of us who care for them need this as well. Well-led organisations can't protect their volunteers and employees from the impacts of vicarious trauma; but they can equip them to live with the impacts and to benefit from a genuine pooling of reflections, skills and resourcefulness to help each other to persist with the work. This book documents how this can be achieved.

Much of the work described in this book arose from the La Trobe University Graduate Certificate and Graduate Diploma in Child and Family Practice Leadership. However all the knowledge and wisdom assembled has universal application. Even place-specific components of the course, such as our local imperative to address the disproportionate over-representation of Aboriginal children in the child protection and care system, carry universal implications. Locally, we have learnt that the safety and healing for Aboriginal children is most durably achieved if the historic impact of invasion, dispossession and family dissolution is recognised through a re-claiming and re-affirmation of connections to culture, country, community and family. Families and communities in other jurisdictions are also likely to benefit from the application of comparable principles to their local circumstances.

I heartily commend this book, as a good 'read-through' and as a leadership resource to be tapped across time. This is a book for the work-site bookshelf!

Ric Pawsey
Director, Take Two
Berry Street
Australia

PREFACE

The impetus for this publication comes from the editors' experiences of teaching leadership in two education programs provided to child and family practitioners in Victoria, Australia between 2009 and 2016. The concept for these courses came from the Victorian Government, Department of Health and Human Services, previously known as the Department of Human Services. These courses were part of a suite of responses to improve the quality of services in the child and family service sector, particularly Child Protection and Family Services, to increase retention of staff and to develop leaders. In addition to improved service outcomes, the initiatives sought to make the sector a first choice for employment. Ultimately, the stronger the leadership, the stronger the practice and, as such, the greater the likelihood of positive outcomes for children and families.

The Department of Health and Human Services tendered out the development and implementation of two education programs – namely, a Graduate Certificate in Child and Family Practice for first line practitioners, and a Graduate Diploma in Child and Family Practice Leadership. The successful team to develop and implement the programs was a consortium comprising: La Trobe University (social work) as the lead partner; the Bouverie Centre for families; the University of Melbourne (social work); a community service organisation, Berry Street Take Two; and an Aboriginal Community Controlled Organisation (ACCO), the Victorian Aboriginal Child Care Agency (VACCA). Dr Bruce Perry of the ChildTrauma Academy USA was a faculty member. The development of the courses is addressed more fully in Frederico, Long, McPherson, McNamara, & Cameron (2016).

Each consortium member was engaged in the development of the curriculum and took responsibility for the delivery of at least one subject. The courses were approved by La Trobe University's Academic Board, and successful students received their qualification from the university. The qualification also provided participants with pathways for study in other academic programs.

The intended participants in the Graduate Certificate were first line practitioners who were identified by their supervisors and managers as high performers. For the Graduate Diploma high-performing middle managers and supervisors were selected as participants. The participants were drawn from Child Protection and Family Services. The aim was not to offer the course as a remedial program, but rather to develop new knowledge about practice and to raise well-performing staff to a higher level of performance. Both courses were taught on a part-time basis so that participants could remain full time in their organisations.

The Graduate Certificate comprised four subjects taught over a year, while the Diploma had eight subjects taught over two years. The courses were taught in block mode (2 days × 2 days × 3 occurrences per subject, with one day less for the Certificate). The teaching model was enquiry-based learning which has a focus on contribution from participants as well as lecturers; and all assessment, whether on theory or skills, focused on relevant work issues for participants. The teaching approach is presented in Chapter 3 of this book. Although leadership was initially only to be formally part of the Graduate Diploma, it was quickly recognised by faculty and course participants that it was important to facilitate the 'doing' of leadership at all levels, and thus leadership content was introduced to the Graduate Certificate. As all participants began to recognise the value of their own leadership contributions, the role of leadership in establishing and maintaining good-quality practice was identified. Over time, the responsibility of all staff to exercise leadership became an active part of the curriculum for first line practitioners as well as managers.

The courses were evaluated, and all stakeholders (participants, supervisors, managers, funders and faculty) were very positive about the courses and the impact they had on practitioners and the organisations, and on improved quality of practice for clients and the role of leadership. Some participants used their qualification to help them gain promotion to leadership positions. Retention of staff improved in child protection. Indicative of evaluation feedback responses received, one CEO reported that following a participant's engagement in the Diploma, an already well-functioning leader improved the functioning of an already well-performing team and transformed a previously poorly functioning team into a strong team.

The motivation for this edited volume was experiencing the value of being engaged in the development and implementation of a course that made a difference to the performance of child and family practitioners and to their leadership. All the chapters' authors were engaged in the program, and the chapter topics are drawn from the content of the Graduate Diploma. An outcome of the courses has been to develop new knowledge and new understandings about Child and Family Practice and the role and application of leadership for the benefit of the vulnerable children and families in the sector.

The concept of this book comes from the experience of developing and delivering an effective education program for the sector. The development and delivery of this program was informed by the work of highly experienced practitioners, leaders and academics as they focused on theory and research as it can better inform leadership and practice with vulnerable and at-risk children and their families.

Margarita Frederico
Maureen Long
Nadine Cameron
Editors

Reference

Frederico, M., Long, M., McPherson, L., McNamara, P., & Cameron, N. (2016). A consortium approach for child and family practice education. *Social Work Education*, 35(7), 780–793. doi:10.1080/02615479.2016.1206520

ACKNOWLEDGEMENTS

The editors would like to acknowledge the following people who shared the journey which has led to this publication:

Faculty colleagues of the Graduate Certificate and Graduate Diploma in Child and Family Practice Leadership, which was the impetus for this publication; Robyn Elliott, Kerry O'Sullivan and Karen Smith (the Bouverie Family Centre); Professor Cathy Humphreys and Dr Menka Tsantefski (The University of Melbourne); Annette Jackson, Sarah Waters and Dr Jen McConachy (Berry Street Take Two); Dr Lynne McPherson and Dr Patricia McNamara (La Trobe University); Adjunct Professor Muriel Bamblett, Dr Peter Lewis and Connie Salamone (Victorian Aboriginal Child Care Agency, VACCA); Dr Bruce Perry (ChildTrauma Academy, CTA); and Dr Robyn Miller, Diana Claxton, Beth Parker and Paula Wilson (Department of Human Services, Victoria, Australia).

The graduates of La Trobe's Graduate Certificate and Graduate Diploma in Child and Family Practice Leadership, whose practice knowledge and commitment to working with vulnerable children and families to achieve best outcomes was inspirational and influenced the development of the curriculum and ongoing development of knowledge of Child and Family Practice.

Janelle Young (La Trobe University) for her invaluable editorial assistance on this book; and Georgia Priestley (Routledge) for her guidance, assistance and support.

1

THE EVER CHANGING CONTEXT OF CHILD AND FAMILY PRACTICE

Robyn Miller and Margarita Frederico

Introduction

Every society places the care and development of children as the highest priority. However children who come into state care, in most societies, do not do well across all areas of their development. Since the mid-2000s, work with children and families in child protection, family services and out-of-home care sectors has become increasingly complex. To improve responses to children and families in need and to achieve positive outcomes for children, many countries have engaged in significant reform legislatively, at a policy level, and within the practice culture. The reform of child and family services into a more co-ordinated and evidence-informed system is the landscape within which this chapter is situated. The aim of the chapter is to set the context for Child and Family Practice, and to highlight the importance of leadership in achieving good outcomes for children and their families. Leadership is required in all areas which impact on children and families. This includes leadership in politics, in shaping legislation in strong policies, in evidence-informed programs adequately funded, in research and in practice. As the following chapters in this book will highlight, practice leadership needs to be provided in a context where risk factors which lead to children coming into care – including poverty, conflict and racism – are addressed at all levels.

This chapter presents an overview of key themes in Child and Family Practice, utilising the Australian context as an example and drawing on international literature and comparisons. The need to have leadership supporting well-trained practitioners who think and engage systemically is an overarching theme in this chapter. It will explore the rationale for early intervention and a public health approach, and the current debate regarding evidence-based and evidence-informed practice.

A paradigm shift

Recent policy settings in the State of Victoria, Australia attempted to shift the practice culture towards a more consistent model of engagement with families, partnering with other services, intervening early in cases of abuse and neglect, and preventing harm to achieve meaningful change for the child. This is in contrast to late intervention and episodic assessment of families, monitoring of perceived risk through a procedural and task-focused approach, and programs which are fragmented and often rigid in operation. The paradigm shift, a key linking theme throughout this chapter, is towards a practice orientation to the child *and* the family. Good practice with vulnerable children and families requires an ecological consideration of the child's development and culture and the impact of trauma on their safety and stability.

While identification and assessment of child abuse and neglect are the initial tasks for child protection practitioners, the ongoing and more complex challenge for systems is how to respond effectively. Frontline practitioners across child and family services engaged with vulnerable children and families are faced with complexity and, not uncommonly, volatile situations where there may be overwhelming distress.

Contemporary context

The contemporary context is one of increased public and political scrutiny (Munro, 2011). In Australia the Royal Commission into Institutional Responses to Child Sexual Abuse has led to increased awareness of the rigor required to be a child-safe organisation. Underpinning these concepts and the reform agenda is the pervasive acknowledgement of the rights of children, families and Aboriginal communities. According to the Australian Institute of Health and Welfare (AIHW), since the mid-2000s the number of children and young people in care in Australia rose from 25,454 in 2006 to 46,448 in 2016 (AIHW, 2007, p. 50; AIHW, 2017, p. 62), an increase of 82 per cent; and in 2015–16, 36 per cent of these children were from Aboriginal and/or Torres Strait Islander backgrounds (AIHW, 2017). The situation in the USA and Canada is similar, with Native American and First Nation children over-represented in care (Trocmé, Knoke, & Blackstock, 2004; Child Welfare Information Gateway, 2016). An attempt to address this over-representation in Australia is the drive to properly resource Aboriginal Community Controlled Organisations (ACCOs) to provide community-based family services. Of critical importance has been support to facilitate the transfer of Aboriginal children and young people from mainstream services to the care of Aboriginal families and communities.

Many children removed from families and communities are staying longer in care, with poorer outcomes than their peers. Reforms are geared towards preventing children and young people entering care, acting more quickly to support family reunification or permanency where indicated, reducing residential care and placing greater emphasis on keeping siblings together (Miller, 2012).

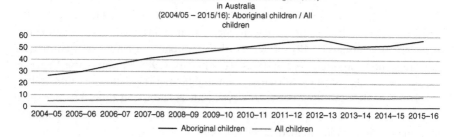

FIGURE 1.1 Number of children in out-of-home care in Australia, 2005/05–2015/16
Note: Aboriginal children = 56.6 per 1,000; all children = 8.6 per 1,000
Source: Halfpenny (2017); data sourced from Australian Institute of Health and Welfare reports 2006–2017

The current approach and need for change

Concurrently, most jurisdictions experience increased societal expectations for stringent scrutiny of systemic compliance to child protection performance measures such as demands to uphold the rights of children to safety and the rights of parents to privacy. There is pressure to identify, document and manage the risk of children being harmed. Consequently, practitioners undertaking this work have insufficient time away from their computers to effectively engage with the children and families.

It is also important to recognise the ongoing tensions between child rescue and child welfare paradigms regarding Child and Family Practice. An analysis of the literature suggests that the social construction of child maltreatment and the views regarding the most appropriate interventions have been influenced by notions of blame and anxiety. British historian Henry Hendrick (1994) argued that the categories of the 'child as a threat and the child as a victim' functioned as dualities in the policies of the late eighteenth century. Scott and Swain (2002) noted that in Australia the child welfare movement refocused and changed around the end of World War I. Later theories were influenced by psychodynamic psychotherapists who conceptualised child abuse primarily as a disorder of the parent–child attachment, with roots in the parent's early childhood experience. Scott and O'Neil (1996, p. 26) critiqued the dominance of this view, noting that from this perspective the problem was seen in terms of the intra-psychic 'wounds' from the parent's own childhood. Of note, by the 1970s, Gil (1970) and Gelles (1973), among others, articulated a strong critique of the parental psychopathology model, and developed a structural model which privileged the prevalence and significance of social circumstances – poverty, unemployment, racism, violence and marginalisation – impacting on children and families involved with statutory services.

Despite the focus on child rescue historically, family practice was always present. Family therapy was influential from the late 1960s (Goding, 1992); and, from an infant mental health perspective, Bowlby's work on attachment theory, and the need for infants to have a stable and secure caregiver, has been prominent since the

1950s. Bowlby was very child-focused, but absolutely clear that in order to have healthy children services must cherish their parents (Bowlby, 1951). Importantly, pioneer social workers in the past were focused on family interventions and family casework (Richmond, 1917). However, the importance of family-centred practice was frequently forgotten, and in 1988 Robin Clark (1988) critiqued the Victorian government policy settings of the day and highlighted the failure of child welfare "to conceptualize the links between services for children and those broader social policies necessary to provide social and economic conditions which enable families to bring up their children adequately" (p. 33).

Similarly, the child protection system in the United Kingdom attracted blame for being wasteful, inadequate and punitive. Spratt and Callan draw attention to the study by Cant and Downie (1994) a decade earlier, demonstrating the inherent waste of resources by systems over identifying large numbers of cases at point of referral as requiring child protection interventions, with a majority "quickly redesignated as not child protection following investigation" (Spratt & Callan, 2004, p. 202). The attempted shift from a child protection to a child welfare orientation in the United Kingdom became known as the 'refocusing debate' (Hearn, 1995).

In the Climbié Report, Lord Laming (2003) also noted, "[it] is not possible to separate the protection of children from the wider support to families" (p. 6). The United Kingdom Government's response to the Climbié Report in 'Every Child Matters' (Department of Health and Social Care, 2003) was to both strengthen child protection and increase the number of children coming to the attention of social workers for reasons of child welfare (Hayes & Spratt, 2009).

It is notable that the United Kingdom Child Protection Review by Professor Munro clarified that previous reforms had not achieved the intended outcomes of the refocusing debate:

> It may seem self-evident that children and young people are the focus of child protection services but many of the criticisms of current practice suggest otherwise. In a system that has become over bureaucratised and focused on meeting targets which reduce the capacity of social workers to spend time with children and young people and develop meaningful relationships with them, there is a risk that they will be deprived of the care and respect that they deserve.
>
> *(Munro, 2011, p. 22)*

Morley (2009) notes that professional legitimacy and competence are linked to scientific, 'objective' knowledge and the quest for certainty. Scarce resources can be devoted to high-risk cases. Low-risk (and unsubstantiated) cases can be referred to community agencies for family support. There are, however, many critics of the surveillance rather than the welfare perspective, who state that they do not achieve the very purpose for which they have been set up: to protect children from harm (Trotter, 2006).

This phenomenon was also observed by Australia's Victorian Child Death Review Committee (VCDRC, 2010, p. 47):

An important factor behind this lack of sufficient information being collected can be that there is not enough direct contact by Child Protection with families. Significantly, there is often even less contact with the child or children who are the subjects of the reported concerns. The committee has previously noted the relative marginalisation of children in the assessment process compared to parents when there is little direct contact with them or observation of them.

A significant aspect of this problem, in human services and also in other professions, is that human beings are reluctant to revise embedded beliefs, biases and assumptions which inform key decisions (Larrick, 2004). This directly impacts on families and children who are engaged with services. Munro (2002) noted that "[t]here is no simple antidote to this weakness. Child protection workers can be aware only of how they are likely to err and consciously try to counteract it" (p. 159). Leadership can provide additional support to workers to help them identify their biases and assumptions.

Impact of research

Inherent tensions exist between understanding the impact of harm on children, selecting the correct reports from intake for investigation, running operations of child protection and setting up systems of family services that protect vulnerable children within communities. The literature on trauma, and the evidence from neuroscience research, was 'news' that both stimulated and further supported change in the approach to Child and Family Practice. For example, Glaser (2000), Perry (2002), Perry (2006) and Shonkoff and Garner (2012) report on the neuro-physiological processes experienced by maltreated children and young people alongside behavioural, cognitive, emotional and relational impacts. What is clear is that the impact of traumatic events at different times in the life cycle has different consequences (Atkinson, 2002; Herman, 1992). Importantly, these researchers also outline evidence that a secure attachment with a primary carer may have a buffering effect and promote healing.

However, while we know more about the impact of harm on the developing child, it is important to acknowledge what we do not know so well – how to reliably predict the most serious cases. Predicting the likelihood of harm and identifying the risk factors associated with child abuse failed to establish clear causal relationships between the variables, or reliably determine what constitutes the inter-relationships between variables posing the highest risk. Parton, Thorpe and Wattam (1997) suggested that it is more appropriate to see child abuse as a result of "multiple interacting factors, including the parents' and children's psychological traits, the family's place in the larger social and economic structure, and the balance of external supports and stresses, both interpersonal and material" (p. 54).

Beginnings of a new approach

Australia, the USA and Canada, generally speaking, are reflecting a policy shift from a limited focus on risk assessment and child rescue to a more holistic understanding that the best interests of the child are served by attention to safety, stability, wellbeing and earlier intervention when a family needs help. A rights-based and developmental focus enables earlier family services intervention, greater collaboration at the local level and a more therapeutically informed care system.

However, these shifts to early intervention are not without critique. Featherstone, Morris, and White (2014) contend that early intervention involves telling parents what to do, not helping them: that it is about 'intervention', not practical 'support' (p. 1737). They believe that families are not supported or listened to, but rather have things delivered or done to them as part of a government program of 'behaviour change' (p. 1740).

This view is challenged by Axford and Berry (2017), who conclude that many evidence-based early intervention programs, including those designed to prevent or reduce maltreatment, are supportive and involve working alongside families. Indeed, failure to do this would render them ineffective.

The consequences of early trauma constitute a major public health problem. Children exposed to violence are more likely to suffer from traumatic stress, depression, anxiety, conduct disorders, learning problems, and substance abuse, and are more likely to engage in violence and criminal behaviour (Lieberman & Osofsky, 2009).

Heckman (2007) demonstrated that early intervention and family support also makes economic good sense. James Heckman, the Nobel Prize-winning economist, discussed a higher financial return from investment in children in the earliest years of their lives. That is, economies would save $17 for every dollar spent on early childhood services. Harvard University's Center on the Developing Child (2007) also found that the cost effectiveness of early intervention child and family investments have a cost benefit ratio range from 2:1 to 17:1 (depending on the program).

In addition, growing empirical evidence, such as by researchers Lieberman and Osofsky (2009), supports the argument that there is a social and economic cost of abuse and neglect resulting in high expenditure on health, social welfare, justice and prisons, and lower economic participation. This is confirmed by the Adverse Childhood Experiences Study (ACE), one of the largest investigations on links between childhood maltreatment and later life health and wellbeing. In this extraordinary study 17,000 participants had comprehensive physical examinations, providing detailed information on childhood abuse, neglect and family dysfunction. The study found compelling evidence that adults who had adverse experiences in childhood showed significantly higher levels of mental and physical health problems, and higher levels of violence and anti-social behaviour, along with academic and economic underperformance. This was graded significantly, with greater negative outcomes directly related to the greater number of adverse experiences (Anda et al., 2006).

Evidence-informed, evidence-based and reflective practice

Hong Chui and Wilson (2006) have commented that "within the literature there are two broad approaches to what contributes to best practice: evidence based and reflective practice" (p. 2). According to them, evidence-based practice is generally considered to have its roots in health care, and aims to use knowledge generated by scientific research to improve the likelihood of obtaining desired outcomes. Despite debate about definitions and applicability in a child protection context, evidence-based practice has significantly challenged authority-based practice, which is characterised by making decisions based on the individual worker's opinions rather than available knowledge (Gambrill, 2003). The latter can be dangerous in a statutory context given the complexity of issues facing practitioners and the potential for cognitive bias under pressure.

Critics of evidence-based practice, such as Webb (2001), argue that a political process that privileges science, positivist research and managerialism over alternative knowledge underpins the epistemology. Webb points out that the nature of social work (and one can add Child and Family Practice) does not easily fit the underlying concepts of evidence-based practice as it is not always possible to demonstrate the effectiveness of family, advocacy and community-based interventions. It is argued that both research-based knowledge and critical reflection (evidence-informed) need to collectively inform practice; and this is where leadership is required and can have a positive impact on practice by supporting workers to find the most effective approach.

Kessler, Gira and Poertner (2005) note that 'evidence-based practice' and 'evidence-informed practice' are often used interchangeably. Munro (2002) notes that empirical evidence also requires judgements about its reliability and its applicability in the worker's own context. Mildon et al. (2011) are inclusive in their definition of evidence-informed practice, as follows: "Evidence informed practice is the use of current best evidence combined with the knowledge and experience of practitioners and the views and experiences of service users in the current operating environment" (p. 175)

Unlike text books, research and policy development or computer systems, Child and Family Practice is much more unpredictable, iterative, dynamic and recursive. It is rarely a linear process with neat end-to-end phases. Good practice with families with complex needs requires skilled engagement that is strength based and forensically astute (Miller, 2008; Miller, 2012). This needs to be informed by a dynamic synthesis of knowledge from theory and research, and contextualised locally. This calls for ongoing critical reflection during practice, and about practice. The debate about evidence-based or evidence-informed practice is one of complementarity rather than dichotomy; a 'both/and' position rather than an 'either/or' position. Child and family practitioners need to not restrict themselves to considering only the research 'gold standard' programs as the only worthy interventions. It is also important to commit resources to growing evidence-based practice in culturally safe ways through rigorous longitudinal evaluation.

Historically, in the social services, practitioners and managers have reported that research is often driven by the researchers and does not meet their own local needs (Walter et al., 2004). Problems of definition and applicability abound. In fact, there is strong contention in regard to what constitutes 'evidence-based practice'. Very few treatment approaches can be strictly considered 'evidence-based'; however, more are considered 'promising'.

Given the seriousness of the issues, the prevalence of family problems and the vulnerability of abused and neglected children, the need for systemic commitment to wise and sustained reform implementation strategies is a critical challenge.

Disparate research, policy and practice communities

Research, policy and practice communities are often disconnected from one another. Practitioners can feel overwhelmed by sometimes contradictory research and emotionally confronting, high-volume issues that demand their attention. The stakes are high regarding their decision-making, and there may be life and death issues at hand that will be closely scrutinised if they make a mistake. They can be too tired to read, and lack the training to integrate how the research evidence should inform or change their practice. Despite this, research is highly valued by child and family welfare professionals. In a survey of 495 child and family welfare professionals in Australia, the majority reported that research was important for informing their work (Holzer et al., 2008). The perceived disconnect between research (evidence) and practice can be changed through education. This was one of the lessons from the Graduate Certificate and Graduate Diploma in Child and Family Practice Leadership formulated by La Trobe University in Australia. As elaborated in the Preface and in Chapter 3 of this book, approaching learning and knowledge development through a model called 'live knowledge', which emphasises a partnership between researchers and practitioners in learning and development of theory, has the impact of truly integrating research and practice for the benefit of vulnerable children and their families.

Supervision and workforce development

The inherent tensions in Child and Family Practice, given the well-publicised risks involved if the wrong decision is made, can make practitioners fearful that they are 'damned if they do and damned if they don't'. This underscores the need for leadership and quality supervision and other opportunities for learning and professional support.

Munro (2002) concluded that most practitioners start their working lives with good intentions; but whether they hold onto them will depend on the culture they find themselves working in. She cautioned that the increasingly common management style that sees the main function of supervision as checking that procedures have been correctly followed, with a punitive approach to errors, undervalues the role of expertise and is hostile to open-minded thinking. She makes the point that a culture must value open-mindedness and the exploration of alternative views.

The capacity of practitioners to synthesise complex data and often conflicting views requires skill and knowledge about the process of information-gathering and analysis, and a commitment to critical thinking. While years of practice are helpful, of itself, experience is not sufficient to ensure good analysis. However, inexperience and poor analytical and written skills can lead to very poor practice outcomes. Healy (2009) also emphasised that the quality of service is impacted by the high turnover of staff reducing access to expertise for both families and inexperienced practitioners – a key issue of concern.

The retention of experienced frontline practitioners and the potential for burnout and vicarious trauma are ongoing issues. The prevalence of often critical and sensational media headlines, in the absence of positive media portrayal and community recognition of child and family services practitioners, can be demoralising. Similarly, the impact of public criticism by external scrutinising bodies conducting inquiries intended to hold practitioners and the system accountable is increasingly challenging. Internationally, leaders in Child and Family Practice have publicly discussed the negative impact and consequences of these issues on the retention of frontline practitioners, which in turn impacts negatively on children and families (Department of Human Services, 2011; Munro, 2004; Scott, 2006).

The problem of embedding thoughtful, relationship-based practice as well as supporting and developing the expertise of inexperienced frontline practitioners is complex. Fiona McColl (2009) strongly challenged the lack of critical reflection in child protection systems as contributing to the retention problems of experienced frontline practitioners, and noted that other community services are becoming "increasingly risk aversive and proscriptive" (p. 128).

Mansell et al. (2011) and Higgins and Katz (2008) have reported the damaging impact of unnecessary statutory intervention on families who may already be marginalised. Unless the system provides proactive strategies to support practice, a more rigid and bureaucratic system can become the reactive response on the ground, when in fact vulnerable children and young people need creative, flexible, dynamic and skilled practice

The importance of professional supervision

The child and family welfare field is beset by the problem of fragmented and procedural forms of supervision that limit the reflective and decision-making abilities of practitioners. Reder and Duncan (1999) and Reder and Duncan (2004) noted this is a recurrent theme in the UK's child death and serious case reviews since the mid-1980s. They also noted that communication problems are recurrent in serious adverse events:

> In some networks, a 'closed professional system' seemed to have evolved, where groups of workers developed a fixed view about the case and became inaccessible to contrary information or observations. Sometimes polarisation

had occurred, with a schism between two groups of workers, whose points of view progressively diverged.

(Reder & Duncan, 1999, pp. 16–17)

In addition, Reder and Duncan (1999) described the phenomenon of the exaggeration of hierarchy where decisions are made by supervisors and others with too little information; role confusion; workers making selective interpretations of the history; failure to note severe family relationship difficulties and inappropriately offering simplistic, concrete solutions. They stress the need for an interactional family perspective, and for quality professional development and supervision. Other research about decision-making has also highlighted the fallibility of decision-makers in child protection and the critical importance of good supervision (Dingwall et al., 1983; Gambrill & Shlonsky, 2000; Munro, 2002; Munro, 2008; Gibbs, 2009).

Towards a public health approach

Scott (2009) advocated for a public health approach to child protection. This requires an understanding of the underlying social determinants of child abuse and neglect, she states: "We need to target our strategies to reduce the risk factors and enhance the protective factors ... to develop empirically based strategies underpinned by good cost-effective data." (p. 14).

Lieberman and Osofsky (2009), when making the point about the significance of violence on human development, cite the President of the American Psychiatric Association, who stated, 'what cigarette smoking is to the rest of medicine, early childhood violence is to psychiatry' (Sharfstein, 2006, p. 3).

Green and Tones note that the 'public health approach' has been marked by a struggle to distance itself from the medical model dominating twentieth-century discourse on health and illness. In contrast, they describe the emergence of the 'New Public Health' approach as an attempt to retreat from an emphasis on individual responsibility for health and health actions and refocus on the factors that collectively influence health status. They argue that a focus on individual prevention does not challenge the increasing disparity in wealth and power within many societies, and that this leads to a conceptualisation of risk that is narrow, ignoring the wider social and environmental determinants of health. They critique attempts to improve health that typically take the form of health education interventions to persuade individuals to adopt healthy behaviours and lifestyles, as they result "in a victim blaming approach in its disregard for the social, environmental and political factors that shape and, indeed, constrain behavioural choices" (Green & Tones, 2010, p. 25). They view this as being inconsistent with two central tenets of health promotion – equity and empowerment.

A public health approach to child protection requires a collective, structural analysis which considers the underlying social determinants of the following: housing, maternal and child health, access to early children's services, employment services and the development of epidemiological intelligence to plan effective responses (Munro & Parton, 2007). As a stark illustration of this, Frederico, Jackson and Jones (2006), in their analysis of effective responses to chronic neglect, found that for the ten children who were the subject of the study, there were collectively 53 notifications to child protection; and all of the children were exposed to multiple types of neglect. Apparent in all cases was structural disadvantage and a high level of complexity, whether relating to the child's needs, the family system, the protective history or the multiple risk factors directly or indirectly associated with neglect. The intersection of the personal vulnerabilities of children, parental psychopathology and the socio-demographic structural issues of disadvantage pervade the lives of many children and families involved with the child protection system.

Head and Alford (2013), in their paper on 'wicked problems', public policy and management, wrote of the importance of leadership. They acknowledged the centrality and importance of collaboration; however, they emphasised that other measures were also required:

> because collaboration alone does not necessarily address all aspects of the complexity challenges. Therefore, we additionally consider two further approaches: broader ways of thinking about variables, options, and linkages; and new models of leadership that better appreciate the distributed nature of information, interests and power. (p. 12)

Graduate Certificate and Diploma in Child and Family Practice Leadership

There was a very active leadership strategy developed within the Victorian Australia DHS Child Protection Program which invested in developing the leadership skills of the team leaders and unit managers. A one-year Graduate Certificate in Child and Family Practice and a two-year Graduate Diploma in Child and Family Practice Leadership were established in 2009. These courses were taught by a consortium of universities and community service organisations, an Aboriginal Community Controlled Organisation (ACCO) and Dr Bruce Perry of the ChildTrauma Academy USA, with La Trobe University as the lead partner. The courses were designed for staff in child protection and community service organisations, and were funded by the Victorian State Government. It has been a very successful initiative in graduating almost 200 practitioners and managers – 96 per cent of whom remain working across sectors in Victoria with vulnerable children and families. It was these courses, described in more detail in the Preface and in Chapter 3, which led to the concept of a book on leadership in Child and Family Practice based upon the curricula of the courses.

Conclusion

When considering the changing context of Child and Family Practice, this chapter has presented the broader historical and professional context and the refocusing to an early intervention, public health approach. We have discussed notions of power, professionalism and partnership, and the need for leadership and accessible support and training for frontline practitioners, linking practice issues to emerging research knowledge and the broader legislative and policy reforms.

Key messages from this chapter

- The increasing complexity of child and family work requires high levels of knowledge and skill at both the organisational and individual practitioner level.
- The new paradigm of Child and Family Practice has a focus on the child and the family, and requires a public health approach including early intervention.
- A properly resourced, culturally informed approach is required to address the over-representation of Indigenous children in the child and family sector.
- The role of leadership is essential in supporting workers to engage in evidence-based and evidence-informed practice to achieve good outcomes with their clients.
- Education for leadership in this sector should be included in education programs for child and family workers.

Questions for further consideration

1. Can you identify examples of how you balance evidence-based practice and evidence-informed reflective practice?
2. How do you assist staff to identify embedded assumptions and biases which impact on their decisions?
3. What is the underlying ideology of the child welfare system you work within, and how does this influence your practice?
4. What are the challenges for leadership if a public health approach is utilised in child and family practice?

References

Anda, R.F., Felitti, V.J., Bremmer, J.D., Walker, J.D., Whitfield, C., Perry, B.D., Dube, S.R., & Giles, W.H. (2006). The enduring effects of abuse and related adverse experiences in childhood: A convergence of evidence from neurobiology and epidemiology. *European Archives of Psychiatry and Clinical Neuroscience*, 256(3), 174–186.

Atkinson, J. (2002). *Trauma trails: Recreating song lines – the transgenerational effects of trauma in Aboriginal Australia*. Melbourne: Spinifex Press.

Australian Institute of Health and Welfare (AIHW). (2007). *Child protection Australia 2005–06*. Canberra, ACT: AIHW. Retrieved from www.aihw.gov.au/getmedia/6568e916-4b41-4ef1-9f97-11b091bd8334/cpa05-06.pdf.aspx?inline=true

Australian Institute of Health and Welfare (AIHW). (2017). *Child protection Australia 2015–16*. Canberra, ACT: AIHW. Retrieved from www.aihw.gov.au/getmedia/bce377ec-1b76-4cc5-87d9-d0541fca586c/20479.pdf.aspx?inline=true

Axford, N., & Berry, V. (2017). Perfect bedfellows: Why early intervention can play a critical role in protecting children – a response to Featherstone et al. (2014) 'A marriage made in hell: Child protection meets early intervention'. *British Journal of Social Work*. doi:10.1093/bjsw/bcx003

Bowlby, J. (1951) *Maternal care and mental health*. Geneva: World Health Organization.

Cant, R., & Downie, R. (1994). *A study of Western Australian child protection data: 1989–1994*. Perth: Department for Community Development.

Centre on the Developing Child. (2007). *A science-based framework for early childhood policy: Using evidence to improve outcomes in learning, behaviour, and health for vulnerable children*. Cambridge, MA: Harvard University Press.

Child Welfare Information Gateway. (2016). *Racial disproportionality and disparity in child welfare*. Washington, DC: US Department of Health and Human Services.

Clark, R. (1988). *Reflecting on child protection decision making* (master's thesis). University of Melbourne, Australia.

Department of Health and Social Care. (2003). *Keeping children safe: The government response to the Victoria Climbie Inquiry report and Joint Chief Inspectors' report 'Safeguarding children'*. London: HMSO.

Department of Human Services. (2011). *Child protection workforce: the case for change*. Melbourne: DHS.

Dingwall, R., Eekelaar, J., & Murray, T. (1983). *The protection of children: State intervention and family life*. Oxford: Blackwell.

Featherstone, B., Morris, K., & White, S. (2014). A marriage made in hell: Early intervention meets child protection. *British Journal of Social Work*, 44(7), 1735–1749.

Frederico, M., Jackson, A., & Jones, S. (2006). *Child death group analysis: Effective responses to chronic neglect*. Melbourne: Office of the Child Safety Commissioner.

Gambrill, E. (2003). Evidence-based practice: Sea change or the emperor's new clothes? *Journal of Social Work Education*, 39(1), 3–23.

Gambrill, E., & Shlonsky, A. (2000). Risk assessment in context. *Children and Youth Services Review*, 22(11–12), 813–837.

Gelles, R. (1973). Child abuse as psychopathology: A socio-logical critique and reformulation. *American Journal of Orthopsychiatry*, 43(4), 611–621.

Gibbs, J. (2009). Changing the cultural story in child protection: Learning from the insider's experience. *Child and Family Social Work*, 14(3), 289–299.

Gil, D. (1970). *Violence against children: Physical child abuse in the United States*. Cambridge, MA: Harvard University Press.

Glaser, D. (2000). Child abuse and neglect and the brain: A review. *Journal of Child Psychology and Psychiatry*, 41(1), 97–116.

Goding, G. (1992). *The history and principles of family therapy*. Melbourne: Australian Association of Family Therapy.

Green, J., & Tones, K. (2010). *Health promotion planning and strategies* (2nd ed.). London: Sage.

Halfpenny, N. (2017). Unpublished internal document. Mackillop Family Services, Victoria, Australia.

Hayes, D., & Spratt, T. (2009). Child welfare interventions: Patterns of social work practice. *British Journal of Social Work*, 39(8), 1575–1597.

Head, B.W., & Alford, J. (2013). Wicked problems: Implications for public policy and management. *Administration & Society*, 47(6), 1–29.

Healy, K. (2009). Critical questions about the quest for clarity in child protection regimes. *Communities, Children and Families Australia*, 4(1), 50–56.

Hearn, B. (1995). *Child and family support and protection: A practical approach*. London: National Children's Bureau.

Heckman, J.J. (2007). The economics, technology and neuroscience of human capability formation. *Proceedings of the National Academy of Science*, 104(3), 13250–13255.

Hendrick, H. (1994). *Child welfare: England 1872–1989*. London: Routledge.

Herman, J. (1992) *Trauma and recovery: The aftermath of violence*. New York: Basic Books.

Higgins, D.J., & Katz, I. (2008). Enhancing service systems for protecting children. *Family Matters*, 80, 43–50.

Holzer, P., Lewig, K., Bromfield, L., & Arney, F. (2008). *Research use in the Australian child and family welfare sector*. Melbourne: Australian Institute of Family Studies.

Hong Chui, W., & Wilson, J. (2006). *Social work and human services best practice*. Annandale, NSW: Federation Press.

Kessler, M., Gira, E., & Poertner, J. (2005). Moving best practice to evidence based practice in child welfare. *Families in Society*, 86(2), 244–250.

Laming, W. (2003) *The Victoria Climbié Inquiry: Report of an inquiry by Lord Laming*. Norwich: HMSO.

Larrick, R.P. (2004). Debiasing. In D.J. Koehler and N. Harvey (Eds.), *Blackwell handbook of judgment and decision making* (pp. 316–337). Malden, MA: Blackwell.

Lieberman, A.F., & Osofsky, J.D. (2009). Poverty, trauma and infant mental health. *Zero to Three*, 30(2), 54–58.

Mansell, J., Ota, R., Erasmus, R., & Marks, K. (2011). Reframing child protection: A response to a constant crisis of confidence in child protection. *Children and Youth Services Review*, 33(11), 2076–2086.

McColl, F. (2009). Where have all the social workers gone? Critical reflection and child protection. *Advances in Social Work and Welfare Education*, 11(1), 127–130.

Mildon, R., Bromfield, L., Arney, F., Lewig, K., Michaux, A., & Antcliff, G. (2011). Facilitating evidence-informed practice: Participatory knowledge translation and exchange. In K. Dill and W. Shera (Eds.), *Implementing evidenced-informed practice: International perspectives* (pp. 173–189). Toronto: Canadian Scholars' Press.

Miller, R. (2008). *Best interests case practice model: Summary guide*. Melbourne: State Government of Victoria.

Miller, R. (2012). *Best interests case practice model: Summary guide* (2nd ed.). Melbourne: State Government of Victoria.

Morley, C. (2009). Developing feminist practices. In J. Allan, L. Briskman, & B. Pease (Eds.), *Critical social work: An Introduction to theories and practices* (pp. 145–159). Crows Nest, NSW: Allen & Unwin.

Munro, E. (2002). *Effective child protection*. London: Sage.

Munro, E. (2004). The impact of child abuse inquiries since 1990. In N. Stanley and J. Manthorpe (Eds.), *The age of inquiry: Learning and blaming in health and social care* (pp. 75–91). London: Routledge.

Munro, E. (2008). *Effective child protection* (2nd ed.). London: Sage

Munro, E. (2011). *The Munro review of child protection: Final report. A child-centred system*. London: Department for Education.

Munro, E., & Parton, N. (2007). How far is England in the process of introducing a mandatory reporting system? *Child Abuse Review*, 16(1), 5–16.

Parton, N., Thorpe, D., & Wattam, C. (1997). *Child protection: Risk and the moral order*. Basingstoke: Macmillan.

Perry, B.D. (2002). Childhood experience and the expression of genetic potential: What childhood neglect tells us about nature and nurture. *Brain and Mind*, 3(1), 79–100.

Perry, B.D. (2006). Applying principles of neurodevelopment to clinical work with maltreated and traumatized children: The neurosequential model of therapeutics. In N.B. Webb (Ed.), *Working with traumatized youth in child welfare* (pp. 27–52). New York: Guilford Press.

Reder, P., & Duncan, S. (1999). *Lost innocents: A follow-up study of fatal child abuse.* London: Routledge.

Reder, P., & Duncan, S. (2004). From Colwell to Climbié: Inquiring into fatal child abuse. In N. Stanley & J. Manthorpe (Eds.), *The age of inquiry: Learning and blaming in health and social care* (pp. 95–114). London: Routledge.

Richmond, M.E. (1917). *Social diagnosis.* New York: Russell Sage Foundation.

Scott, D. (2006). Towards a public health model of child protection in Australia. *Communities, Children and Families Australia,* 1(1), 9–16.

Scott, D. (2009). *Seminar Report: A public health approach to child protection.* Adelaide: Australian Centre for Child Protection.

Scott, D., & O'Neil, D. (1996) *Beyond child rescue: Developing family-centred practice at St Lukes.* Sydney: Allen & Unwin.

Scott, D., & Swain, S. (2002). *Confronting cruelty, historical perspectives on child protection.* Melbourne: Melbourne University Press.

Sharfstein, S. (2006) New task force will address early childhood violence. *Psychiatric News,* 41(3), 3.

Shonkoff, J., & Garner, A. (2012). The lifelong effects of early childhood adversity and toxic stress. *Pediatrics,* 129(1): e232–e246.

Spratt, T., & Callan J. (2004). Parents' views on social work interventions in child welfare cases. *British Journal of Social Work,* 34(2), 199–224.

Trocmé, N., Knoke, D., & Blackstock, C. (2004). Pathways to the overrepresentation of Aboriginal children in Canada's Child Welfare System. *Social Service Review,* 78(4), 577–600.

Trotter, C. (2006). *Working with involuntary clients: A guide to practice* (2nd ed.). London: Sage.

Victorian Child Death Review Committee (2010). *Annual report of inquiries into the deaths of children known to child protection 2010.* Melbourne: Office of the Child Safety Commissioner.

Walter, I., Nutley, S., Percy-Smith, J., McNeish, D., & Frost, S. (2004). *Improving the use of research in social care.* London: Social Care Institute for Excellence.

Webb, S. (2001). Some considerations on the validity of evidence-based practice in social work. *British Journal of Social Work,* 31(1), 57–79.

2

SKILLS AND KNOWLEDGE FOR CHILD AND FAMILY PRACTICE

Maureen Long

Introduction

This chapter discusses the foundational skills and knowledge required to work effectively with vulnerable children and their families. It includes a brief overview of neurobiology and the impacts of trauma on children. Skills and knowledge develop along a trajectory of practice commencing from beginner level through to advanced practice and, finally, leadership level in a complex and ever-changing way. Child and Family Practice covers a breadth of practice settings – including statutory child protection, mental health, out-of-home-care, family violence and substance abuse – and the intersection of these contexts across both statutory and community contexts.

The introduction of early intervention and therapeutic approaches to working with families with children at risk of harm has become increasingly important as adverse experiences in early life can contribute to long-term negative outcomes for adult survivors. This is noted by Bromfield, Sutherland & Parker (2012, p. 16), who state that "trauma has its most profound impact during the first decade of life and when experienced interpersonally". Different skills are required in different child and family settings, from primary prevention through to tertiary intervention. These will be discussed with recognition of the often long-term, entrenched disadvantage of families involved within the Child and Family Practice context.

Who are the families?

Increasingly, the families comprising the Child and Family Practice context and child protection populations have multiple and complex needs. Many experience considerable economic disadvantage, with poverty and homelessness being strong indicators of involvement with child protection (Berger et al., 2015, p. 300;

Dworsky, 2014). Additional mental health, family violence and drug and alcohol issues often compound these structural factors (Bromfield et al., 2012). However, within this group there is considerable diversity, and these families do not comprise a homogeneous group. Responding to families as if they are all 'the same' has, as suggested by Mitchell and Campbell (2011), contributed to social work's least effective outcomes. They argue that "the tendency to lump all 'vulnerable families' together without distinguishing differences leads to poor engagement, high dropout rates and low achievement of desired outcomes for excluded families" (p. 422). Skilled practitioners acknowledge the uniqueness of individual families without stigma and work with them in a flexible manner, responding to their different needs.

Arguably, social work is least effective with excluded families, despite a wealth of experience with them and many attempts to develop effective interventions. There is often a mismatch between what excluded families need and official resources, timelines, targets and programs, despite some programs demonstrating that a more targeted approach brings better results (White, Hall, & Peckover, 2008). And while poverty, racism and discrimination are integral for excluded families, services continue to be delivered without tackling these forces.

Developing skills

Practice theory, knowledge and skills are learnt through formal education, but how they are integrated is grounded in an individual's 'use of self' and their personal style developed over time. Klein (2000, as cited in Munro, 2011, p. 88) articulates four key ways in which expertise is developed:

> i. engaging in deliberate practice, and setting specific goals and evaluation criteria; ii. compiling extensive experience banks; iii. obtaining feedback that is accurate, diagnostic, and reasonably timely; and iv. enriching experience by reviewing prior experiences to derive new insights and lessons from mistakes.

Munro (2011) considers this model as "crucial for thinking about how both individuals and the profession as a whole can be supported to develop their knowledge and skills in helping children and families" (p. 88). Bogo (2006) continues this theme by stressing that mastering social work practice "involves the integration of the knowledge and value base of the profession and a set of core interviewing skills with the 'personal self' of the social worker" (p. 3). At the advanced practice level, it is expected that practitioners will have considerable "practice wisdom" built through "repeated practice experience" (Connolly & Morris, 2012, p. 129). Knowledge can also be seen as an exchange between the client and the practitioner, with an acknowledgment that clients are the experts in their lives and that they have learnt their parenting and interpersonal skills through their formative early life experiences.

Trevithick argues that "social work knowledge refers to many components: theory, models, wisdom and specialised knowledge". This theoretical knowledge includes knowledge of structures in society; theories that derive from psychological and social theories as well as "practice models and their related intervention techniques". She acknowledges that although our knowledge will always be 'incomplete', the importance of building a sound theoretical and skill base from which to practice is fundamental (Trevithick, 2011, pp. 4, 5).

Munro's (2011) review of child protection practice in the United Kingdom recommends that, at a minimum, the capabilities to deliver competent Child and Family Practice are:

- knowledge of child development and attachment and how to use this knowledge to assess a child's current developmental state;
- understanding the impact of parental problems such as domestic violence, mental ill-health and substance misuse on children's health and development at different stages during their childhood; and
- knowledge of the impact of child abuse and neglect on children in both the short and long term and into adulthood (p. 96).

Each of the authors above makes explicit the importance of having a comprehensive knowledge base that traverses a range of theoretical frameworks inclusive of recognition of context and awareness of the importance of practising from a sound ethical framework. Additionally, without sound knowledge of children's development, workers can be at risk of dangerous practice that will not be responsive to children's wellbeing and safety.

Foundational skills

This section will explore the foundational skills upon which good practice is built. These interpersonal skills include: engagement, forming the working relationship, non-verbal and direct communication, critical reflection, and imparting hope. "Knowledge about skills can be developed at arms-length, but skills are only developed in the doing of practice" (Flaskas, 2011, p. 3). This quote reinforces the importance of a sound knowledge base, identifying that the transformation of knowledge into skills is achieved through practice. The 'doing' is not a one-off event, of course, skill-building is an ongoing activity, and even the most experienced of practitioners up-skill regularly, accessing new approaches and reviewing and fine-tuning their work. Having strong interpersonal skills is of course the cornerstone for the development of more advanced practice skills. The ability to relate to and engage service users in the development of the working relationship are essential skills. Engagement involves more than just developing a friendly rapport; it is a focused activity. Workers need to be honest and transparent in their work with families and clearly identify their purpose and role, including how they will respond if they consider children remain unsafe within the family. Within the child protection context, it needs to be made clear with families that the risk factors that brought them to the attention of statutory authorities have to be addressed.

Engaging parents notified to child protection agencies can be more challenging as families may feel victimised, misunderstood and blamed; and, due to previous poor experiences with workers and services, they may have lost any sense of hope for their futures. This can be very difficult terrain for new workers to navigate, especially in trying to instil in parents a positive sense of self as a parent, facilitating a con-nectedness between parent and child and stemming the intergenerational trans-mission of hopelessness.

Practitioners have a key role in facilitating hope within families. The Home-builders' model developed in the US in the 1970s identified the importance of practitioners generating hopefulness. The program was underpinned by the principles that "troubled families can change" (Kelly, 1995, p. 8). This is not to suggest promulgating an unrealistic (and potentially dangerous) hopefulness, but building families' self-esteem and sense of possibility for the future. In previous research undertaken by the author (Long & Frederico, 2014, p. 79), service users participating in family preservation interventions cited the importance of hope, which they attributed "to the way their workers engaged with them". This engagement was delivered authentically to create the possibility of change. Experienced workers also recognise that it is important to assist families to create some happy memories – to support families to have fun together and enjoy each other. This can be achieved in simple ways, such as spending time playing together in the park. Sometimes, workers need to model 'how to play' and have fun, and much therapeutic work has been done while pushing children on swings in playgrounds.

Workers' respect for service users is demonstrated by commitment to punctuality, showing reliability and following through on what they say they will do. Nothing diminishes client trust more than workers not being true to their words and actions. Clarifying your role, and not denying the authority that exists within your role, using inclusive language that clients can readily understand and maintaining a professional self are all part of the process of engagement (Healy, 2012). Such role clarification requires workers to make explicit the rationale for involvement and service delivery approaches. Many families within the Child and Family Practice context have limited social networks (Mitchell & Campbell, 2011), to the extent that the weekly home visit by the worker is the only visitor received each week. This highlights the importance of being clear that the practitioner role is not that of a friend, and that the relationship is not an ongoing one. Though families often accept workers who 'own' their mistakes, they have little time for workers who are not honest. Parents in the child welfare system want 'honest' workers who have clarity of purpose, do not 'beat around the bush and are 'straightforward' (Altman, 2008, p. 49). "Parents felt that dealing with workers who were empathic, reliable and supportive helped them to engage in services" (p. 50). Practitioners should steer away from the use of jargon, which often serves to increase the divide between worker and client. Being a skilled communicator means having the capacity to work with diversity and across contexts, and, most importantly, to be 'on message' so that families know where they stand.

Families in 'the system' may also be well versed in feigning compliance. This can make already vulnerable children increasingly so, as their safety and wellbeing can be further compromised. This is sometimes difficult for beginning level child and family practitioners to understand as they focus on compliance and miss other behaviour and attitudes that may indicate superficial compliance. This can be addressed in supervision through case discussion to help strengthen beginning level practitioners' assessment and listening skills.

What non-verbal communication demonstrates to clients is also 'highly influential' (Healy, 2012, p. 27). A practitioner's demeanour and facial expressions may belie non-judgemental language. Service users well entrenched in the Child and Family Practice context are finely tuned to workers' nuances, having experienced the styles of multiple workers, some of whom may not have delivered effective service. It is important for beginning practitioners to learn that reflecting on and being alert to what non-verbal communication conveys to clients – facial expressions, posture, tone of voice – are all important. Making direct eye contact within a western context demonstrates the listener's attention; not to look directly may suggest disinterest. This is not how all cultures interpret eye contact, and workers need to be alert to the sensitivities of non-western cultures (discussed in detail in Chapter 8). Misinterpretation of culture can result in miscommunication and inappropriate or inaccurate interpretations and judgments that are likely to negatively impact the agency–family relationship and case decisions (Healy, 2012, p. 73). The SOLER model proposed by Gerard Egan (2014) is one approach to helping workers focus on their non-verbal communication. SOLER an acronym for: "sitting squarely, open body posture, leaning towards the other, eye contact, relaxed" (pp. 77–78). Such positioning sets an invitational pose demonstrating that the worker is present, available and there to listen to the client.

Critical reflection

Critical reflection is perhaps the most difficult skill to learn. It requires engaging in all the behaviour described above, plus a thorough understanding of theory as well as gathering information from the client and family. The ability to practise critically is an important part of developing professional competence. It is the capacity to 'stand back' and reflect on what actions the worker is taking (doing), the why and the how, as well as the outcomes aimed for and achieved. This is challenging for workers in a time of decreasing resources yet increasing demand and complexity. "Critical reflection involves social and political analyses which enable transformative changes, whereas reflection may remain at the level of relatively undisruptive changes in techniques or superficial thinking" (White, Fook, & Gardner, 2006, p. 9). In this context, Gardner (2014, p. 24) asserts that critical reflection "is both a theory and a process" that "involves a deeper look at the premises on which thinking, actions and emotions are based".

Critical reflection also implies an awareness of worker responses to clients, a capacity to critically engage with our practice and identify areas that may pose particular challenges to us as practitioners because of our own personal values and lived experience. It can be challenging as a worker to identify and critically reflect on practice, particularly if the work environment does not support a workplace culture accepting of mistakes as something to learn from without attributing blame. More experienced practitioners can support beginning practitioners to adopt critical reflective practice by creating a safe environment in which to reflect.

Munro (2011, p. 87), quoting Oakeshott (1989, p. 133), "draws attention to the limitations of a 'crowded' life where people are continually occupied and engaged but have no time to stand back and think. A working life given over to distracted involvement does not allow for the integration of experience". In a highly demanding work context with unremitting demands, it can be difficult to take time out to review, reflect and consider practice. However, not doing so can lead to rote-like practice that struggles to view clients' uniqueness; or even to dangerous practice that is inured to the risks posed to children. The importance of workers critically reflecting on their practice is essential to making "well-evidenced decisions and recommendations, including when a child cannot remain living in their family either as a temporary or permanent arrangement" (Munro, 2011, p. 95).

Munro (2011) writes about 'intuitive expertise', which is "built up through pattern-recognition and this has implications for how social workers should be trained, managed, and provided with a career path that values and promotes the continual development of expertise" (p. 91). Intuitive expertise helps the worker feel confident and comfortable in the role; however, it should not exist without challenge, and should exist in an openness to new experiences that may conflict with patterns from the past. Entry-level workers need to learn how to explore their intuition and understand what is influencing their perceptions.

Working with children

Entry-level practitioners sometimes express trepidation about working with children. In working in Child and Family Practice, it is imperative that workers have a sound understanding of normative child development; an awareness of when children's development is compromised as well as understanding risk and/or harmful behaviour (Munro, 2011, p. 95). Working with children can also increase the likelihood of worker burnout due to the emotional toll of delivering services to such a vulnerable population. Workers may feel anxiety around their communication with children and require further support and training to effectively communicate with children who have experienced trauma. To work effectively with children, workers need to have a repertoire of skills built upon knowledge and theory. Working with a child who is traumatised, the worker may initially find the child difficult to engage. Modelling safety includes being able to sit with children's distress and support them while remaining calm; adapting communication styles to ensure that the workers are communicating appropriately with the child's developmental age; and being creative in the use of stories and play to help children talk about what is happening for them. The ability to interpret observations of children at play and/or in their interactions with family is also an important skill in undertaking assessments of children's wellbeing and safety. Many tools are available to assist in working with children, such as cards that depict the various emotions, as well as toys such as dolls' houses and puppets.

Trauma-informed practice

Best practice in Child and Family Practice requires workers to have a sound understanding of trauma and to adopt a 'trauma-informed' paradigm that incorporates knowledge and awareness of how trauma impacts people's lives. There is increasing awareness of how childhood adversity such as exposure to abuse and neglect impacts children's development and wellbeing, with exposure to multiple traumatic events in childhood compounding long-term implications for later mental health. "Understanding the experiences of adversity in childhood such as sexual or other abuse as trauma is now recognised to be an important concept for human service delivery sectors" (Wall, Higgins, & Hunter, 2016, p. 2). Workers need to be aware that within Child and Family Practice, parents who have harmed their own children may have grown up in abusive situations. Though children's safety cannot be jeopardised, recognition of the early-life trauma experiences of the adults in the family requires a compassionate response. Such a response includes supporting the family to address this trauma and to be able to care for the child in a manner that recognises the trauma and seeks to reduce its impact on the life of the child. Most currently taught courses teach trauma theory, which underpins much of Child and Family Practice.

Assessment

Though Child and Family Practice has moved away from the deficit-saturated models of previous times, and strength-based approaches that recognise family resources and capacities have replaced them, undertaking assessments within the child and family/child protection contexts need to ensure a child-focused lens and awareness of risk factors. Children's safety is paramount in all situations. It is important to adopt an ecological framework that enables the worker to consider the "complex interplay of factors in human development and across human relationships" (Connolly & Harms, 2015, p. 51). This approach identifies the relationships within and outside the family and the levels of support (or lack of support) that surround the family. The roles that people play within the family as well as the impacts at the macro level of structural conditions – such as access to housing, employment, health services to support families – are important factors. Within Child and Family Practice, the importance of assessments to consider the capacities of parents to nurture their children, protect them and keep them safe is also paramount. Experienced practitioners can manage multiple stakeholders and gaps in information, often developing multiple intervention options that can be implemented as needed.

Case planning and implementation

The goal of case and/or service planning is to develop an individualised, strengths-based, needs-driven case plan that addresses the unique needs of children and their families as identified through assessment. At the same time, it needs to meet the standards of professional social work practice and the safety and permanency requirements of federal and state mandates. Service implementation involves providing ongoing support for families and children through brokering, facilitating, monitoring, coordinating, connecting, developing and/or providing services identified in the case plan, as well as reporting relevant information to the courts and working with administrative reviewers. "A family-centred and strengths-based approach to planning and implementation results in a worker-family relationship and plan for services that will best enhance the safety, permanency, and well-being of individual children, youth, and their families" (Mallon & Hess, 2014, p. 49).

Families with multiple and complex needs may experience numerous, chronic and interrelated problems. As discussed earlier, these families do not constitute a homogenous group, and should not be labelled or assumed to be 'forever' in this state. There is significant diversity among these families, which indicates the complexity and multi-dimensional nature of the problems they experience and the need for individualised, tailored and flexible approaches to assist them.

Most families in need are also affected by poverty and housing problems (Delfabbro, Kettler, McCormick, & Fernandez, 2012). The practitioner must therefore be aware of how these needs intersect, and acknowledge that where certain basic needs are not met it may be impossible for a family to change, albeit not through lack of motivation or desire. The practitioner, as part of their assessment and case planning, must try to address these needs where possible or refer to other services where required. It is not possible to solely work with the family around your specific area of practice without acknowledging or seeking to address their other needs. A practitioner working with a family without seeing them in their context will never be able to implement or effect long-term change.

Evidence-based practice

In an era of diminishing resources, the importance of demonstrating the efficacy of services has never been greater. The requirement for programs to demonstrate their 'evidence base' has never been stronger. Munro (2011) defines evidence-based practice as "the conscientious, explicit, judicious, use of current best evidence in making decisions about the care of individual patients" (p. 92). However, evidence-based practice can be contentious within the Child and Family Practice field for its inability to capture the more subtle nuances of effective practice – such as the role that the worker–client relationship contributes to achieving desired outcomes and social constructs and contexts.

Gray, Plath, and Webb (2009) argue that "evidence-based practice requires that practitioners inform clients when no scientifically tested treatments are available"

(p. 7). This requires an openness of dialogue with clients and a recognition that, at times, the family and practitioner may attempt strategies that do not yield the outcomes they were anticipating. The practitioner must assist the family in remaining hopeful despite perhaps making many attempts to change without success. "Learning to use evidence-based approaches requires a combination of training, explicit analysis of family strengths and difficulties, and well-developed skills in observation and understanding" (Munro, 2011, p. 93). Connolly and Morris (2012) argue that evidence-based practice is used alongside multiple sources to support practice, and is not the only one. They state that "frameworks based on research findings, ethical principles, natural justice and human rights will help to clarify and reinforce practice behaviours that support good outcomes for children and their families" (p. 48). To be able to use and identify many practice styles and possibilities with a family is key to providing flexible and individual services.

A key challenge in Child and Family Practice and child protection practice is workforce retention, given that the work is often highly emotional, stressful and confrontational. As Munro (2011) notes:

> Being exposed to the powerful, and often negative, emotions found in child protection work comes at a personal cost. If the work environment does not help support workers and debrief them after particularly traumatic experiences, then it increases the risk of burnout which, in the human services, has been defined in terms of three dimensions: emotional exhaustion, depersonalisation (or cynicism), and reduced personal accomplishment. (p. 91)

In recognition of the impact that 'self-care' has on practitioners, it has been added to worker education and training within the field over the past few years. Though self-care was not discussed when the author was a new child protection worker many years ago, the forming of supportive, trusting, collegial relationships proved a very helpful protective factor in managing the work. Being able to discuss the work with a trusted supervisor also played a role in the author's informal self-care plan. As Munro (2011) warns, "the emotional dimension of working with children and families plays a significant part in how social workers reason and act. If it is not explicitly discussed and addressed then its impact can be harmful" (p. 138). To ensure practice is of a high standard and reasoning is sound requires workers to effectively manage themselves and seek the necessary support if they feel their judgement and decision-making may be impaired. Burnout for new workers often comes from the emotional distress incurred from working with children and families in very difficult circumstances, as well as from the sense, at times, of not knowing what to do next in complex situations. For more experienced workers, burnout may occur due to feeling overwhelmed by a sense that their work makes little difference – that there are too many troubled families and that they do not have the resources to improve their lives. Whatever the causes or levels of worker experience, worker fatigue needs to be addressed not only in the interests of the worker's well-being but also in respect of the families in need of quality services.

Finally, although this is a chapter about the development of foundational skills, if leaders are to help practitioners develop the many skills discussed, they need to be able to articulate what the basic blocks of good practice are for their staff, and to model them in practice.

Summary

Work in Child and Family Practice is indisputably complex and challenging, demanding much of practitioners. As noted earlier, formal education and training can provide the foundation knowledge and theories, "but skills are only developed in the doing of practice" (Flaskas, 2011, p. 3). To develop from an entry-level practitioner into a highly skilled one requires solid foundations which, if nurtured and supported, can lead to expert practice. Reaching expert level requires a commitment to life-long learning, an awareness of self and the capacity to manage one's emotions and responses. Practitioners with openness to learning and access to quality supervision, professional development opportunities and the ability to critically reflect upon their capacities and position within the welfare space can work effectively with families, which can lead to better outcomes in the long term.

Key messages from this chapter

- Child and Family Practice is complex and involves working with individuals and their relationships.
- It requires practice-based skills such as assessment, case planning and the adoption of trauma-informed approaches.
- It also, as does all social work, requires critical reflection and an awareness of self and the inherent power of the role.
- Working with children is unique and requires a different skill set to working with adults.
- Child safety is paramount and can never be compromised.

Questions for further consideration

1. How would I articulate my approach to working with families? What underpins this approach?
2. How often in my 'crowded life' do I reflect upon my practice? How could I build in more opportunities for reflection?

References

Altman, J. (2008). Engaging families in child welfare services: Worker versus client perspectives. *Child Welfare, 87*(3), 41–61.

Berger, L., Collins, M., Font, S., Gjertson, L., Slack, K., & Smeeding, T. (2015). Home foreclosure and child protective services involvement. *Pediatrics,* 136(2), 299–307. doi:10.1542/peds.2014-2832

Bogo, M. (2006). *Social work practice: Concepts, process and interviewing*. New York: Columbia University Press.

Bromfield, L., Sutherland, S., & Parker, R. (2012). *Families with multiple and complex needs: Best interests case practice model specialist practice resources*. Melbourne: Victorian Government Department of Health and Human Services.

Connolly, M., & Harms, L. (2015). *Social work: From theory to practice*. Port Melbourne: Cambridge University Press.

Connolly, M., & Morris, K. (2012). *Understanding child and family welfare*. Basingstoke: Palgrave Macmillan.

Delfabbro, P., Kettler, L., McCormick, J., & Fernandez, E. (2012, 26 July). The nature and predictors of reunification in Australian out-of-home care. Paper presented at the 12th Australian Institute of Family Studies Conference: Family transitions and trajectories, Melbourne.

Dworsky, A. (2014). Families at the nexus of housing and child welfare. Chicago: State Policy Advocacy and Reform Center. Retrieved from http://childwelfaresparc.org/wp-content/uploads/2014/12/Families-at-the-Nexus-of-Housing-and-Child-Welfare.pdf

Egan, G. (2014). *The skilled helper: A problem-management and opportunity-development approach to helping* (10th ed.). Belmont, CA: Cengage Learning.

Flaskas, C. (2011). *What is advanced social work practice?* Canberra: Australian Association of Social Workers.

Gardner, F. (2014). *Being critically reflective*. Basingstoke: Palgrave Macmillan.

Gray, M., Plath, D., & Webb, S. (2009). *Evidence-based social work: A critical stance*. Abingdon: Routledge.

Healy, K. (2012). *Social work methods and skills*. Basingstoke: Palgrave Macmillan.

Kelly, S. (1995). Our challenge: Strong families/safe children. Paper presented at Proceedings of the Second National Family Preservation Conference, Melbourne, 14–17 February.

Klein, G. (2000). *Sources of power: How people make decisions*. Cambridge, MA: MIT Press.

Long, M., & Frederico, M. (2014). What parents say about their experiences of family preservation programmes. *Children Australia*, 39(2), 74–80. doi:10.1017/cha.2014.3

Mallon, G., & McCartt Hess, P. (2014). *Child welfare for the 21st century: A handbook of practices, policies, and programs* (2nd ed.). New York: Columbia University Press.

Mitchell, G., & Campbell, L. (2011). The social economy of excluded families. *Child and Family Social Work*, 16, 422–433. doi:10.1111/j.1365-2206.2011.00757.x

Munro, E. (2011). *The Munro review of child protection: Final report. A child-centred system*. London: Department for Education.

Oakeshott, M. (1989). *The voice of liberal learning*. New Haven: Yale University Press.

Trevithick, P. (2011). *Social work skills and knowledge: A practice handbook* (3rd ed.). Maidenhead: Open University Press.

Wall, L., Higgins, D., & Hunter, C. (2016). *Trauma-informed care in child/family welfare services*. Melbourne: Australian Institute of Family Studies.

White, S., Fook, J., & Gardner, F. (2006). Critical reflection: A review of contemporary literature and understandings. In S. White, J. Fook, & F. Gardner (Eds.), *Critical reflection in health and social care* (pp. 3–20). Maidenhead: Open University Press.

White, S., Hall, C., & Peckover, S. (2008). The descriptive tyranny of the Common Assessment Framework: Technologies of categorization and professional practice in child welfare. *British Journal of Social Work*, 39, 1197–1217.

3

A DYNAMIC APPROACH TO DEVELOPING KNOWLEDGE AND SKILLS THROUGH CURRICULUM AND TEACHING AND LEARNING APPROACHES

Nadine Cameron and Margarita Frederico

Introduction

This chapter looks at the concept of live knowledge: the idea that knowledge is contextual and ever evolving at both conscious and unconscious levels, and the level of the individual practitioner and institution. It also considers its utility for child and family practitioners with respect to their acquisition, development and use of knowledge. The chapter discusses the concept and its capacity to support Child and Family Practice through: encouraging practitioners' reflective engagement with theory; increasing the status of practitioner knowledge; informing the teaching and learning process; and creating a rationale for closer collaboration among practitioners, academics and policymakers. The concept of live knowledge also provides a strong argument for a specific conceptualisation of the learning organisation that has a more democratic interpretation of knowledge exchange. On this basis, we create an argument for leaders of Child and Family Practice organisations establishing mechanisms and a workplace culture consistent with the principles of live knowledge.

Child and family practitioners' under-utilisation of theory

There is considerable evidence that child and family practitioners have inadequate exposure to, or draw minimally on, theoretical knowledge, even where they have undertaken related tertiary study (for example, Brandon, Sidebotham, Ellis, Bailey, & Belderson, 2011). There is also evidence that fruitful exchange among child and family practitioners, researchers and policymakers is limited (see Holzer, Lewig, Bromfeld, & Arney, 2007). Both are problems that undermine the effectiveness of practitioners.

Despite the plethora of education programs in Child and Family Practice, as Osmond and O'Connor (2006) report, social workers' and child and family practitioners' marginal usage of theory has persisted for several decades. They interviewed child protection workers who appeared not to have "an explicit, comprehensive, coherent research/theory base" underpinning their practice (p. 17). Explanations for the lack of engagement by social workers and child and family practitioners with theory include that they lack time to read research reports or keep abreast of new knowledge (Walter, Nutley, & Davies, 2003). From a different perspective, the provision of time for their professional learning is inadequately prioritised by their workplaces (Barratt, 2003). Other possible reasons for the lesser use of theoretical knowledge by child and family practitioners include practitioners' lack of understanding of the purpose of research. For example, in a large study of child and family practitioners, Barratt found that practitioners were uncertain even about what kinds of evidence constituted 'research findings'.

Rutter and Fisher (2013, p. 8), considering practitioners in community organisations more broadly, suggest that another form of discouragement might be that research findings often reflect the interests of policymakers or funding bodies rather than those of practitioners (see also Walter, Nutley, Percy-Smith, McNeish, & Frost, 2004; Small, 2005). Shonkoff (2000) argues that, within Child and Family Practice, policy, research and practice constitute three distinct cultures with unique perspectives and concerns. The 'cultural' differences between these three domains, Lewig, Arney and Scott (2006) claim, result in a lack of institutional frameworks to link researchers and stakeholders, mutual mistrust and other related problems.

Problems with practitioners' under-utilisation of theory

Another consequence of the existence of the different cultures is that knowledge from these different parts of the sector is treated hierarchically. Knowledge from one domain – in most cases, research – is seen to have greater validity or relevance than knowledge from other domains. Fox, Martin and Green (2007), for example, argue that practitioner knowledge is routinely 'downgraded' by bodies such as the National Health Service (NHS) against research findings gleaned through the experimental studies of full-time researchers (p. 93). Gould (2000) reports that practitioners in one UK child care agency found that managers of their organisation treated their knowledge as inferior to that of people who were commissioned to undertake research on the organisation. The existence of the three cultures also invokes a false distinction between those who should, or do, create knowledge as opposed to consuming knowledge.

Evidence-informed and evidence-based practice

A number of advances have been made in recent years in the conceptualisation of practitioners' use of knowledge that undermines the hierarchy between practitioners and theoreticians, and usefully blurs the distinction between the producers and creators of knowledge. Such advances include the development of the concept of 'evidence-informed practice', variously characterised as an extension or a version of the concept of evidence-based practice that initially emerged within medical research discourse (Sackett, Richardson, Rosenberg, & Haynes, 1997).

Evidence-based practice is popularly understood within Child and Family Practice contexts as "the conscientious, explicit and judicious use of current best evidence in making decisions regarding the welfare of service-users and carers" (Sheldon, 2003, as cited in Mullen & Streiner, 2004, p. 113). In other words, it is an approach to practice that requires the adoption of approaches that have been evaluated as effective through methodologically robust methods (Kessler, Gira, & Poertner, 2005). Evidence-based practice has attracted a number of critics (Webb, 2001; Gray, Plath, & Webb, 2009). Their concerns include that the approach involves unreflexive and uniform application of research findings to clients who in fact require tailored and nuanced responses. Another concern is that it relies on an unjustified level of confidence in research evidence. Others have, in turn, criticised 'narrow' interpretations of evidence-based practice, arguing that it had always implied the use of evidence tailored to the needs of individual clients (see, for example, Gibbs & Gambrill, 2002).

The terms 'evidence-based practice' and 'evidence-informed practice' are considered by some theorists to be interchangeable (Shlonksy & Ballan, 2011). Others, however, argue that an evidence-informed practice approach differs from an evidence-based approach in conceptualising theoretical knowledge as just one of several knowledge sources practitioners might draw on. For those such as Nevo and Slonim-Nevo (2011), an evidence-informed approach accepts that, in an area such as Child and Family Practice, no theoretical knowledge is perfect, and that data on which theories are based are always interpreted through the biased lens of a researcher or theoretician. They believe it also makes more explicit than does an evidence-based approach the uniqueness of clients' problems. This has the consequence that no 'proven' practice approaches, alone or even in concert, can be sufficient to address a client's circumstances. It also leaves the practitioner having to decide on the best mix of approaches. They believe this approach also allows that what constitutes the most appropriate intervention for a client will evolve with the client's circumstances, preferences and ways in which they understand their own conditions. An evidence-informed approach, thus, suggests a broader role for practitioners' experiential or professional knowledge in the selection and application of interventions than an evidence-based approach. Nevo and Slonim-Nevo (2011) indicate that the model additionally recognises the importance of client expertise, so "the constructive and imaginative judgements" of both practitioners and clients are included (p. 1178).

Models of learning with organisations

Of interest here is not just the kind of knowledge that is utilised by practitioners but also the means by which practitioners acquire, maintain and use knowledge as this, too, has a bearing on the effectiveness of practice. And, just as ideas pertaining to how theoretical knowledge is ideally used by practitioners have evolved, so have ideas regarding where or with whom knowledge resides within an organisation. Walter et al. (2004) refer to three ways in which knowledge or responsibility for its acquisition might be distributed. First, a research-practitioner model makes a practitioner within a welfare organisation ultimately accountable for their own learning while placing expectations on management to support their attainment of knowledge. Second, an 'embedded' research method describes a model where policymakers and organisational managers design systems and programs that take account of current research. Third, an organisational excellence model has been adopted by those agencies for whom constant adaptation of organisation-wide knowledge is a priority. This latter model overlaps with the concept of the learning organisation first developed by Senge (1990) and since then elaborated in different directions of relevance to community organisations (see, for example, Argyris & Schön, 1996; Gould & Baldwin, 2004).

Broadly speaking, a learning organisation is one in which staff share the understanding that an appropriate standard of service requires employees' constant acquisition of knowledge (in its broadest sense) and the pooling thereof among stakeholders. Different elaborations of the learning organisation vary in the extent to which they emphasise bottom-up, top-down or more equitable means of knowledge generation and transmission (Johnson, Spicer, & Wallace, 2009). Beddoe (2009, p. 725), however, argues that, in practice, too often the learning organisation's imperative is interpreted by community organisations as a requirement that staff undergo continual training, where their learning goals are "decided far away from the learners and the consumers" of an agency. Fielding (as cited in Beddoe, 2009) argues that Senge, in his initial discussion of learning organisations, skirts around issues of power, failing to locate the learning organisation "within a reality which is socially, politically and historically contested" (p. 725). Beddoe argues that workers are keen to be involved in active workplace learning but need to feel "engaged in the processes, including deciding what to learn. They need to feel heard, respected and acknowledged for the practice wisdom they develop in the field" (p. 730).

Live knowledge: the volatility of practitioners' knowledge

The theory of live knowledge, introduced here, extends the notion of the contingent nature of knowledge per se and of what may be considered best or state-of-the-art knowledge, as introduced within the evidence-informed practice model. It expands on the idea of the dispersed nature of knowledge expounded in various models of the learning organisation. In so doing, it highlights that practitioner contributions to the development of theory are equally important as those of academics. It also better represents the complexity of knowledge acquisition and use. Ultimately, it suggests a role for leaders in the Child and Family Practice arena to bring theoreticians and practitioners together.

This theory has been developed in part from the experience of the writers in conducting and evaluating the Graduate Certificate and Graduate Diploma in Child and Family Practice Leadership courses offered to child and family practitioners at La

Trobe University in Melbourne, Australia (discussed in more detail in the Preface). The Graduate Certificate and Diploma largely drew on case study and enquiry-based learning pedagogies, discussed in more detail below. How the participants and, in fact, all stakeholders learnt from each other was more complex and nuanced than can be captured by outcomes associated with these models. This realisation by the authors drew attention to the lack of theories that adequately explain the complexity of how individuals learn and use knowledge. Live knowledge is the first tentative step towards providing such a theory.

The concept of 'live knowledge' takes as its starting point that all theoretical knowledge is in constant flux at the level of an individual practitioner, an organisation and a professional sector. It is compatible with the current understanding that the sector's requisite knowledge base pertains to phenomena – from individual client circumstances through to child protection legislation and policy – that are themselves constantly changing and influencing each other. Live knowledge highlights that it is not only the suite of information that practitioners require that is subject to constant revision, but also how that knowledge itself is constructed.

In the context of a practitioner drawing on a given theory, his or her more fine-grained understandings thereof – how it constructs a 'strength' or 'risk', for example – can shift rapidly with alterations in environment or exposure to new information or ideas. Such modifications are often made unconsciously. A number of researchers have found that what individuals are able to recall of a wide range of information, and how they appraise and conceptualise it, can be impacted by myriad and often unexpected factors. These span the mood that individuals are in through to room temperature (Siemer, 2001; Clore & Huntsinger, 2007; Woike, Bender, & Besner, 2009; Smith, Glenberg, & Bjork, 1978; Miles & Hardman, 1998; Kihlstrom, Dorfman, & Park, 2007). The neural mechanisms underlying these effects are just starting to be identified (see, for example, Hayes, Nadel, & Ryan, 2007; Hayes, Baena, Truong, & Cabeza, 2010). Other research has shown how individuals' exposure to new figures of speech and linguistic constructs impacts how they conceptualise a broad range of phenomena ranging from money to time itself (Casasanto et al., 2004; Boroditsky, 2003). It can thus be assumed that conversations with others will produce shifts in the way individuals understand minor through to large objects and concepts.

This is to say that, at the most detailed level, individuals' ideas about a theory likely vary not only from one usage to the next but also across the length of a single usage. In this way, individuals are creating a particular version of a theory in every moment. Närhi (2002) states that one cannot consider knowledge separately from the context in which it is being used and produced. Put another way, it cannot be understood completely outside of the moment in which it is being used.

How practitioners subsequently translate theoretical knowledge into action is also determined by factors as broad as their current frame of mind, organisation protocols and client circumstances, values and preferences (Närhi, 2002). These are factors that, themselves, tend towards rapid change. There are many ways in which theoretical knowledge can be used, or translated, for practice. Eraut (1985), for example (citing Broudy), claims that knowledge may be applied in one of four main ways: in a largely automatic or 'replicative' mode; in ways requiring a little through to considerable professional judgment (applicative or interpretive modes); or in an 'associative' mode which involves lateral or creative use of a theory. Fargion (2006) distinguishes between social workers who take an 'enlightenment' versus a 'romantic' approach to knowledge usage; where the former view theories as formal guidelines for action, the latter see them more as 'stimuli to reflection' (p. 269). How a practitioner uses theory, i.e. undertakes praxis, may also vary from moment to moment. How practitioners apply theoretical knowledge can, in turn, impact how they assess its efficacy or further modify their understanding of it more generally.

An individual's broader understanding of a theory may undergo a slower kind of evolution in addition to that which occurs in situ and often unconsciously. This latter kind of change is the result of deliberate processes such as a practitioners' reflection on their practice and its effect, discussion with others or reading related material (D'Cruz, Gillingham, & Melendez, 2007). When practitioners share their (explicit) knowledge with colleagues – and especially where that knowledge has broader utility, i.e. is less context-bound – this can contribute to the development of a new, more general set of understandings about a particular theory across an organisation or profession.

In summary, practitioners' theoretical knowledge and application thereof in complex areas such as Child and Family Practice are continually evolving as a result of both conscious and unconscious processes, and including responses to contextual stimuli. Some of these 'micro' shifts may become the basis of more conscious reformulation of ideas. Just as complexity theory has recognised that multiple variables interact in complex ways to produce often unpredictable outcomes for clients of child and family services (Stevens & Cox, 2008), live knowledge emphasises the unpredictable ways in which knowledge can combine and manifest. Practitioners' broader perspectives on theories tend to evolve more slowly, and more detailed understandings can occur rapidly and often. Practitioners are presented with a considerable challenge in identifying which knowledge is useful for one context only and which might have broader or more ongoing applicability of some kind.

Organisations and live knowledge

An organisation's theoretical knowledge is likewise constantly and rapidly changing at the 'invisible' level as practitioners and managers adapt their own understandings of theories. (The same can be said for the knowledge of teams and other units within an organisation.) It is also changing more slowly at an aggregate and visible level, as represented by an organisation's evolving policies and other documentation. An organisation's knowledge can also be considered live in the sense that each time its constituents collectively discuss or draw on a particular theory, what is recalled by the group, what interpretations they make of it and how they translate it will be impacted by the kinds of contextual factors mediating individuals' thinking, as discussed above.

Researchers and live knowledge

That researchers' knowledge is subject to constant revision is, in some respects, more taken for granted. The explicit goal of research in Child and Family Practice, or social work more generally – whether exploratory, descriptive or explanatory in nature (Strydom, 2013; Marlow, 2001; D'Cruz & Jones, 2004) – is to advance (i.e. change) knowledge relevant to practice. Less well appreciated has been that changes in researchers' knowledge are likely to occur not only as a result of their considered analyses of data sets and other information. (This is a process that has, in any case, been long understood to be impacted by various biases, for example, Hammersley & Gomm, 1997.) Ideas that researchers have about phenomena ranging from theories through to very small units of data – a single observation, or statement made by a participant, for example – will vary at the very detailed level each time the researchers revisit them. Researchers' thinking – no different to that of practitioners or the broader population – will be continually impacted by many contextual factors, including research literature and others' conceptual thinking. It is arguably even more important for researchers than practitioners, however, to identify what of their knowledge will have more sustained or general relevance.

The implications of live knowledge for Child and Family Practice

Live knowledge arguably has particular relevance for Child and Family Practice, in which practice outcomes matter particularly; practitioners work with the most vulnerable clients and in volatile circumstances. There are a number of important implications for Child and Family Practice relating to knowledge being under constant revision at various levels and within different domains. The first of these is that practitioners need to develop awareness of the broad range of factors (climate, mood, type of room they are in, etc.) that can impact their thinking, and that much of their knowledge will 'look' different in different contexts. They also need to develop strategies for identifying which parts of their knowledge will have only fleeting or specific versus general and ongoing utility.

Another important implication of knowledge constantly evolving at different levels is that where best or state-of-the-art theoretical and practice knowledge might be considered to reside shifts continually between direct practice and research contexts. Researchers often have the benefit over practitioners of possessing more data from which broad rules about 'what works', or trends in various phenomena, can be inferred. Practitioners, on the other hand, have fresher knowledge about the evolving circumstances of clients, and opportunity to test the utility of current theories (or their particular understanding thereof). Additionally, given that practitioners continually adjust their own understandings of theories, client issues and so on – and that their views often comprise the data from which researchers draw their conclusions – research knowledge can be quickly rendered out of date. In any case, knowledge of researchers and practitioners alike needs to be treated as highly tentative where "expertise becomes a result of negotiation, and knowing becomes a process rather than a product" (Jones & Joss, 1995, cited in Närhi, 2002, p. 334).

That the location of state of the art practice knowledge is constantly under revision should in turn, diminish policymakers' inclination towards, and rationale for, automatically privileging researcher over practitioner knowledge. Additionally, that practitioner and researchers' interpretations of policy elements (as for other theoretical content) can be expected to frequently fluctuate highlights the need for policymakers to stay in close communication with both professional groups.

At the same time, the concept of live knowledge underscores the need for a more equitable interpretation of the learning organisation. Underpinning a top-down model of knowledge transmission are the beliefs that the most important knowledge emanates from a single location and evolves slowly. By contrast, a learning organisation based on the principles of live knowledge would recognise that all stakeholders in the organisation gain or adapt knowledge in every moment, some of which will have utility for the organisation as a whole. One way such dialogue can be achieved is through collaboration around the design and delivery of professional development and higher learning curricula, an example of which is provided below.

Innovative practice built on an appreciation of the principles of live knowledge

The Graduate Certificate and Graduate Diploma in Child and Family Practice, while not explicitly designed on the principles of live knowledge, demonstrated appreciation for the rapidness with which learners generate and adapt knowledge. The courses and their evaluation lent significantly to the development of the concept of live knowledge.

The courses, as stated, officially drew on enquiry-based and problem-based learning and case study pedagogies, both 'inductive' approaches to teaching. Inductive approaches provide students with "a set of observations or data to interpret, or a complex real-world problem" for which they are required to gather or develop "facts, procedures and guiding principles" (Spronken-Smith, 2012). Case-based teaching saw students in the Graduate Diploma and Graduate Certificate using specific real-world scenarios as a jumping-off point for identifying their current knowledge and value bases and clarifying their personal approaches to practice. (See Snyder & McWilliam, 2003; McCollum & Catlett, 1997; Lundeberg, Levin, & Harrington, 1999 for more on case-based learning.) Enquiry-based learning involved students working together in groups to identify problems relevant to their current professional work and resources required for addressing these. (See Preston, Harvie, & Wallace, 2015; Kahn & O'Rourke, 2005 for more on enquiry-based learning.)

These pedagogical approaches were selected because they have been found to support learners' richer engagement with theoretical material and their development of analytical abilities (Prince & Felder, 2007; Spronken-Smith, 2012). They have also been shown to enhance opportunities for the sharing of knowledge among learners. They do, however, possess shortcomings, particularly in relation to their treatment of knowledge. Like other pedagogies, they privilege extant knowledge; i.e. treat such knowledge as that which is to be retrieved and assimilated or, in other words, as answers that are 'out there'. Relatedly, they treat the pooling of knowledge among learners – often a feature of inductive pedagogies – as an additive proposition rather than something more complex.

The broader design of the Graduate Diploma and Graduate Certificate reflected an appreciation that students do not merely retrieve knowledge, but continually and rapidly create and recreate it. This process occurs through students bringing together the knowledge offered them by teaching staff and their co-learners with their pre-existing knowledge and learning experiences. Learning experiences take place in the classroom as well as students' workplaces where they can test the utility of various theoretical frameworks for different client groups and situations. Students were frequently given opportunities to feed back to each other about their evolving thinking and praxis. Appreciation for students' *co*-creation or '*co*-adaption' of ideas was demonstrated through the range of opportunities they were given to not only work together but also to *collectively* revisit the products of their collaborations.

Staff also showed an awareness of the importance of students' knowledge per se, and vis-à-vis their own, through their willingness to make broad-based amendments to their own theoretical thinking and teaching in response to feedback provided them by students.

Further – and this speaks to the uniqueness of the course designs – throughout the development and delivery thereof, there was frequent interaction between academic staff and a range of other individuals from the other two 'cultures' of research and policy. The Diploma course was, in the first place, designed around the Department of Human Services Child and Family Practice leadership capabilities (Atkinson Consulting, 2008). This, itself, represents a rare level of collaboration between academia and government. That regular communication of this kind occurred ensured that each domain remained aware of any broad-based or more general evolutions occurring in the theoretical thinking of the other.

Below is a comprehensive list of avenues of knowledge exchange among practitioners, academic staff and Community Service Organisations/CSOs (the consortium) and government that were supported by the course (also shown in graphic form in Figure 3.1):

- Provision, by the Department of Human Services (DHS), of information about challenges facing the child and family sector at a policy level to the academic consortium delivering the course
- Sharing by consortium members with DHS of the theoretical and practice-related content with which practitioners need to be familiar
- Discussion, between academic staff (consortium members) and leaders of Child and Family Practice organisations about organisational needs and suitable course participants
- Sharing by consortium members with each other about substantive issues requiring presentation in the course as well as about good collaboration and process

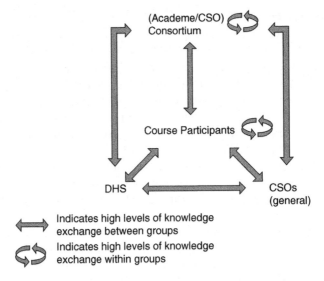

FIGURE 3.1 Knowledge exchange supported by the Graduate Certificate and Graduate Diploma program

Source: Frederico et al. (2016)

- Sharing by the consortium with students those research findings and practice approaches of relevance to practice
- Discussion among course participants about the structure, operations, values and practice models of their own and other organisations, as well as about their own theoretical thinking and explorations in praxis
- Feedback to consortium members from course participants about the success in their workplaces of implementing theories discussed with them in class (in turn, able to be shared by consortium members with Department staff)
- Sharing by course participants of their newly developed knowledge with their colleagues and other professionals.

Evaluation undertaken of these courses indicated that the courses boosted participants' sense of confidence in their work; their interest and proficiency in the use of theory; and their sense of hopefulness (Frederico et al., 2016). Importantly, the courses also positively impacted participants' decision to stay in the sector. Staff also found their involvement in the courses highly fulfilling, with one member saying it was the best teaching experience they had had.

Implications of live knowledge for the practice of leaders in Child and Family Practice

The concept of live knowledge, being a new theory of knowledge, suggests new roles for leaders of Child and Family Practice organisations. These include helping practitioners understand not only what theories they are already drawing on but also how their theoretical knowledge might be evolving and what the catalysts for this might be.

Leaders would also assist practitioners in understanding that their 'knowledge work' extends beyond the attainment of practice wisdom to incorporate actual development of theoretical knowledge. This is one strategy by which practitioners might be encouraged to take more interest in theory as a whole. Leaders would also assist practitioners in understanding the different models for translating a particular theory into practice and how different approaches, in yielding different results, can in turn impact their thinking about the theory.

Leaders of live knowledge-informed organisations would also assist practitioners to share with others not just their knowledge per se but also their thinking around the processes of adapting and recreating knowledge and identifying its specific versus general utility. Their idea of the learning organisation would create more opportunities for discussion not only of theory but also of how practitioners can make more formal contributions to sector-level theoretical development.

Leaders would also take advantage of the fact that different contexts encourage different kinds of thinking processes and conceptualisations. They would, for example, allow theoretical discussions at the organisational level to occur in a variety of settings. Knowing that the conceptual environment also has a significant impact on the evolution of ideas, they would also alternate with whose ideas a discussion commenced.

Leaders of the live knowledge-informed learning organisation in the child and family domain would also ensure that dialogue is retained among themselves and the other two cultures of research and policy. One way they could achieve this is through collaboration around higher learning projects.

Conclusion

The insufficient use of theory by child and family practitioners and contact with researchers and policymakers can be remedied where organisational leaders adopt the principles of live knowledge. Live knowledge recognises that the 'shape' of individuals' knowledge is ever evolving; that context continually impacts, at the subtle and unconscious level, how individuals conceptualise and, subsequently, implement knowledge. This is in addition to any conscious, broader-based adjustments individuals make to their thinking. Acknowledging that all practitioners are themselves constant creators and adaptors of theoretical knowledge can encourage their more engaged relationship with it and creative implementation thereof. Emphasising practitioners' role in the development of theory can also increase the status of their overall knowledge, including vis-à-vis that of researchers, and encourage their interaction with the 'cultures' of research and policy. Leaders of child and family organisations therefore have a role in incorporating the idea of live knowledge into their organisational processes.

Key messages from the chapter

- Context impacts how individuals recall, conceptualise and use theoretical knowledge. In this way, knowledge about a given theory is being created slightly anew each time it is accessed. Thus, we can consider knowledge to be 'live'.
- The concept of live knowledge is especially relevant to the child and family sector given that this arena is otherwise characterised by volatility. There are constant changes within the circumstances of individual clients and clients as cohorts – and therefore what theories might, broadly, be considered relevant to practice – right through to within the policy environment.
- Practitioners, in constantly adjusting or recreating knowledge, can be said to be directly involved in the development of theory. Understanding this is likely to encourage practitioners' ongoing use of, and learning about, theory.
- That practitioners are involved in 'theory work' creates a rationale for the higher valuation of practitioner knowledge vis-à-vis research knowledge, and for stronger ongoing relationships between the three cultures of practice, research and policy.
- Leaders of child and family agencies need to incorporate live knowledge principles into the practice of their organisations.

Questions for further consideration

1. How does your organisation conceptualise knowledge development? Have you accounted for the range of sources that can impact how employees recall, conceptualise and implement their knowledge?
2. What strategies can you implement that will allow employees to consider the evolution of their knowledge and identify which changes in their thinking may have enduring utility for their own practice and/or the practice of their organisational or sector colleagues?
3. Do your reflective and supervision sessions also focus on changes to knowledge?
4. Can you identify which learning contexts are most conducive for employees' clear recall of theoretical knowledge and capacity for useful exchanges with each other or other organisations?
5. What mechanisms could you implement that would allow your organisation to have regular exchanges of thinking with academia and policymakers about knowledge per se?

References

Argyris, C., & Schön, D. (1996). *Organizational learning II: Theory, method, and practice.* Reading: Addison-Wesley.

Atkinson Consulting. (2008). *Development framework for child protection frontline managers: capabilities, foundation knowledge and skill, and work culture.* Melbourne: Department of Human Services.

Barratt, M. (2003). Organizational support for evidence-based practice within child and family social work: A collaborative study. *Child and Family Social Work*, 8, 143–150.

Beddoe, L. (2009). Creating continuous conversation: Social workers and learning organisations. *Social Work Education*, 28(7), 722–736.

Boroditsky, L. (2003). *Linguistic relativity*. In L. Nadel (Ed.), *Encyclopedia of cognitive science* (pp. 917–921). London: Wiley.

Brandon, M., Sidebotham, P., Ellis, C., Bailey, S., & Belderson, P. (2011). *Child and family practitioners' understanding of child development: Lessons learnt from a small sample of serious case reviews*. Research report DFE-RR110. London: Department for Education.

Casasanto, D., Boroditsky, L., Phillips, W., Greene, J., Goswami, S., Bocanegra-Thiel, S., & Gil, D. (2004). How deep are effects of language on thought? Time estimation in speakers of English, Indonesian, Greek, and Spanish. In K. Forbus, D. Gentner, & T. Regier (Eds.), *Proceedings of the 26th Annual Conference Cognitive Science Society* (pp. 575–580). Hillsdale, NJ: Erlbaum.

Clore, G., & Huntsinger, J. (2007). How emotions inform judgment and regulate thought. *Trends in Cognitive Sciences*, 9, 393–399.

D'Cruz, H., Gillingham, P., & Melendez, S. (2007). Reflexivity: a concept and its meanings for practitioners working with children and families. *Critical Social Work*, 8(1), 1–18.

D'Cruz, H., & Jones, M. (2004). *Social work research: Ethical and political contexts*. Thousand Oaks, CA: Sage.

Eraut, M. (1985). Knowledge creation and knowledge use in professional contexts. *Studies in Higher Education*, 10(2), 117–133.

Fargion, S. (2006). Thinking professional social work: Expertise and professional ideologies: Social workers' accounts of their practice. *Journal of Social Work*, 6(3), 255–273.

Fox, M., Martin, P., & Green, G. (2007). *Doing practitioner research*. London: Sage.

Frederico, M., Long, M., McPherson, L., McNamara, P., & Cameron, N. (2016). A consortium approach for child and family practice education. *Social Work Education: The International Journal*, 35(7), 780–793.

Gibbs, L., & Gambrill, E. (2002). Evidence-based practice: Counterarguments to objections. *Research on Social Work Practice*, 12, 452–476.

Gould, N. (2000). Becoming a learning organisation: A social work example. *Social Work Education: An International Journal*, 19(6), 585–596.

Gould, N., & Baldwin, M. (2004). *Social work, critical reflection and the learning organization*. Burlington, VT: Ashgate.

Gray, M., Plath, D., & Webb, S. A. (2009). *Evidence-based social work: A critical stance*. New York: Routledge.

Hammersley, M., & Gomm, R. (1997). Bias in social research. *Sociological Research Online*, 2(1). Retrieved from www.socresonline.org.uk/2/1/2.html

Holzer, P., Lewig, K., Bromfield, L. M., & Arney, F. (2007). *Research use in the Australian child and family welfare sector*. Melbourne: Australian Institute of Family Studies.

Hayes, S., Baena, E., Truong, T., & Cabeza, R. (2010). Neural mechanisms of context effects on face recognition: Automatic binding and context shift decrements. *Journal of Cognitive Neuroscience*, 22(11), 2541–2554.

Hayes, S., Nadel, L., & Ryan, L. (2007). The effect of scene context on episodic object recognition: Parahippocampal cortex mediates memory encoding and retrieval success. *Hippocampus*, 17, 873–889.

Johnson, C., Spicer, D., & Wallace, J. (2009). *An empirical model of the learning organization*. Bradford: Bradford University. Retrieved from www2.warwick.ac.uk/fac/soc/wbs/conf/olkc/archive/olkc6/papers/id_251.pdf

Jones, S., & Joss, R. (1995). Models of professionalism. In M. Yelloly & M. Henkel (Eds.), *Learning and teaching in social work: Towards reflective practice* (pp. 19–33). London: Jessica Kingsley.

Kahn, P., & O'Rourke, K. (2005). Understanding enquiry-based learning. In T. Barrett, I. Mac Labhrainn, & H. Fallon (Eds.), *Handbook of enquiry and problem-based learning* (pp. 1–12). Galway, Ireland: CELT.

Kessler, M. L., Gira, E., & Poertner, J. (2005). Moving best practice to evidence-based practice in child welfare. *Families in Society*, 86(2), 244–250.

Kihlstrom, J., Dorfman, J., & Park, L. (2007). Implicit and explicit memory and learning. In L. M. Velmans & S. Schneider (Eds.), *The Blackwell companion to consciousness* (pp. 525–539). Oxford: Blackwell.

Lewig, K., Arney, F., & Scott, D. (2006). Closing the research-policy and research-practice gaps: ideas for child and family services. *Family Matters*, 74, 12–19.

Lundeberg, M., Levin, H., & Harrington, H. L. (Eds.). (1999). *Who learns what from cases and how? The research base for teaching and learning with cases.* Mahwah, NJ: Erlbaum.

Marlow, C. (2001). *Research methods for generalist social work* (3rd ed.). New York: Wadsworth Brooks/Cole.

McCollum, J., & Catlett, C. (1997). Designing effective personnel preparation for early intervention: Theoretical frameworks. In P. J. Winton, J. A. McCollum, & C. Catlett (Eds.), *Reforming personnel preparation in early intervention: Issues, models, and strategies* (pp. 105–125). Baltimore, MD: Brookes.

Miles, C., & Hardman, E. (1998). State-dependent memory produced by aerobic exercise. *Ergonomics*, 41(1), 20–28.

Mullen, E., & Streiner, D.L. (2004). The evidence for and against evidence-based practice. *Brief Treatment and Crisis Intervention*, 4(2), 111–121.

Närhi, K. (2002). Transferable and negotiated knowledge: Constructing social work expertise for the future. *Journal of Social Work*, 2(3), 317–336.

Nevo, I., & Slonim-Nevo, V. (2011). The myth of evidence-based practice: Towards evidence-informed practice. *British Journal of Social Work*, 41, 1176–1197.

Osmond, J., & O'Connor, I. (2006). Use of theory and research in social work practice: Implications for knowledge-based practice. *Australian Social Work*, 59(1), 5–19.

Preston, L., Harvie, K., & Wallace, H. (2015). Inquiry-based learning in teacher education: A primary humanities example. *Australian Journal of Teacher Education*, 40(12), 73–85.

Prince, M., & Felder, R. (2007). The many faces of inductive teaching and learning. *Journal of College Science Teaching*, 36(5), 14–20.

Rutter, D., & Fisher, M. (2013). Knowledge transfer in social care and social work: Where is the problem? PSSRU Discussion Paper 2866. London: London Personal Social Services Research Unit. Retrieved from www.pssru.ac.uk/archive/pdf/dp2866.pdf

Sackett, D., Richardson, W., Rosenberg, W., & Haynes, R. (1997). *Evidence-based medicine: How to practice and teach EBM.* New York: Churchill Livingstone.

Senge, P. (1990). *The fifth discipline: The art and practice of the learning organization.* New York: Doubleday/Currency.

Shonkoff, J. (2000). Science, policy, and practice: Three cultures in search of a shared mission. *Child Development*, 71(1), 181–187.

Shlonsky, A., & Ballan, M. (2011). Evidence-informed practice in child welfare: Definitions, challenges and strategies. *Developing Practice: The Child, Youth and Family Work Journal*, 29, 25–42.

Siemer, M. (2001). Mood-specific effects on appraisal and emotion judgements. *Cognition and Emotion*, 15(4), 453–485.

Small, S. A. (2005). Bridging research and practice in the family and human sciences. *Family Relations*, 54(2), 320–334.

Smith, S. M., Glenberg, A., & Bjork, R. A. (1978). Environmental context and human memory. *Memory & Cognition*, 6(4), 342–353.

Snyder, P., & McWilliam, P. (2003). Using case method of instruction effectively in early intervention personnel preparation. *Infants & Young Children*, 16(4), 284–295.

Spronken-Smith, R. (2012). Experiencing the process of knowledge creation: The nature and use of inquiry-based learning in higher education. Paper prepared for International Colloquium on Practices for Academic Inquiry, University of Otago, New Zealand. Retrieved from https://akoaotearoa.ac.nz/sites/default/files/u14/IBL%20-%20Report%20- %20Appendix%20A%20-%20Review.pdf

Stevens, I., & Cox, P. (2008). Complexity theory: Developing new understandings of child protection in field settings and in residential care. *British Journal of Social Work*, 38(7), 1320–1326.

Strydom, H. (2013). An evaluation of the purposes of research in social work. *Social Work/ Maatskaplikewerk*, 49(2), 149–164.

Walter, I., Nutley, S., & Davies, S. (2003). *Research impact: A cross sector review*. St. Andrews: University of St Andrews, Research Unit for Research Utilisation.

Walter, I., Nutley, S., Percy-Smith, J., McNeish, D., & Frost, S. (2004). *Improving the use of research in social care practice*. London: Social Care Institute for Excellence.

Webb, S. (2001). Some considerations on the validity of evidence-based practice in social work. *British Journal of Social Work*, 31, 57–79.

Woike, B., Bender, M., & Besner, N. (2009). Implicit motivational states influence memory: Evidence for incidental learning in personality. *Journal of Research in Personality*, 43, 39–48.

4

DEVELOPING EFFECTIVE LEADERSHIP IN CHILD AND FAMILY PRACTICE

Types of leadership

Margarita Frederico

Acknowledgements

The author acknowledges the contribution of the following leaders who were interviewed for this chapter: Dr Allison Cox (Director Berry Street Take Two), Angela Forbes (General Manager UnitingCare Australia), Julie Edwards (CEO, Jesuit Social Services) and Paul McDonald (CEO, Anglicare Victoria).

Introduction

Leadership is no longer the province of the sole leader who, with heroic behaviour, leads followers to achieve seemingly impossible outcomes. Leadership is now much more complex than in the past. Moreover, contemporary culture requires an inclusive, almost democratic, approach to leadership. Few followers will accept a leader's direction without holding an understanding of the purpose of the action being taken and the outcome sought. It can be argued that in human services effective leadership is at least as challenging as leadership in other areas, if not more so. This is highlighted by Tate (2009), who states, "In child protection work there is a complex and unpredictable human system of interpersonal relationships ... there are procedures to follow, of course; but each family situation is unique, bringing a need for discretionary judgment and a tailored response" (p. 44). In Child and Family Practice, challenges and complexity arise from what is uncertain and unknowable in relation to the lives of vulnerable children, families and communities who are engaged with this sector. As Austin (1995, as cited in Rank & Hutchinson, 2000) states, "the human services executive operates under conditions of ambiguity and paradox" (p. 488). The level of ambiguity inherent to the sector is one reason that positive outcomes with clients demand strong leadership. The child and family sector is subject to legislation and policies which aim to provide greater certainty in practice implementation. However, as all practitioners and leaders in the sector are aware, whilst legislation and policies provide guidelines for decisions, these policies and guidelines need interpretation when applied in practice. Good decisions in practice are made through utilising discretion. Decisions should be based on the best information available and the knowledge and skill of the practitioner (practice wisdom), within a legislation and policy frame, and meeting the goals set by the organisation. Strong leadership is required to guide frontline workers in these decisions. Due to the complexity and inherent uncertainties of Child and Family Practice, provision of manualised policies and procedures provide essential but not sufficient guidance for practitioners.

In reviewing the approaches of formal enquiries into child protection, Munro (2009, para. 4) suggests that "we might consider if there is any point in repeatedly asking why staff do not follow procedures, and ask instead what hampers them from doing so". Munro was highlighting the importance of moving the focus away from blaming the practitioner for negative outcomes and recognising the importance of the role of the system in providing support to the practitioner. In the Munro Review report (Munro, 2011), she identified the importance of leadership that challenges current organisational systems and leads change to build organisations which support the good practice of the workers.

The focus of this book is about leadership within the different contexts of Child and Family Practice and within different theoretical frameworks for practice. This chapter focuses on leadership theories and skills that inform and create effective leadership in Child and Family Practice.

Preparation for leadership in Child and Family Practice

Leaders in social work and other disciplines in Child and Family Practice frequently have to rely on their own practice experience and practice wisdom to guide their leadership approach. Leadership is rarely taught in formal Child and Family Practice education programs (see Chapter 6). Yet it is practitioners who are promoted to leadership positions. The Graduate Diploma in Child and Family Practice Leadership (see Preface; Chapter 3) is one educational program which was designed around leadership and provided to aspiring Child and Family Practice leaders (Frederico, Long, McNamara, McPherson, & Cameron, 2014). The focus of the Diploma was on learning leadership within the Child and Family Practice context. The organisational context was held as a critical component to be addressed. The developing leaders who were employed in the child and family sector learnt about leadership in a way that they could relate immediately to their practice (see Chapter 2).

Building on the work of Hall & Donnell (1979), Fisher (2009) highlights that "managers who conform to the tenets of one leadership theory or another versus none at all achieve more in their own eyes and the eyes of their workers" (p. 347). However, McDonald and Chenoweth (2009) suggest that social work, a key profession in Child and Family Practice, "has been less proactive and even reluctant in taking on leadership as an issue for theory and practice" (p. 105). This chapter aims to address this gap.

Theories of leadership

The concepts of leadership and management are often used interchangeably, but there are differences. The focus of leadership is change, and the focus of management is implementation. Heifetz and Linsky (2002) note that both leadership and management are required to meet the desired outcomes of service. The relationship between the two concepts in leadership is identified by Wooding (2007), who states that, "in practice, managers spend some of their time leading and leaders spend some of their time managing. Deciding within a situational context when to manage or to lead is the critical factor determining the success of each" (p. 42).

This chapter is written with the assumption that in Child and Family Practice a person will also take on management activities in the exercise of leadership. Child and Family Practice personnel in leadership positions are continually faced with the tension between leadership and management. Whilst promoting a vision of change and hope for families, leaders need to ensure that workers operate within legislation and policy guidelines. Leadership theories provide the leader with knowledge and skills to help the worker focus on analysing the case situation and implementing the intervention whilst ensuring the safety of the child.

Leadership theories have developed over time, usually reflecting the cultural context of the time. A traditional list of leadership theories from a chronological perspective reflects changes in society and corresponding changes in expectations of leaders. Such a list normally commences with the Great Man theory of leadership, first promoted by philosopher and writer Thomas Carlyle in 1840 (Carlyle, 1888), or the born to lead approach (Grinin, 2010), where one person is a leader because of their naturally held characteristics for leadership and the ability to achieve change through leadership.

Other early leadership theories which still have currency today are trait theories (Stogdill, 1958; Goldberg, 1990), which hold that individuals have to possess certain naturally given traits to become leaders. These trait theories led to the design and implementation of leadership courses which focused on developing the desired leadership skills. Contingency theories (Fiedler, 1967) hold that the type of leader required is contingent on the situation to be addressed. A variation of contingency leadership is situational leadership (Hersey & Blanchard, 1972), where the leader determines their approach dependent on the situation. Other leadership theories include behavioural theories of leadership (Follett, 1927), where individuals are trained or educated to be leaders and to learn the traits and skills that earlier theories held were possessed by natural born leaders.

Over time, theories of leadership and management have been integrated. These theories include transactional and transformational theories of leadership (Bass, 1985; Burns, 1978). It is transformational leadership theories and distributive leadership (Pearce, 2015) which have been claimed as appropriate for Child and Family Practice. However, before accepting these theories as the most relevant to the sector, it is important to explore the issues to be addressed in Child and Family Practice in relation to leadership as this provides an understanding of what is required of today's leadership.

The value of leadership

Why is it that leadership is important? What it is that leaders can contribute to a situation? These questions are particularly relevant in the service industry. It could be argued that as practitioners have the knowledge and skills to practise, they should be able to operate without requiring leadership. However, as has been identified in the literature (e.g. Rank & Hutchinson, 2000; Gellis, 2001) and in formal enquiries (e.g. Munro, 2011), leadership has a crucial role in supporting good practice. The assumption in this chapter is that leadership is required to support staff to achieve good outcomes with their clients.

One element of leadership that supports staff has been discussed above: that is, assisting workers to address the complexity and uncertainty inherent in practice itself. For example, a challenge for the worker is to identify what is a 'good' outcome in a given situation. This question is not simple in Child and Family Practice. The growing emphasis on child wellbeing as an outcome requires that it is the child's best interests that drive the intervention. However, the practitioner has to interpret the child's best interests in each situation. Wellbeing is an individual measure and, whilst there are wellbeing indicators, application of the measures in each situation requires an ability to assess the situation. For example, a 'good' outcome in one case may be the removal of a child to out-of-home care to ensure their safety, whilst in another situation it is keeping the child with their own family. Moreover, conditions do not remain static, and practitioner decision makers always need to have alternative intervention plans to be ready to respond in a timely manner if client circumstances change. The application of outcome indicators still requires discretion and judgement from the individual practitioner. Alongside this is the importance of utilising evidence-based and evidence-informed practice. It is analysis and judgement, as well as the practitioner's skills, knowledge and behaviour, that will achieve the best outcome for the child.

Leadership impacts on more than direct practice in the organisation. It impacts on worker satisfaction, on recruitment and retention of good staff, and on worker morale and organisational culture. It also impacts on the reputation of the organisation, its ability to influence powerful stakeholders and promote change in the social issues bringing children into the sector. Leadership also impacts on fundraising and achieving appropriate budgets in government organisations.

Organisational support for leadership

Leaders in Child and Family Practice are both guided and at times constrained by government and institutional policies. Legislation provides the legal framework, and government policies provide directions for programs to implement the legislation. However, as noted above, these can only guide decisions, and application of interventions in the real world requires judgement. It is the leader who can support practitioners to make the best decisions with families. For leadership to be effective and achieve the overall goals and mission of an organisation – which in Child and

Family Practice should be the wellbeing of children and families – the organisation needs to be structured in a way to support leadership. As the Sanctuary Model has demonstrated (Bloom & Farragher, 2013), a whole of organisation approach is most effective in supporting good practice. A whole of organisation approach is one in which all components of an organisation – including its governance, staff and clients – are committed to the values and purpose of the organisation. This approach does not make leadership less important. Rather, it highlights the role leaders can play when supported by organisational systems. Moreover, a whole of organisation approach to leadership supports the implementation of a trauma-informed approach (Bloom & Farragher, 2013), a desired approach for many organisations. This approach recognises that trauma affects not only the clients who have experienced trauma, but also the staff and the entire organisation. It is not only the leader who needs to be aware of this; it is also the role of the supervisors to provide support to practitioners. The role of supervisors is discussed in greater depth in Chapter 5. Another organisation-wide approach is Heroic Leadership, based upon the Jesuit religious order as described by Lowney (2003). This theory promotes the role of a values-driven culture with a clear organisational mission which is known and accepted by all staff of the organisation.

Leadership theories for Child and Family Practice

Transformational leadership approaches have been identified as the most effective and also the most preferred by workers in social work (Rank & Hutchison, 2000; Gellis, 2001; Tafvelin, Hyvo, & Westerberg, 2014), nursing (Cummings et al., 2010) and teaching (Lynch, 2014b). Originally developed by Burns (1978) and later expanded by Bass (1985), it has been updated by numerous authors.

Transformational leadership is described by Bass (1985) as leadership that motivates others (staff) to ignore self-interests and work for the greater good of the organisation to achieve significant outcomes for the organisation and its clients. It is also about motivating others to do more than they originally intended, and often more than they thought they were capable of doing. To achieve outcomes within a transformational leadership approach, the leader focuses on the development of the individual worker. With this approach, leaders also seek to develop good insight into their own ontology (personal values and beliefs) and ways of working. This is needed to be able to take an unbiased approach and help workers reflect on their own approach.

Transformational leadership and neoliberalism

Although transformational leadership has been shown to be a preferred and effective leadership approach in social work (Rank & Hutchison, 2000; Gellis, 2001; Tafvelin et al., 2014), there is scepticism as to whether this approach can counteract the overriding impact of neoliberalism in management. Neoliberalism introduced a new set of values based upon market forces. As Lynch (2014a, p. 5) notes:

When managerialist practices achieve hegemonic control within organizations, they parasitize and weaken those very values on which the organization depends [and] ... the difficulty with managerialism is that it does not just prioritize efficiency, it suppresses other organizational values so that they become incidental to the running of public bodies.

A challenge that faces leaders in Child and Family Practice is how they can use transformational leadership in the light of the new managerialism whose key features include: "an emphasis on outputs over inputs; the close monitoring of employee performance and the encouragement of self-monitoring through the widespread use of performance indicators, rankings, league tables and performance management" (Lynch, 2014b, para. 3). Thus new managerialism ignores the important role of a strong, value-based organisational culture which supports workers as they are confronted with the trauma and challenges of Child and Family Practice. Findings from interviews with current leaders, which are presented later in this chapter, demonstrate that it is possible for leaders to neutralise the negative components of new management.

Challenges to be addressed by leaders in Child and Family Practice

New managerialism is not the only challenge to leadership in this field. The way the environment supports or does not support the work of Child and Family Practice is an important factor in the effectiveness of the work and impacts upon the influence of the leader.

The lack of a coordinating framework between the service sectors – including child and adult mental health services, family violence and substance abuse sectors – increases the difficulties of Child and Family Practice. Frequently, it appears that the onus is on child and family workers to effectively negotiate across these sectors for their clients. Thus the leader's attention to external stakeholders to promote effective working between sector boundaries is important.

Another area of increased complexity is the seemingly exponential development of knowledge within the area of neurobiology. Understanding the area of trauma and neurobiology of the brain adds to the practice knowledge required of the worker. The need to know and utilise evidence-based practice and keep ahead of new developments can be challenging for workers. At the same time, this developing area of knowledge assists in explaining the impact of trauma and abuse on the child, and can guide interventions. Leadership can support practitioners to hold and utilise this knowledge and improve outcomes for clients.

Leaders are important in supporting workers as they deal with the emotionally charged practice context and management of their own responses to the case situations they are dealing with. Morrison (2007) highlights the impact of trauma and emotional aspects of the work on practitioners. Leaders are responsible for the climate of the organisation. The organisational culture can also be what staff are attracted to, and can support recruitment of good staff as well as influencing retention of staff.

All of these elements have to be addressed by the leader in Child and Family Practice. The work of the sector takes place within a legislation framework which is open to change, including changing political philosophies as different political parties win government and introduce new policies. Another external challenge is the role of the media in conveying messages to the public regarding the perceived success or failure of Child and Family Practice. It is the leader's role to be aware of the impact of the media and to 'protect' workers from negative portrayals of Child and Family Practice. Rather than be reactive to negative stories, the leader needs to take the initiative and present the positive message of the work, using the media to inform the community of the issues which need to be addressed. It is the role of the leader to translate the purpose of Child and Family Practice to government and to the public. The challenge to leadership is seen in the situation where the practice itself, whilst it needs to be informed by research and current knowledge of the wellbeing of children and families, still remains "messy, unpredictable and chaotic", influenced by "organisational hierarchies" and yet a "human, active and contingent process" (Hughes & Wearing, 2007, p. 78).

An approach to effective leadership in Child and Family Practice

For a leader in Child and Family Practice, juggling the demands and tensions described above can be perceived as an impossible task. However, as many leaders have demonstrated, effective leadership in Child and Family Practice is both possible and influential in achieving positive outcomes for children and families. There are a number of publications based on research which give guidance on leadership in this area. One example is the concept of engaged leadership developed by Wooding (2007). The elements of this approach include:

> Working collaboratively and in partnership between the prescribed boundaries and beyond the traditional authority of public service organisations;
>
> Engaging stakeholder communities including the public service workforce, the service user, other providers and the citizen in a co-productive, meaningful relationship;
>
> Developing new technologies to manage the tension and dynamic between risk, governance, creativity and innovation;
>
> Finding ways to make sense of the, process for others and to influence outcomes and meaning beyond the realm of immediate control. (p. 44)

There are also other elements identified in the literature which have relevance to leadership in Child and Family Practice. The roles of emotional intelligence and social intelligence are important attributes of leaders (Goleman, 2005; Goleman, 2006). Emotional intelligence addresses the importance of knowledge of self, an element in transformational leadership styles. Social intelligence is about understanding and collaborating with others. This concept can be seen to fit with engaging others and in the relationship theories of leadership that are transformational approaches. More recently, Goleman (2013) has been promoting the value of mindfulness in leadership. Mindfulness is a Buddhist practice of being in touch with one's self and present surroundings. It requires reflection of the individual's own immediate experience. Goleman (2013) has identified an important role of mindfulness (focus) in effective leadership.

Another type of leadership which has relevance for Child and Family Practice is distributive leadership (Spillane, 2006). Distributive leadership holds that it is important for leadership to be distributed across the organisation so that individuals with expertise in relation to specific areas of practice can take the lead when that expertise is required. As the need for specialised knowledge increases in relation to child development and the impact of trauma and attachment problems, it is important for the leader to facilitate experts to take the lead in decisions in their areas of specialisation. This leadership approach is particularly useful in providing support for direct service practitioners who strive to utilise evidence-informed practice but find it challenging to keep up to date with the knowledge. Finally leadership in Child and Family Practice needs to find a way to bring clients into the change process as key stakeholders. The children and their families are key stakeholders in Child and Family Practice, and the leader needs to ensure that their voices are heard.

The leadership approaches required in Child and Family Practice fit well with an approach to leadership identified by Groysberg and Slind (2012), who noted how modern organisations are impacted by globalisation and new technologies. They state that changes in how companies create value and interact with customers require a new approach to leadership. This new approach is identified as effective communication. According to Groysberg and Slind (2012), the new leadership is a 'leadership conversation'. They identify the form of this conversation as being personal and direct, reflecting value, trust and integrity. The focus is on open communication and an organisational system that staff experience as supportive.

Implications for leadership: leadership in practice

Theoretical discussion of leadership is important to provide a basic foundation for understanding the concepts and dynamics of leadership. However, how this knowledge is translated and new learning for leadership is identified provides another key to understanding how to lead effectively in this sector.

Four current leaders in Child and Family Practice were invited to individually respond to six questions focusing on their approach to and understanding of leadership. The leaders interviewed were: Dr Allison Cox of Berry Street Take Two, a trauma-informed therapeutic program for children traumatised by abuse; Angela Forbes, General Manager, Eastern Victoria, UnitingCare Australia, one of the country's largest providers of community services; Julie Edwards, CEO Jesuit Social Services, a social change organisation working at the sharp end of social justice; and Paul McDonald, CEO Anglicare Victoria and former Executive Director of the Children, Youth and Family Division for the DHS. All of these interviewees are known in the sector as effective leaders. The interview questions sought to explore the respondents' use of leadership theories; their leadership style and major challenges to leadership; how they evaluated their leadership impact; their perception of the influence of leadership on client outcomes; and messages drawn from their experiences for aspiring leaders. The purpose of these conversations was to explore knowledge translation in the realm of leadership and the learning identified through the practice of leadership.

Theoretical foundation

All four leaders had moved beyond simply working with a specific leadership theory. Whilst they had all undertaken specific training in leadership, as one leader put it: "The more expert you become, the less able to articulate the theories!" However, without the leaders necessarily naming transformational leadership, elements of this theory were present in the descriptions each gave of their leadership approach. These elements included a focus on development of staff, modelling desired behaviour and values, and self-reflection. This approach was identified as key to a relational approach to leadership. Two leaders specifically mentioned other formal theories: one being the Ignatian, which is based on the leadership philosophy of St Ignatius Loyola, the founder of the Jesuits; and the other being psychoanalytic. As one leader stated, leadership theories could provide knowledge, but "unless you can make these purposeful to people and relevant to their beliefs" it will be difficult to be effective. Learning leadership styles from leaders who had been admired was important for some leaders. The role of the leader in setting the organisational culture was identified as a core component of leadership. As identified in the following discussion, the style of these leaders is similar to the leadership conversations described by Groysberg and Slind (2012).

All four leaders held the belief that leadership requires attention to multiple areas of organisational life. It was suggested by one leader that a risk for leaders is to focus too much on administrative processes (management) to the detriment of the vision and policies. Whilst the leader should not ignore the organisational systems and administrative processes, the reality is that the staff learn these quickly through documentation and supervision. "It is the leader's role to make the system humane for the worker", and thus for the clients. Being aware of the environment and managing the message in the media and 'speaking the truth to power' (that is to political and other influential and decision-making leaders in the community) were seen as important areas for the leader to focus on in providing effective leadership and in advocating for staff and for clients.

Leadership style

Each leader described their leadership approach differently; however, the similarities were stronger than the differences. Whilst it was clear that each leader had developed their own theory which guided a purposeful leadership approach, the following elements could be identified in the approach of each. The elements of effective leadership that were identified include:

- *Leadership is relational.* Relationship was seen as the core of leadership. The relational aspect was specifically discussed, and was also present in the examples each provided to demonstrate good leadership. An example of good leadership was the importance for the leader to know and be known by staff. It was held that the leader should have an understanding of what motivates staff, and for staff to know what motivates the leader. This element includes recognising that staff in Child and Family Practice will have their own vision for the sector and want to make a difference. It is important that staff can see how their vision can fit with the mission of the organisation. Two leaders specifically mentioned how they utilised orientation programs for new staff to provide the key messages of the vision and mission of the organisation, inviting staff to find their place in the organisation
- *Positive values and behaviour.* The role of the leader in modelling positive values and behaviour was constant in the presentation of each leadership style. Modelling congruence, integrity and desired behaviour was identified as important in influencing staff behaviour and outcomes for clients. Being prepared to engage in difficult conversations with staff when necessary was also recognised as an important part of being congruent and modelling value-driven behaviour.
- *Achieving trust.* Integral to the relational approach for the leader was gaining the trust of the staff: 'trust has to be won and is easily lost' was an important aspect of effective leadership. To achieve trust, the leader needs to be congruent and authentic in their own behaviour, 'walking the walk' of their own values and ensuring that the organisational system, through managers and supervisors, encourages openness and feedback.
- *Reflection and knowledge of self.* What was notable was that all the leaders were aware of their own values and how these led their work. Engagement in reflective practice was an important component of their leadership styles. Each was very self-aware within their role of leader. Each spoke of a strong commitment to the underlying mission of their organisation and to society. It also appeared that each of the leaders was practising mindfulness, even if they did not mention this concept. In part, the context of child and family and the vision to achieve a more just community were drivers in their behaviour.
- *Developing a positive organisational culture.* Developing and maintaining a culture which fosters hope and optimism were outcomes of modelling desired values and behaviours. It was considered that this provided a positive structure and framework that supported staff in undertaking the challenging work of Child and Family Practice. Ensuring the climate created also provided light and shade and that staff could enjoy their work and have fun was suggested by

one leader as acknowledging the importance of connectedness in ways of working.

- *Organisational structure.* The four leaders also referred to the importance of the organisational structure supporting the work of the organisation (see, e.g., Munro, 2011), and the crucial role of managers and supervisors. The leaders identified that managers and supervisors needed to understand the bigger picture of the work and its purpose in the community and of the role of the organisation so that they could assist other staff to do so. The leaders' acknowledgment of the difficult and emotionally demanding practice in child and family work was a driver in striving to provide an organisational structure that was supportive and which facilitated staff to achieve their own potential. The leaders also highlighted that staff needed to feel safe to speak up if something was going wrong.
- *Investing in information and knowledge sharing.* Investing in training for all levels of the organisation, and appropriately sharing knowledge with boards of management/directors, operational and administrative staff and volunteers are crucial to promote a whole organisation approach and achieve organisational goals.
- *Attention to specific requirements.* There were also specific behaviours which leaders took on in their work. These included managing clinical risk, fundraising and developing a leadership team.

Knowing if your leadership is effective

The leaders' ways of knowing if their leadership was effective included self-reflection and a commitment to feedback from all levels of staff. It was seen as important that the organisational structure independently supported this feedback. However, as one leader stated, if you are effective, the feedback "should not tell you what you don't already know". The degree of staff optimism and willingness to take on new challenges were identified by one leader as indicators of the leader's effectiveness. All leaders acknowledged that mistakes will be made; however, mistakes could open creative ground. As one leader expressed it, "the only mistake is not learning from mistakes".

Challenges to leadership

When asked to identify challenges to leadership in Child and Family Practice the leaders interviewed responded by focusing on the challenge of supporting staff in a difficult environment. Recognition of the impact of trauma and the awareness of unmet needs on workers influenced the leaders' approach. Examples of how this challenge was addressed by leaders included those relating to the leaders' response to significant negative outcomes for clients. Leaders identified the importance of actively supporting staff as well as exploring the factors that led to the incident. Assisting staff to work within their sphere of influence was seen as a way of supporting staff to not become overwhelmed by unmet needs in the sector.

Does leadership make a difference for clients?

As one leader stated, "Leadership is incredibly important at all levels." There was a strong expression that leadership makes a difference for clients in Child and Family Practice, and that this is the aim of leadership. As one leader noted, it was important that throughout the organisation there was a line of sight from the vision to all areas and activities of the organisation. This trajectory should be documented in program logic. It was also suggested that everyone in the organisation needs to take a leadership role in their area. Leadership can also influence the practice of evidence-informed practice. If staff feel safe and know the vision of the organisation they are more able to implement evidence-informed practice. If staff have realistic levels of confidence in their work they can work better with clients, which can then lead to better client outcomes. Moreover, the sector requires advocacy for staff and clients, and this requires leaders to model advocacy to staff.

Messages to new and current leaders

The interviews concluded by asking each leader what messages they would give to aspiring leaders based upon their leadership experiences. These included:

- It is important for each person to discover what leadership approach works for them.
- Be congruent and behave according to your values. Congruency is essential.
- Transparency is not always possible as organisations go through changes. It is important that staff can trust the leader to be true to organisational values.
- Be well informed.
- Recognise the importance of relationships in getting all tasks done.
- Make connections internally and externally – all actions are taken within the context of relationships.
- Value diversity – listen to feedback and act from a place of good intent. Do not be defensive. Be conscious of your response to feedback. Always ask yourself if your response is driven more by your own career ambitions rather than the mission and vision of the organisation and your values which you promote in the organisation.
- Be bold and courageous – fight for what is important.
- Hold your own vision of what you want to achieve.
- Understand that work is a social environment. Staff need colour and movement. People need to have fun at work.
- Recognise that all staff come into the sector wanting to do well and make things happen positively for their clients. Not all will gain senior leadership positions, but all still want to make a difference.
- Advocacy for clients and for staff is important.
- Staff wellbeing is crucial to ensure provision of high-quality services.

- Leaders evaluating not only the outcome of their leadership but also what they do and how they do it are critical leadership behaviour.
- Do more to engage consumers and find new ways to assist clients to be heard in the services system. Voices of children are often devalued, and it is the leader's role to ensure the child's voice is heard.

Summary

To summarise the style of these leaders is to identify that they were in constant authentic conversation with their staff and external stakeholders, and strove to be connected to those in their networks. Their leadership styles, whilst demonstrating elements of transformational leadership, also had elements of distributive leadership. Elements of emotional intelligence and social intelligence were also present. This analysis suggests that theories can be useful in providing direction for the child and family leader. However, more is required. By identifying effective leadership as an authentic conversation, Groysberg & Slind (2012) provide a good conceptualisation to apply to effective leadership in this sector. Engagement in self-reflection, modelling values and behaviour, and being courageous for staff and clients, are all aspects of effective leadership.

Key messages from this chapter

- Knowledge of leadership styles and theories are important in developing an effective leadership approach in Child and Family Practice.
- A whole of organisation approach is required to support effective leadership.
- Leaders need to be reflective and able to model this behaviour to their workers.
- A relational leadership approach, such as a transformational approach, has been shown to be preferred and effective in Child and Family Practice. A relational approach can assist in neutralising the negative elements of New Management.
- Participatory and distributive leadership approaches both recognise the high degree of complexity of Child and Family Practice, and the degree of specialised expert knowledge which is required to keep up with knowledge developments.
- Effective leadership can bring results in all areas of practice and organisational work. It supports the best outcomes for the client, not only in direct practice but also in facilitating a positive culture and encouraging recruitment and retention of good staff.
- A trauma-informed approach is beneficial as it facilitates engagement with the characteristics of the clientele.
- Leadership needs to be taught to Child and Family Practice workers. The high degree of complexity which leaders in this area have to address cannot be learnt solely through the experience of undertaking good practice.

Questions for further consideration

1.   How do you describe the leadership approach in your organisation? What are the theoretical foundations of the approach?
2.   How does your leadership promote safety in the organisation and support staff to reach their potential?
3.   Is there an identifiable trajectory from organisational vision to practice and to client outcomes in your organisation?
4.   What is an example of a good leadership conversation in your organisation?

References

Austin, D. (1995). Management overview. In R.L. Edwards (Ed.), *Encyclopaedia of social work* (19th ed., pp. 1642–1658). Washington, DC: NASW Press.

Bloom, S., & Farragher, B. (2013). *Restoring sanctuary: A new operating system for trauma informed organisations.* New York: Oxford University Press.

Bass, B.M. (1985) *Leadership and performance beyond expectations.* New York: Free Press.

Burns, J.M. (1978). *Leadership.* New York: Harper & Row.

Carlyle, Thomas. (1888). *On heroes, hero-worship and the heroic in history.* New York: Fredrick A. Stokes & Brother.

Cummings, G.C., MacGregor, T., Davey, M., Lee, H., Wong, C.A., Lo, E., Muise, M., & Stafford, E. (2010). Leadership styles and outcome patterns for the nursing workforce and work environment: A systematic review. *International Journal of Nursing Studies, 47,* 363–385.

Fiedler, F.E. (1967). *A theory of leadership effectiveness.* New York: McGraw-Hill.

Fisher, E.A. (2009). Motivation and leadership in social work management: A review of theories and related studies. *Administration in Social Work, 33*(4), 347–367. doi:10.1080/03643100902769160

Frederico, M., Long, M., McNamara, P., McPherson, L., & Cameron, N. (2014). *An evaluation of the graduate certificate in Child and Family Practice and Graduate Diploma in Child and Family Practice Leadership: A study of an academe and industry partnership.* Bundoora, Australia: Department of Human Services Victoria and La Trobe University.

Follett, M. (1927). Leader and expert. Paper given in the Bureau of Personnel Administration annual conference series, April and November. Reprinted in E. Fox & L. Urwick, *Dynamic administration: The collected papers of Mary Parker Follett* (pp. 212–234). New York: Hippocrene Books, 1973.

Gellis, Z.D. (2001). Social work perceptions of transformational and transactional leadership in health care. *Social Work Research, 25*(1), 17–25.

Goldberg, L. (1990). An alternative 'description of personality': The big five factor structure. *Journal of Personality and Social Psychology, 59,* 1216–1229.

Goleman, D. (2005). *Emotional Intelligence.* New York, NY: Random House.

Goleman, D. (2006). *Social intelligence: The new science of human relationships.* New York, NY: Random House.

Goleman, D. (2013). *Focus: The hidden driver of excellence.* London, UK: Bloomsbury.

Grinin, L. (2010). The role of an individual in history: A reconsideration. *Social Evolution & History, 9*(2), 95–136.

Groysberg, B., & Slind, M. (2012). Leadership is a conversation. *Harvard Business Review, 90*(6), 76–84.

Hall, J., & Donnell, S.M. (1979). Managerial achievement: The personal side of behavioural theory. *Human Relations*, 32(1), 77–101.

Heifetz, R., & Linsky, M. (2002). *Leadership on the line: Staying alive through the dangers of leadership.* Boston, MA: Harvard Business School Press.

Hersey, P., & Blanchard, K.H. (1972). *Management of organizational behaviour utilizing human resources* (2nd ed.). Englewood Cliffs, NJ: Prentice-Hall.

Hughes, M., & Wearing, M. (2007). *Organisations and management in social work.* Los Angeles, CA: Sage.

Lowney, C. (2003). *Heroic leadership: Best practices from a 450-year-old company that changed the world.* Chicago, IL: Loyola.

Lynch, K. (2014a). New managerialism: The impact on education. *Concept*, 5(3), 1–11. Retrieved from http://concept.lib.ed.ac.uk/index.php/Concept/article/viewFile/271/255

Lynch, K. (2014b, 16 September). New managerialism in education: The organisational form of neoliberalism [Blog post]. Retrieved from www.opendemocracy.net/kathleen-lynch/ 'new-managerialism'-in-education-organisational-form-of-neoliberalism

McDonald, C., & Chenoweth, L. (2009). Leadership: A crucial ingredient in unstable times. *Social Work & Society*, 7(1), 102–112.

Morrison, T. (2007). Emotional intelligence, emotion and social work: Context, characteristics, complications and contribution. *British Journal of Social Work*, 37(2), 245–263.

Munro, E. (2009, 4 November). Beyond the blame culture. *The Guardian.* Retrieved from www.theguardian.com/commentisfree/2009/nov/03/serious-case-review-child-p rotection

Munro, E. (2011). *The Munro review of Child Protection: Final report. A child-centred system.* London: Department for Education.

Pearce, C. (2015). The future of leadership: Combining vertical and shared leadership to transform knowledge work. In B. Shamir (Ed.), *Emerging Approaches to Leadership.* Vol. 1, *Collective Leadership.* London: Sage.

Rank, M.G., & Hutchison, W.S. (2000). An analysis of leadership within the social work profession. *Journal of Social Work Education*, 36(3), 487–502.

Stogdill, R. (1958). Personal factors associated with leadership: A survey of the literature. In C. Brown & T. Cohn (Eds.), *The study of leadership.* Danville, IL: The Interstate Printer and Publishers Inc.

Spillane, J.P. (2006). *Distributed leadership.* San Francisco, CA: Jossey-Bass.

Tafvelin, S., Hyvonen, U., & Westerberg, K. (2014). Transformational leadership in the social work context: The importance of leader continuity and co-worker support. *British Journal of Social Work*, 44(4), 886–904.

Tate, W. (2009, 10 November). Sometimes it's the workplace that's stupid, not the staff. *The Guardian.* Retrieved from www.theguardian.com/commentisfree/2009/nov/11/systems-procedures-management-child-protection

Wooding, N. (2007). Engaged leadership: The new public service managerialism. *Journal of Finance and Management in Public Services*, 7(1), 39–51.

5

LEADERSHIP AT TEAM MANAGER LEVEL

Lynne McPherson

Introduction

This chapter considers key messages from the theoretical and research literature in relation to supervisors of Child and Family Practice teams, also known in some agencies as coordinators or team leaders. Considering the contemporary context, the unique aspects of the role of team supervisor in child protection practice are explored. Issues of role ambiguity and role tension emerge as key considerations where, in spite of international moves toward preventative, more holistic practice in this field (Munro, 2008; Munro, 2011; Wonnacott, 2012), the reality may be a demand for increased accountability and reporting. These can be experienced as onerous and a detraction from reflective practice. It is within this complex and contested context that team leaders are charged with the responsibility of leading and developing their practitioners, requiring an awareness of the socio-political, community and organisational context within which they operate. Having presented and discussed the supervision literature and the socio-political context within which the supervisor operates, the chapter concludes with key considerations for contemporary supervisory practice.

Definitions and key terms

The terms 'supervisor' and 'team leader' are used interchangeably throughout the chapter to denote those professionals engaged in the management and supervision of a team of practitioners engaged in Child and Family Practice. The terms 'child protection' and 'Child and Family Practice' are used interchangeably to denote case work practice with vulnerable children and their families. This includes statutory child protection practice and prevention and support practices undertaken by government or non-government organisations (NGOs).

Theorising supervision

Supervision in Child and Family Practice is a 'hot topic', with a wealth of literature having been published this century. The majority of these are primarily theoretical texts (Brown & Bourne, 1996; Carroll, 2008; Davys & Beddoe, 2010; Gardner, 2006; Morrison, 2005; Wonnacott, 2012). Models influencing contemporary supervision include those of reflective practice and critically reflective supervision (Carroll, 2008; Gardner, 2006; Wonnacott, 2012). Developmental theory is also drawn on in supervision; and this, in turn, can relate to theories of social learning when applied to the supervisee experience (Carroll, 2008; Davys & Beddoe, 2010; Hawkins & Shohet, 2000) and to solution-focused theories (Lohrbach & Sawyer, 2004). These latter approaches represent a paradigm shift away from traditional ideas about knowledge and learning where the supervisor was identified as the holder of all expertise and the supervisee the recipient of their supervisor's wisdom. Solution-focused ideas challenge these assumptions, suggesting that supervisees bring their own lived experience and learning to the supervisory relationship. When these approaches underpin supervision, case practitioner 'success' in a given situation is identified and celebrated with an assumption that small gains and successes can be built upon (Davys & Beddoe, 2010). In a field of practice with a focus on trauma, abuse and neglect, solution-focused ways of working have been described as offering new possibilities for assessment and intervention at the frontline of casework and, in turn, within the supervisory relationship.

The concept of power, and its use and misuse, is a theme emerging in the supervision literature. Typically, supervisors are in a hierarchical relationship, administrating workload and employee performance whilst charged with the responsibility to educate and support their staff (Brown & Bourne, 1996; Hawkins & Shohet, 2000). This potential for role conflict is raised by some authors (for example, McPherson, Frederico, & McNamara, 2015), who point to the ultimate purpose of supervision as a means of resolving this tension. In short, whilst some theorists suggest that supervision is primarily oriented toward the supervisee's need to learn (Davys & Beddoe, 2010), others concur with the seminal work of Alfred Kadushin in defining the ultimate purpose of supervision. Kadushin identified it as a means of enhancing the service received by clients in this field: vulnerable children and their families (Kadushin, 1976; see also Kadushin & Harkness, 2002). This subtle but critical distinction enables supervisors of child protection practice to maintain, first and foremost, a focus on the identified child, and to direct efforts toward the development and support of the case worker in order to enhance the service offered. Related to issues of power within the supervisee/supervisor relationship are those of authority and power in case practice where, in child protection, consideration of culture, diversity and anti-oppressive practice is central (Hair & O'Donoghue, 2009; Hawkins & Shohet, 2000). Cultural approaches to supervision have been described as a means of privileging the local indigenous knowledge, and consequently enhancing relevant and culturally competent practice (Hair & O'Donoghue, 2009).

A 'really good' supervisor does far more than merely supervise staff in accordance with agency policy. As Wonnacott (2012) noted, a highly skilled supervisor will also "inspire, motivate and act as a leader of social work practice" (p. 30). This implies that supervisors are also leaders of practice, which brings us to the issue of leadership theory.

Leadership as a concept is discussed elsewhere in this book. In summary, however, it would appear that, of these theories, transformational models are the most relevant to supervision. They have been found to promote, within Child and Family Practice, collaboration, consultation and effective and transparent communication (Zwanenberg, 2010). The transformational supervisor is one who motivates and inspires others, rather than merely focusing on process and procedure. Consequently, a leader is capable of influencing organisational culture and communicating the values and mission of the organisation (Skinner, as cited in Zwanenberg, 2010). More recently, new knowledge in relation to neuroscience and relationship has been identified as offering useful ideas about models of supervision that can calm and contain, yet motivate staff. Leadership based on this emerging knowledge has a focus on relationship and using this relationship to lead professional social and emotional behaviour in the workplace (Rock, 2009).

Messages from research

Turning to the available research in relation to supervision in Child and Family Practice, three areas of focus are identified and have been outlined in detail elsewhere (McPherson et al., 2015). In summary, these included, first, a focus on the supervisee/supervisor relationship, where studies identified case worker competence as being positively influenced by a supervisor demonstrating certain attributes within the professional relationship, including warmth, humour, integrity and loyalty, and the ability to communicate complex ideas (Bogo & McKnight, 2006; Hensley, 2003). The second area was related to supervisors' capacity to manage and contain anxiety and to respond proactively to the trauma inherent in the work and the workplace (Bowers, Esmond, & Canales, 1999; Gibbs, 2001; Harrison & Westwood, 2009). These studies were typically small and exploratory. The growing body of literature on stress and burnout (Coffey, Dugdill, & Tatersall, 2004; Collins, 2008; Figley, 2002) has contributed to thinking about how supervision might effectively prevent the experience of vicarious trauma in the workplace (see also Bloom & Farragher, 2011).

Finally, the bulk of research in relation to supervision in practice involves the impact of supervision on workforce attrition. Large-scale studies, mostly conducted in North America, have examined the relationship between professional case workers' decisions to resign from their role and the influence that supervision may have on those decisions (Barth, Lloyd, Christ, Chapman, & Dickenson, 2008; IASWR, 2005). In short, many of these studies identified an association between a practitioner's decision to remain in their role and the experience of effective supervision, in particular where the management of emotion is a central concern

(Barth et al., 2008; Chen & Scannapieco, 2010; Ellett, Ellis, Westbrook, & Dews, 2007; Faller, Grabarek, & Ortega, 2010). Whilst these studies offer some insight into the importance of supervision in Child and Family Practice, they do not offer a detailed analysis of the nature of supervision that is experienced as supportive, containing and educative. What follows is an analysis of the historical and contemporary context within which supervisors practise in contemporary child and family work, using Australia as a case example.

The context for supervising Child and Family Practice using Australia as a case study

Child and Family Practice in Australia includes both statutory and non-governmental services offered to vulnerable children and their families. Central to the work is the nature of the service user's relationship with the helping professional. Historically, agencies such as the Children's Protection Society in Victoria, Australia, and the National Society for the Prevention of Cruelty to Children (NSPCC) in the United Kingdom were charged with the responsibility of 'protecting' children from abuse and neglect by their parents or caregivers. The essence of the relationship between parents and professionals was involuntary, and has been dominated by a 'child rescue' paradigm for practice which, for some, involved a sense of blaming and shaming parents. The nature of relationships with parents of 'rescued' children could be seen as adversarial, with case practice emphasising detection, investigation and protection as opposed to 'social' work, with an emphasis on social justice, collaboration and connection.

In recent years a significant international paradigm shift has changed the way that vulnerable children and their families are perceived and responded to by that service system designed to protect children (Munro, 2011). There has been a growing understanding of the importance of relational social work in terms of client outcomes; a greater appreciation of the complexity of intergenerational trauma and the potential constraints for parents who may struggle under adverse circumstances; and at the same time a recognition of the limitations of a child rescue paradigm in effective lasting change (Munro, 2011). Major reform efforts across the western world are endeavouring to cement the 'pendulum swing' from blame, shame and rescue to a stronger family focus which identifies and builds upon 'signs of safety' for children and their families (Turnell, 2012). This approach is one which moved away from an exclusive focus on problems and risks to children to incorporate thinking about prevailing strengths within families as indicators of safety that might be worked with. Implications for the supervision of contemporary, more holistic case practice which works with what continues to be essentially an 'involuntary' service user–professional relationship are potentially profound. Before examining implications for supervision and supervisors, however, we will first examine the context for Child and Family Practice in recent years and the socio-political environment within which the new paradigm for practice is located.

TABLE 5.1 Number of notifications (reports) to child protection in Australia, 1995–2015

Year	Total number of reports
1995–96	91,734
2000–01	115,471
2014–15	320,169

Australian Institute of Health and Welfare, *Child Protection Australia 2014–2015*.

In spite of calls to strengthen preventative, relationship-based practice (Munro, 2011; Turnell, 2012) the demand for statutory child protection services in Australia has escalated at what could be described as an alarming rate. Taking a snapshot of reports made to the statutory child protection service in Australia since the mid-1990s, we can see that the number of reports more than tripled, in this time. Table 5.1 indicates the number of these ever-increasing reports of suspected child abuse and neglect, including throughout recent times where the practice paradigm has shifted to one of greater family support.

The number of reports made to the child protection agency is not indicative of the number of matters that were confirmed or substantiated. In addition, these figures do not indicate the number of matters presented to the Children's Court resulting in court orders and an ongoing requirement for statutory intervention. What they do indicate is the initial demand for a statutory child protection response, which in Australia has more than tripled in less than 20 years. Workforce data indicating the relative size of the Australian child protection workforce are not publicly available; however, few would imagine that the available practitioner resource has tripled in the past 20 years.

International comparisons are difficult to make. There are differences in child protection and Child and Family Practice systems, legislative requirements and data gathering procedures. What is evident, however, is a common theme that across the United Kingdom, Australia and Canada there has been continuous growth in reported rates of child abuse and neglect requiring a child protection response. In the United Kingdom, for example, public contact with the National Association for the Prevention of Cruelty to Children (NSPCC) helpline in relation to suspected emotional abuse of children increased by 70 per cent between 2011/12 and 2016/17 (Bentley et al., 2017, p. 3). Whilst the NSPCC notes that there are no official government sources identifying trends in respect of reporting rates of child abuse in the United Kingdom, it reports on a series of publicly available indicators such as calls to the helpline and recorded offences against children (p. 29). Sexual offences against children in Scotland, for example, have increased by 68 per cent since the mid-2000s (p. 29). In Canada, as in Australia, data in relation to suspected child abuse and neglect are publicly available from the Public Health Agency of Canada. A snapshot of investigations there following concerns in relation to suspected child abuse between 1998 and 2008 indicates an increase from an estimated 135,261 in 1998 to 235,842 investigations in 2008 (Trocmé et al., 2008). In the

United States of America the picture is a little less clear. Data revealing how many children had received a child protection investigation or 'alternative response' indicate an increase that appears to be relatively modest, at 3,171,616 visits across all 52 states in 2012 and 3,3587,347 visits in 2015 (Administration for Children and Families, 2017). What is clear, however – and consistent with available data from the United Kingdom, Australia and Canada – is an upward trend in recent years.

In the context of increases in reported concerns about children internationally, and in spite of efforts to change the practice paradigm, neoliberal approaches to the development of procedures and policies to govern child protection and Child and Family Practice have dominated. Managerialism, defined as discourses and practices that look to big business techniques to ensure efficiency and effectiveness (Zwanenberg, 2010), has been a dominant influence in formulating system-wide responses. The emphasis on reporting requirements, which were dominated by quantitative measures, replaced what were seen as less strategic methods of management throughout the states and territories responsible for delivering child protection services (Markiewicz, 1996). Since the 1980s, government approaches have been embedded in a neoliberal approach to public policy, with a foundational belief that the free market is the best way to transact any activity. Its basic tenets include that government should be restricted to creating and protecting free markets and distinguishing between the role of government as funder or contractor and the role of community-sector organisations as service providers only (Paterson, 1988). The fundamental attributes of this approach embrace "performance measurement, performance improvement, program based organisational structures, program budgeting, corporate planning, senior executive service, program evaluation, effectiveness review, performance payment, cash limits, devolution, financial management and so on" (Paterson, 1988, p. 288). The underpinning ideology – which might be considered at odds with professional, reflective practice – is a set of beliefs which fundamentally assume that better management will prove an efficient solvent for a wide range of social ills. Whilst an interest in 'metrics' may be an aid to good governance, this ideology can dominate at the expense of professionalism and the development of contemporary professional knowledge.

In summary, whilst research literature has been shown to be limited in terms of guiding supervisory practice, the contextual challenges faced by supervisors appear to have spiralled. Theoretical literature, however, promotes the significance of the supervisory relationship in the context of trauma and an ultimate focus on the service user experience. Whilst, on the one hand, contemporary practice paradigms promote the value of relationship-based professional practice (Munro, 2011), organisations responsible for the delivery of the service (at least in Australia) demand adherence to metrics which may privilege efficiency over effectiveness. Supervisors of practice may be charged with frontline management responsibilities to report on efficiency metrics whilst, at the same time, supporting, enabling and educating their practitioners.

An ecological approach to contemporary supervision

Models of supervision require attention to the multiplicity of roles in various contexts that are held by the supervisor, and the inherent tensions within those roles. Supervision can be usefully conceptualised as responding systemically and, in turn, influenced at various 'levels' by an ecological perspective (Belsky, 1980). A diagrammatic representation of this conceptualisation of supervision is shown in Figure 5.1.

The conceptual framework for supervision proposed here is based on an adaptation of Belsky's multi-dimensional analysis of the phenomenon of child abuse in which divergent layers are presented as integrated or 'nested' (Belsky, 1980). It is beyond the scope of this chapter to consider the role of the macro system, which in this context would involve an examination of community attitudes and beliefs in relation to Child and Family Practice. At the outer layer in this model, the significance of the exo-system is identified in terms of the employer organisation and operating policies that sanction or mandate supervision. These policies can only take effect where they are accompanied by an organisational culture promoting quality supervision, continuous learning and 'sanctuary' (Bloom & Farragher, 2011). This reference to sanctuary implies that those organisations designed to help, heal and offer a safe place for vulnerable people could also be places of safety for their professional employees. An additional implication at this level would be for senior executives governing organisations to demonstrate

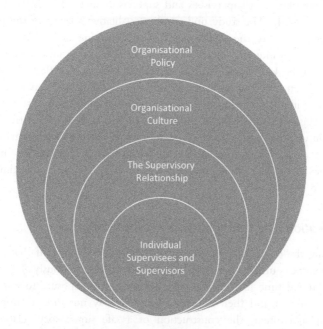

FIGURE 5.1 An ecological representation of supervision
Source: McPherson (2014)

leadership that was consistent with transformative and distributive practices (Zwanenberg, 2010).

At the next level, the professional relationship between supervisor and supervisee maintains the service user as the central focus of supervision. Supervision promotes supervisee wellbeing and safety, informed by the neurobiology of trauma and relationship. It facilitates learning and growth, leads and inspires and manages fairly. Supervision integrates each of these functions and leads change processes, advocating strategically on behalf of the workforce and service users. Finally, the third, foundation layer involves the individual supervisees and supervisors who consider, respect and work with each other's values, beliefs about parenting and childhood, resilience, knowledge development, and identity and development as leaders (McPherson, 2014). This consideration includes personal and professional growth and the developmental issues relevant to understanding what each individual brings to the supervisory relationship. Clearly, as is the case in the Bronfenbrenner model (1979) and Belsky's adaptation of it, individual 'levels' within this conceptual framework should not be considered in isolation. What follows is a focus on the knowledge, skills and attributes of supervisors within this ecological context.

Supervisor knowledge and skills

Having located key aspects of supervision within an overarching ecological framework, what follows draws from a small exploratory, Australian study drawing on the lived experience of supervisees and supervisors in Child and Family Practice (McPherson, 2014). The study undertook a qualitative analysis of the perspectives of professionals where the construction of the meaning of 'effective supervision' was the subject of inquiry. Ethical clearance was granted to undertake this research by the La Trobe University Human Ethics Committee (11–082). Aspects of this study have been reported elsewhere (McPherson, 2014; McPherson et al., 2015); however, the implications for supervisor knowledge and skill are presented here. In summary, this study highlights the significance and complexity of the supervisory relationship as pivotal to 'effective supervision'. Five core dimensions of effective supervision are proposed as integrative and each having implications for supervisor knowledge and skills (McPherson, 2014, p. 205). Each of the dimensions is summarised as follows.

1. Co-creation of a safe supervisory relationship

Considering the contextual analysis offered earlier, it is apparent that practitioners may experience unsafe practice contexts, with continuously high workload demand, limited time for reflection and learning, and exposure to trauma experienced by children and their families. Whilst it may not directly impact on the socio-political context, the construction of a safe supervisory relationship may alleviate these distressing experiences for the practitioner. It requires supervisees and supervisors to collaborate, share accountability and work toward a transparent and non-judgemental approach to practice. Within the relationship, supervisors require the skills to work with issues of power, gender, culture and difference. A calm and well-regulated supervisor, prepared to identify the needs of the supervisee, may empower staff to manage complexity, ambiguity and uncertainty. Emerging knowledge in relation to the neurobiology of relationship (Perry, 2009; van der Kolk, 2005; Rock, 2009) informs supervisor knowledge and skill development, with clear implications for supervisors to create and maintain a calm and calming workplace that holds minimal psychological, emotional or physical 'threat' to the supervisee. Within the context outlined earlier, this may require an extraordinary level of competence in interpersonal leadership and self-knowledge on the part of the supervisor.

2. Knowledge and skill development

The findings of this study suggest that supervisees are best placed to learn when a calm and safe supervisory relationship exists. Supervisors can be seen as knowledge leaders who are responsible for the development of the supervisee in a manner which is collaborative and matched to the unique identified learning needs of the practitioner. Three areas of knowledge are identified as required by the supervisor for contemporary supervision. These are:

i   expert theoretical knowledge of practice, supervision and leadership;
ii   knowing policy, process, procedure and organisational awareness; and
iii practice wisdom and self-knowledge.

In the first area – expert theoretical knowledge of practice, supervision and leadership – supervisors additionally need to understand diversity and be sensitive to 'difference' in models of child rearing. Wider theoretical knowledge, in particular complexity theory and ecological developmental theory, inform the way that supervisors approach the work, enabling a wide perspective on child abuse and neglect which draws upon a multi-dimensional systemic approach. The body of knowledge informing supervision, leadership and management includes emotional intelligence and self-knowledge, models of leadership including transformational leadership.

The second area of knowledge required is procedural knowledge, which involves a working knowledge of policy, legislation, procedure and process requirements to undertake the work.

The third area of knowledge relates to professional experience in the work itself as a practitioner, and demonstrating a sense of practice wisdom on the basis of that experience. Practice wisdom and personal maturity are seen as the ingredients that make an important contribution to the capacity to develop an effective supervisory relationship.

Knowledge development involves the supervisor and supervisee critically reflecting on aspects of practice. Models of reflection are complex and can incorporate different levels, including technical reflection, practical reflection, critical reflection and process reflection. Actively incorporating the four levels of reflection in the context of Child and Family Practice may involve anxiety, distress and 'messiness' (Gardner, 2006).

3. Leadership and management

Leadership skills for supervisors are those behaviours that demonstrate and integrate expert theoretical knowledge in the workplace. Skills include approaches that create a reflective learning space for supervisees to conceptualise their practice in partnership with supervisors. Leadership skills underpinning effective supervision include transparent and consistent behaviour, modelling self-regulation and self-awareness as well as distributed power and authority. Values such as integrity, honesty, a commitment to social justice and natural justice principles are fundamental to the creation of a mutually respectful supervisory relationship and the demonstration of effective leadership. Leadership skills that are congruent with social work values are identified as those skills used in the promotion of social justice. 'Emotionally intelligent' leaders are described in the literature as visionaries – democratic yet pace-setting and commanding (Cherniss & Goleman, 2001), adapting their leadership style to the particular context. In summary, the powerful impact that modelling leadership behaviours may have in the workplace – in particular transparent decision-making practices and sound communication and personal leadership attributes, including self-knowledge self-regulation – are noted. In relation to management skills, the organisational requirements to manage the 'business of …' may create tension in the supervisory relationship. Within a managerialist context, reporting requirements, 'business' rules and measures of performance may undermine the capacity of the supervisory relationship to remain a collaborative space where the child is at the heart of reflection and where learning and reflection are paramount (Munro, 2011). It is proposed here that effective supervisors are those who can embrace the opportunities presented by efficient operating 'systems' yet strive to 'balance' the dimensions of supervision in a complex environment. The management dimension coexists with leadership and includes the management of this sense of balance, facilitated by keeping the child, in Child and Family Practice, at the heart of supervisory reflection.

4. Advocacy

Advocacy, as a core component of supervision, involves the supervisor as advocate operating at the micro level of the supervision relationship, at the mezzo level across the organisation and at the macro, wider community level. The skill set required is to strategically identify issues of concern and to 'manage up' as appropriate and advocate as an agent of change. Supervisors may need to make strategic judgements about mediating between supervisee and the wider organisation as issues present themselves. The inclusion of 'advocacy' as one of the dimensions of supervision grounds the model in the historical roots of social work, a profession whose members have traditionally been viewed as 'agents of change'.

5. Placing the child at the centre of all supervisory considerations

The primary objective of supervision is to focus on the service delivered to the child, who is seen in the context of their family and community. To that end, the vulnerable child is central to the supervisory relationship. Whilst the other dimensions of supervision focus on supporting, developing, managing and leading and advocating for supervisees, this work is undertaken not as an end in and of itself, but to strengthen the quality of practice that the child experiences.

Effective supervisors in Child and Family Practice endeavour to have a sustained focus on the safety and wellbeing of the client child. This implies a focus on the quality of the relationship that the supervisee has developed with the child, including evidence of the supervisee's level of empathy with the child. Supervisory reflections might consider issues faced by the child, intervention strategies to be trialled and desired outcomes for the child, whilst facilitating a deepening of an empathetic response to the child.

Key messages from this chapter

- This chapter has highlighted some core themes emerging from the supervision literature and a recent Australian study reporting on the concept of 'effective supervision' in Child and Family Practice.
- A contextual analysis of the contemporary child and family workplace within which supervision takes place reveals both unrelenting increases in workload and a continued dominance of a managerialist paradigm.
- Supervisors are charged with responsibility for navigating the inevitable tensions that arise, supporting and developing practitioners and maintaining an ultimate focus on vulnerable children. The chapter concludes by reporting on the outcomes of a small, exploratory study and implications for supervisor knowledge and skill. Five integrated dimensions of supervision in Child and Family Practice are proposed as each having implications for supervisor knowledge and skill. Key messages for the supervisory relationship include the co-creation of a safe relationship and facilitation of learning and growth. The learning process is a critical function of supervision (Wonnacott, 2012), where practitioners may creatively conceptualise new approaches and practice strategies. Knowledge is defined broadly as encompassing empirical and theoretical knowledge, procedural knowledge and self-knowledge and practice wisdom (Thompson & West, 2013). A supervisee who is a motivated learner brings a willingness to consider, reflect and explore new knowledge in the context of their practice. The supervisor, in collaboration with the supervisee, is a facilitator of development and the acquisition of new knowledge (Gibbs et al., 2009).

- Areas for knowledge development are potentially vast, reflecting advances in research and complexity of context (Snowden & Boone, 2007). In partnership with supervisees, supervisors need to identify the existing strengths and priority areas for learning and continuous development. In doing so, they identify the developmental 'stage' of their supervisees, with supervisee development described as moving through various levels of experience and competence (Davys & Beddoe, 2010).
- Finally, the proposed model recognises the complex nature of the work and the range of contemporary leadership, management and advocacy dimensions that need to be effectively 'balanced' by supervisors in what can be experienced as a turbulent environment.

Questions for further consideration

1. Reflecting on your current experience as a team supervisor, to what extent have you been able to co create a safe supervisory relationship? What factors assisted you to achieve this? What were the barriers or constraints?
2. In looking at the three core areas of knowledge identified, undertake a 'knowledge audit' identifying strengths and your current areas for further development. How will you address your development needs?

References

Administration for Children and Families. (2017). *Child Maltreatment 2015.* Retrieved from www.acf.hhs.gov/cb/research-data-technology/statistics-research/child-maltreatment

Australian Institute of Health and Welfare. (2015). *Child Protection Australia 2014–2015.* Canberra: AIHW.

Barth, R., Lloyd, C., Christ, S., Chapman, M., & Dickenson, N. (2008). Child welfare worker characteristics and job satisfaction: a national study. *Social Work,* 53(3), 199–209.

Belsky, J. (1980). Child maltreatment: An ecological integration. *American Psychologist,* 35(4), 320–335.

Bentley, H., O'Hagan, H., Brown, A., Vasco, N., Lynch, C., Peppiate, J., … Letendrie, F. (2017). *How safe are our children? The most comprehensive overview of child protection in the UK.* London: NSPCC. Retrieved from www.nspcc.org.uk/globalassets/documents/research-reports/how-safe-children-2017-report.pdf

Bloom, S., & Farragher, B. (2011). *Restoring sanctuary: Toward the evolution of sane societies.* New York: Oxford University Press.

Bogo, M., & McKnightK. (2006). Clinical supervision in social work: A review of the research literature. *Clinical Supervisor,* 24(1–2), 49–67.

Bowers, B., EsmondB., & Canales, M. (1999). Approaches to case management supervision. *Administration in Social Work,* 23(1), 29–49.

Bronfenbrenner, U. (1979). *The ecology of human development.* Cambridge, MA: Harvard University Press.

Brown, A., & Bourne, I. (1996). *The social work supervisor: Supervision in community, day care, and residential settings.* Buckingham: Open University Press.

Carroll, M. (2008). Supervision and transformational learning. *Psychotherapy in Australia,* 14(3), 38–45.

ChenS., & Scannapieco, M. (2010). The influence of job satisfaction on child welfare worker's desire to stay: An examination of the interaction effect of self-efficacy and supportive supervision. *Children and Youth Services Review*, 32(4), 482–486.

Cherniss, C., & Goleman, D. (2001). *The emotionally intelligent workplace*. San Francisco: Jossey-Bass.

Coffey, M., Dugdill, L., & Tattersall, A. (2004). Research note: Stress in social services: Mental well-being, constraints and job satisfaction. *British Journal of Social Work*, 34(5), 735–747.

Collins, S. (2008). Statutory social workers: stress, job satisfaction, coping, social support and individual differences. *British Journal of Social Work*, 38(6), 1173–1193.

Davys, A., & Beddoe, L. (2010). *Best practice in supervision: A guide for the helping professions*. London: Jessica Kingsley.

IASWR. (2005). *Factors influencing retention of child welfare staff: A systematic review of research*. Washington: Institute for the Advancement of Social Work Research.

Ellett, A., Ellis, J., Westbrook, T., & Dews, D. (2007). A qualitative study of 369 child welfare professionals about factors contributing to employee retention and turnover. *Children and Youth Services Review*, 29(2), 264–281.

Faller, K., Grabarek, M., & Ortega, R. (2010). Commitment to child welfare work: What predicts leaving and staying? *Children and Youth Services Review*, 32(6), 840–846.

Figley, C. (2002). Compassion fatigue: psychotherapists' chronic lack of self-care. *Journal of Clinical Psychology*, 58(11), 1433–1441.

Gardner, F. (2006). *Working with human services organisations*. South Melbourne: Oxford University Press.

Gibbs, J. (2001). Maintaining front-line workers in child protection: a case for refocusing supervision. *Child Abuse Review*, 10(4), 323–335.

Gibbs, J., Dwyer, J., & Vivekananda, K. (2009). *Leading practice: A resource guide for child protection frontline and middle managers*. Melbourne: Victorian Government Department of Human Service.

Hair, H., & O'Donoghue, K. (2009). Culturally relevant, socially just social work supervision: Becoming visible through a social constructionist lens. *Journal of Ethnic and Cultural Diversity in Social Work*, 18(1), 70–88.

Harrison, R., & Westwood, M. (2009). Preventing vicarious traumatization of mental health therapists: Identifying protective practices. *Psychotherapy Theory, Research Practice, Training*, 46(2), 203–219.

Hawkins, P., & Shohet, R. (2000). *Supervision in the helping professions* (2nd ed.). Maidenhead: Open University Press.

Hensley, P. (2003). The value of supervision. *Clinical Supervisor*, 21(1), 97–110.

Kadushin, A. (1976). *Supervision in social work*. New York: Columbia University Press.

Kadushin, A., & Harkness, D. (2002). *Supervision in social work* (4th ed.). New York: Columbia University Press.

Lohrbach, S., & Sawyer, R. (2004). Creating a constructive practice: Family and professional partnership in high risk child protection case conferences. *Protecting Children*, 20(2–3), 78–92.

Markiewicz, A. (1996). The child welfare system in Victoria: Changing context and perspectives 1945–1995. *Children Australia*, 21(3), 32–41.

McPherson, L. (2014). *Supervision in Child and Family Practice: What works?* (Unpublished doctoral thesis). La Trobe University, Melbourne.

McPherson, L., Frederico, M., & McNamara, P. (2015). Safety as a fifth dimension in supervision: Stories from the frontline. *Australian Social Work*, 69(1), 67–79.

Morrison, T. (2005). *Staff supervision in social care: Making a real difference for staff and service users* (3rd ed.). Brighton: Pavilion.

Munro, E. (2008). *Effective child protection* (2nd ed.). Los Angeles: Sage.

Munro, E. (2011). *The Munro review of child protection: Final report. A child-centred system.* London: Department for Education.

Paterson, J. (1988). A managerialist strikes back. *Australian Journal of Public Administration*, 47(4), 287–295.

Perry, B. (2009). Examining child maltreatment through a neurodevelopmental lens: Neurosequential model of therapeutics. *Journal of Loss and Trauma*, 14(4), 240–255.

Rock, D. (2009, August). Managing with the brain in mind. *Strategy and Business*, 56. Retrieved from www.strategy-business.com/article/09306?gko=5df7f

Snowden, D.J., & Boone, M.E. (2007). A leader's framework for decision making: A leader's framework for decision making. *Harvard Business Review*, 85(11), 68–76.

Thompson, L., & West, D. (2013). Professional development in the contemporary educational context: Encouraging practice wisdom. *Social Work Education: The International Journal*, 31(1), 118–133.

Trocmé, N., Fallon, B., MacLaurin, B., Sinha, V., Black, T., Fast, E., ... & Holroyd, J. (2008). *Rates of maltreatment-related investigations in the CIS-1998, CIS-2003, and CIS-2008.* Retrieved from www.phac-aspc.gc.ca/cm-vee/csca-ecve/2008/cis-eci-07-eng.php

Turnell, A. (2012). *Signs of Safety: A comprehensive briefing paper.* Perth: Resolutions Consultancy.

van der Kolk, B. (2005). Developmental trauma disorder: Toward a rational diagnosis for children with complex trauma histories. *Psychiatric Annals*, 35(5), 401–408.

Wonnacott, J. (2012). *Mastering social work supervision.* London: Jessica Kingsley.

Zwanenberg, Z. (2010). *Leadership in social care: Research highlights.* London: Jessica Kingsley.

6

LEADERSHIP IN DIRECT PRACTICE

Bruce D. Perry, Annette L. Jackson and Sarah Waters

Introduction

Leadership is sought after and avoided, sometimes in equal measure and at the same time. It may come with a perception of prestige and power and control. It may also represent an opportunity to fail publicly and to hold responsibility for decisions without actual authority to enact the desired change.

A well-loved Australian children's classic tells the tale of a *magic pudding* named Albert. No matter how often or how fast he was eaten this magical pudding would be as though not one bite had been taken. Grumpy as Albert was, he was always ready when his companions' hunger next struck, and could become a different dish every time (Lindsay, 1918).

Leadership has its magic pudding moments. As more and more is asked of leaders, there is often an unspoken expectation of continuous regeneration. As with the magic pudding, when all others are exhausted, the leader is often relied upon to be the one whose energy remains unabated regardless of how depleted they feel. Needless to say, we are not magic puddings.

Leadership is fine in theory, but what happens in practice? Many books have been written about leadership, with steps to guarantee success or other such promises. Some are based on sound principles with useful hints, whilst others have little relevance to lesser mortals.

This chapter draws on different experiences in leadership. Although we have each played various leadership roles over the years, here we focus on particular vignettes and explore some of the themes. As with other chapters in this book, our focus is on leadership in the context of vulnerable and at-risk children and their families.

Dr Bruce Perry writes from the perspective of a neuroscience-informed clinician. Annette Jackson writes about the aftermath of a child death and the responsibilities of leadership that follow. Sarah Waters reflects on salient lessons from supervision and leadership from others before she became a leader.

Stories and reflections

Reflections from a clinical neuroscientist (Bruce Perry)

My professional training as a neuroscientist and physician (general and child and adolescent psychiatry) involved no formal or informal training in leadership. Scientists and physicians typically focus on reducing issues into component parts: the neuroscientist often hones in on the brain, neurons, synapses, receptors, genes – with each level of analysis more granular. Physicians tend to learn and solve problems the same way – find symptoms and physical signs and focus on the organ system and physiology to identify pathology to address. My few experiences with leadership were from sports and school, where I saw the positive power of optimism, encouragement and acknowledgement, as well as the destructive impacts of shaming, scapegoating and humiliation from a coach or teacher.

Despite the lack of training, academically successful young physicians are often given important leadership roles requiring skills well beyond their education or experience; this 'promotion without protection' occurs in the Child and Family Practice context as well. And so it was with me. Two years out of my training, I was the Chief of Psychiatry at the largest paediatric hospital in the United States, the head of the Trauma Recovery Program at a Veterans Administration (VA) hospital and the Vice-Chairman for Research in the Department of Psychiatry at a major medical school. I went from 'leading' a handful of technicians and graduate students in my laboratory to leading peers and colleagues in three different systems – each with a different set of explicit and implicit rules and traditions. Over the next few years I learned dozens of powerful, and often painful, lessons regarding leadership.

Humans are a social species. We have complex and pervasive neural networks continually 'at work' monitoring the social milieu: sensing, processing, interpreting and responding to the verbal and non-verbal cues of those around us. This social monitoring process is very sensitive to social dominance and power. A primary challenge in leadership is mastering the transition from being 'one of the group' to 'leader' of the group. In child welfare, high rates of staff turnover often involve rapid promotion: front line workers are quickly promoted to unit supervisors, unit supervisors to program supervisors. These shifts in designation can dramatically change relationships with peers, colleagues, supervisees and others. Due to the increase in the 'power differential' between the leader and those s/he leads, the new leader will often underestimate the 'power' of their words and actions.

When I was originally promoted to senior leadership roles, I had little under-standing of these concepts. I quickly learned that any minor criticisms or constructive suggestions to existing program or practice activities were perceived as 'major overhauls'. By way of example, I wanted to keep track of the incoming consultation requests on an electronic database rather than a paper accounting ledger. The staff and other physicians ultimately insisted on a 'meeting' to discuss these drastic changes. I was able to explain my reasoning; their objections were duly noted and over the next several months the transition took place. They insisted on keeping their nineteenth-century accounting ledger as we introduced the electronic database, but after a few weeks decided that it was not necessary to hand write the same information they typed into the database.

A leader's whispers are often perceived as shouts. I learned to become a better listener; to solicit the group's input on areas for improvement and focus on slower rates of transition. The parallel processes between an individual's and an organisation's capacity to learn new things and change are remarkable. Both are bound by 'state-dependent' functioning (see Chapter 10): a sense of safety and predictability facilitate the introduction of new content (e.g., changes in practice and program). For the individual and the group, novelty induces a default defensive response; change is perceived as threatening until proven otherwise. Systems in economic distress, experiencing major leadership transitions or with high rates of personnel turnover are not capable of effectively internalising innovations.

A second major lesson regarding leadership – from a neurosociology perspective – is the power of relational contagion; and, due to the unique position of the leader, this contagion tends to flow from the leader to the group. A calm, optimistic leader can inspire and motivate; a pessimistic, frustrated or angry leader can destabilise a group, immobilise progress and undermine the fundamental work of the group.

One of the most powerful examples of this I experienced was with a complex child welfare situation in Gilmer, Texas in the mid-1990s. There were accusations of satanic child abuse, including ritualised murder. There was a multidisciplinary group of caseworkers, law enforcement personnel, mental health clinicians and a special prosecutor assigned to investigate. They all believed that there was a powerful evil group at work. The leaders in all of these arenas fed on each other's fears, leading to a level of paranoia and distorted thinking which itself began to become destructive to all involved. When our team was asked by the State's Attorney General to get involved, I sent two of our experienced clinicians to the area to get some preliminary information. They returned and told stories of 'being followed' and seeing a 'dead black cat' – that was a clear sign to stay away. They both told stories of strange, almost supernatural occurrences (a branch struck their car just as they were getting close to the place where a girl had disappeared). Their paranoia and fear were palpable. One of our most dependable clinicians requested to not be involved in this case. The contagion of fear – coming primarily from the leaders of this multidisciplinary team – distorted their perceptions and cognitions.

I went up to Gilmer. The fear, suspicion and paranoia were pervasive (anyone who was not a believer was immediately suspected of being part of this powerful and secret satanic group). At one point, I was accused of being a leader of this satanic group and a local police officer who expressed doubt was actually charged with murder, jailed and also accused of being a key part of the cult. In the end, a team from the Attorney General's office led by a very pragmatic, calm leader and our team were able to sort through the mess. By staying regulated, focused and calm, I helped the members of our team – and those we interacted with – start to feel safer. Their 'thinking' became more rational, and we were able to sort out a terrible mess (for more see Perry & Szalavitz, 2017, Chapter 7). There are of course many other examples of the power of a leader's emotional state to help create a sense of safety, optimism and purpose for a group. This powerful potential may be a leader's strongest tool. In order to get the most potential from the group – their creative and productive potential – the members of the group need to feel safe and valued and have a sense of purpose (see sections on state-dependent functioning in Chapter 10). This is one of the leader's primary responsibilities.

Reflections from a child protection senior manager (Annette Jackson)

I was one of those social workers who became a child protection manager too early (as discussed earlier by Dr Perry). At the age of 25, I realised that if I continued in management at this time I would miss out on valuable learning in Child and Family Practice. Stepping out of that trajectory, I worked in non-leadership roles in residential care and family preservation before resuming a leadership position a few years later. I then returned to leadership roles in Child and Family Practice and then in therapeutic services, out-of-home care and related fields. Thirty years on, my working life has always been in fields of practice in Victoria, Australia, with a focus on children who have experienced abuse and neglect – reflecting intra-familial trauma and deprivation, separation and loss, and cultural and societal dislocation and marginalisation.

We are often drawn to success stories in the face of difficult or complex problems. There is much to gain from reflecting on positive leadership. Yet, we also learn from situations where there are no obvious solutions and when there is sadness and confusion, including when the worst possible circumstances have occurred, with or without mistakes.

In the field of Child and Family Practice in particular, there is often an emphasis on errors at the individual and/or system level, as in the event of a child death. There is much to learn from this type of analysis; however, mistakes do not need to be made for there to be a tragedy or a major crisis. This is a frightening reality of this field of work.

One case in point was when, as an experienced senior manager in Child and Family Practice, I case planned a two-year-old boy, Todd, and his five-year-old sister to return to their mother's and her boyfriend's care. A few weeks later, the boyfriend killed Todd. Despite a thorough assessment, regular home visits (including on the day of Todd's death), involvement of a family preservation service, and an experienced and competent child protection worker who worked collaboratively and proactively with the family, carers and the family preservation program, this unspeakable event occurred. A consistent view of judges and magistrates throughout coronial hearings, committal hearings and a Supreme Court murder trial was that, even with the benefit of hindsight, there were no indications that this man would commit a heinous violent act – let alone kill a child. There were still system and practice issues to be considered and lessons learned, but I want to focus on a rarely discussed issue impacting on leadership – what happens the day after a child dies?

I cannot imagine what it is like for a mother the morning after her child has been beaten to death by someone she trusted. Her never-ending day started the night before. Returning from the shops, she discovered her two-year-old son had died. The ambulance took her little boy away. Child protection took her daughter away. She and her boyfriend were then taken to the police station, where he was later charged with murder.

The next morning, whilst driving to work, I heard over the car radio that the police were investigating the death of a two-year-old. In Child and Family Practice, every time you hear such a news report you are not only saddened, but also a latent anxiety begins. Then I received the dreaded call from the regional manager to tell me of Todd's death. My heart sank; my mind went numb.

As I walked into the child protection office, staff were in tears. The direct worker was concentrating on what had to be done, doing what he could to hold it together. His colleagues, left with nothing to do to make the situation better, were distraught. This was a child and family known to everyone. This was also a fear felt by everyone. Their observable distress reminded me of just one of my responsibilities – to support them. It also highlighted one of the most potent messages: none of us are on our own, although we probably all felt as if we were.

The morning consisted of speaking to staff and more senior management, quickly re-reading the client file and being interviewed by homicide detectives about the minutiae of what I knew, what I did and what I decided. The police were respectful, empathic and thorough. It was exhausting. It was 11.00am and the day had barely begun.

Whilst the team leader, worker and I focused on this intense task – to be as clear and accurate as possible – we needed others to think and act on behalf of the best interests and immediate safety of the sister who had just witnessed her brother's death. Another manager took on this task with fortitude and compassion, knowing that all decisions were being watched and questioned by countless others. Nonetheless, she was determined to make decisions in this little girl's best interests, not necessarily ones that were easy to justify to a system baying for assurance and retribution. She also ensured that the mother and remaining child had emotional and financial support, and that the child protection teams continued to focus on their work with other children and families. This was a leadership team in action.

One of the first things my regional manager asked me – after the inevitable questions she needed to ask on behalf of the larger bureaucracy, politicians and the media – was 'How are you?' She told me I would not be asked to make any decisions for the next couple of weeks. This did not add to my self-doubt, but offered reassurance and a buffer. Not only was the immediate pressure removed, but it also reduced my fear of what else could go wrong. In other words, although I was a senior manager with a high degree of responsibility and commensurate expectations, I was treated as a human being who had experienced loss and trauma and who needed support, kindness and scaffolding during this terrible time. My manager couldn't rescue me from the police interrogations, numerous court hearings, the need to reassure everyone involved and the inevitable self-doubt and burden of duty. So she removed and buffered what she could.

My day ended with exhaustion, sapped of all energy. I had maintained self-control. I had not wept. I had tried to be whatever others needed me to be during this horrible day. But on my return home there was my father pottering around my garden. "I heard what happened on the radio and thought you must have had a bad day," he said. Embraced in a hug by a loving father, no longer needing to be strong for others, now I could cry. This was my safe haven.

Literature about child death reviews and filicide rightfully focus on what the service and legal system can learn from such tragedies. This often includes the role of leadership in decision-making, ensuring collaborative and effective communication and systems thinking (Frederico, Jackson, & Dwyer, 2014). Human nature suggests that professionals under heightened scrutiny after a child death are likely to gloss over possible errors or gaps in practice. It can be difficult to explore other themes due to the inevitable defensiveness in the face of the intense and oftentimes public examination. Also, they are often less able to retrieve memories when in a heightened state of anxiety. Exploring what happens after such an event (not just what preceded the event) can be indicative of how a leader or a leadership team responds when things go horribly wrong.

One such theme is the state-dependent functioning of a leader during and following an adverse event such as a violent child death. As mentioned earlier, all human functioning, including leadership, is state-dependent (Gaskill & Perry, 2014). In addition to genetics and experiences, we have good and bad days and good and bad moments. When under threat, tired or ill we do not function as effectively and efficiently compared to when we are calm, refreshed and well.

Leadership is not just about knowledge, experience and capacity; it is also about day-to-day functioning, including when faced with a worst case scenario. When overwhelmed in the face of a tragic event, neuroscience suggests we are less able to take in new information or try new ideas, less confident in ourselves or others. We may have a restricted or distorted sense of time; be unable to think of anything beyond the immediate situation; less able to integrate our internal and external worlds; less able to be calm and self-regulate, and less able to calm or regulate someone else (see Chapter 10 for further discussion). Recognising this in a pre-emptive and empathic way can not only provide support to the leader but also prevent the broader situation deteriorating into a crisis-laden fog.

Equally, there is value in reflecting on mistakes and mishaps in day-to-day situations, not just when tragedy strikes. Such 'benign' mistakes may be uneventful, involve near misses or lead to situations with negative but less dire consequences. A focus on these types of errors can be preventative as even relative minor but cumulative errors may snowball, leading to catastrophic outcomes (Reder & Duncan, 1999).

Creating an organisational culture where it is safe and encouraged to discuss mistakes, dilemmas and stuckness is an interesting challenge. Munro (2008) wrote that the single most important way to minimise errors is to admit when you are wrong.

When delivering leadership workshops for child protection senior staff in the state of Victoria, one of my co-authors, Sarah Waters, and I developed a training activity called 'Mistakes Anonymous'. We asked participants to reflect on mistakes such as in thought, opinion, attitude, decisions, implementation, actions and relationships. Rich examples – sometimes funny, sometimes excruciating – taught us a lot about ourselves and leadership.

Reflections of the power of supervision and leadership (Sarah Waters)

My journey towards leadership is, and always will be, a work in progress, and can best be described as an ongoing struggle to achieve the appropriate balance between heart and mind. As Peter Senge (1990) says, writing on one of his five disciplines for building learning organisations, "personal mastery is not something you possess. It is a process. It is a lifelong discipline" (p. 142). We learn to lead from those around us, and develop a catalogue of experiences of being led through challenging and often transformative situations. We form our own template of ourselves as leaders, and consciously and unconsciously choose approaches that resonate with us and discard those that do not accord with the image of the leader we aspire to be. So whilst the perfect balance between heart and mind may be forever elusive, we gain competency in walking the tightrope.

The following example pinpoints an occasion, early in my career, where the balance between my heart and my mind was challenged, and supportive leadership helped me develop the skills to resolve the immediate challenge and to build my catalogue of positive leadership experiences. I was working as a foster care worker in a non-government agency in Melbourne, Victoria. In this context, my primary interface with leadership was through my supervisory relationship with my team leader. The direct guidance, as well as the organisational and system context, was navigated through this important working relationship.

Sam was three and a half years old when he was admitted with a ruptured spleen to intensive care at a large hospital. Upon discharge, he was placed into foster care. The child protection report suggested that Sam had been thrown across the room and against a wall by his mother as punishment for wetting his pants. She was subsequently charged with assault.

Sam was a pale, underweight child with large searching brown eyes. In the early days of his foster placement he avoided eye contact, spoke little and was frightened of everyday things like an iron and a garden hose. His speech was severely delayed, and he was not toilet trained.

The court ordered Sam and his mother to have contact three times a week for two hours at a time. As a young, passionate social worker who had seen the long surgical scar on this little's boy's body and the fear in his eyes, I was incredulous.

Whenever the word 'mum' was mentioned Sam would retreat behind furniture and become very still and quiet, usually sucking his thumb. How could we subject this little boy to contact with the person charged with inflicting his injuries, someone he clearly feared?

Sam's mother was unimpressed that the contact was supervised. I would be lying if I said my disposition as the access supervisor was friendly and welcoming. At best it was professional. Sam would refuse to enter the room ahead of me, and held onto the back of my clothes. His mum would reach out; Sam would retreat further behind me. Mum would complain that she could not see Sam as he was behind me. I would pick Sam up and place him on my knee facing her. Sam would turn around and face me and stroke my hair, over and over again. If I attempted to turn him around he would press himself into my chest and whimper. Mum was clearly unhappy with what she was seeing and would pace the room. She complained that if I wasn't in the room Sam would be 'fine'.

This was not why I was in social work. I wanted to make things easier for traumatised children, not harder! What 'rights' did this woman have given what she had done to her child? What about Sam's rights?

My supervisor was able to hear and tolerate my rage. As a leader she created a safe space for me to vent and lament the frustrations I was feeling towards 'the system' and to acknowledge my distress for Sam. She was also clear that it had to be about more than that. The energy I discharged was acknowledged and validated and, through her supportive leadership, transformed. We looked at the meaning behind my behaviour. I was angry and upset, that much was clear; but what else was lurking underneath? Certainly a fear of not being in control of decisions about this little boy's welfare and powerlessness in my capacity to protect him and to influence 'the system'. And a sense of deep disquiet about being in a room on a regular basis with a woman who had allegedly done terrible things to her child. Holding that in mind whilst also seeing that she wanted a relationship with this little boy. She sang a favourite nursery rhyme in an attempt to bring a smile to his face. She exercised restraint in reaching out and approaching him as she was aware he was frightened. She would pass me bags of clothing and toys to give to the carer. How to reconcile this with the template of the 'evil' mother?

Leadership supported me to see that reconciliation on my behalf was essential to supporting Sam, and that I need to hold the 'end-goal' in mind. I have come to realise that leadership often means being the one to change the 'dance' when the existing steps are not working. Could I accept the circumstances I could not control, and define and work with the elements I could influence? I was the adult in the room who Sam trusted. Could I demonstrate that I could keep him safe but not undermine his relationship with his mother? I realised I could not do this without developing a relationship with his mother. Could I reach out and initiate an adult discussion about creating the best possible contact environment for Sam? Could I utilise the contact as an opportunity to honestly and professionally record my observations about the interaction between Sam and his mother?

It was difficult to make that initial telephone call, and I was surprised when Sam's mother agreed to meet. Framed in the context of wanting to draw on her knowledge and understanding of Sam to make their time together as enjoyable as possible, we began to really talk. Taking the lead in this situation actually involved relinquishing some control and remaining open to news of difference. I heard about how when Sam was distressed she would sometimes take him outside and push him on the swing. She talked about some of the items she had brought to give to the carer and why they were important to Sam. One was a book they would occasionally read at night that made Sam smile.

Over the coming weeks we relocated contact to a park nearby, and Sam allowed his mother to push him on the swing. At the end of each session his mother read the book that Sam had previously enjoyed. At the beginning of each session, I gave Sam's mother an update on his activities from the last few days, and Sam could hear me talk about his swimming lessons, his love of brushing the carer's dog, and that he had made friends with the neighbour's children. I felt more comfortable with how the contact was progressing and reflected that part of taking the lead to change a situation sometimes involves giving up some control.

I wish I could say the relationship blossomed. Sam's mother was impatient when he wanted to swing for what she regarded as 'too long'; she read to him in a monotone and became frustrated when he would disengage from the story. But his fear response was less, and I can safely say we reduced the re-traumatisation.

When I received a witness summons to the children's court, good leadership provided what I needed to prepare and literally take the stand for Sam. The outcome was to maintain the placement with his carers, reduce the contact with his mother and plan towards long-term care. My evidence alone did not lead to this outcome and I am aware that sometimes, despite our very best efforts, decisions are made that are not in the child's best interests. On this occasion I felt that I not only had some influence but also that I had been on an invaluable learning journey.

Initially overwhelmed by a sense of powerlessness in the face of decisions made by the system, I needed skilled leadership to assist my focus on the important things such as the nature of contact between Sam and his mother and the way in which careful observation and recording of the contact could support future decisions being made in Sam's best interests.

Covey's (1989) concept of the Circle of Influence helps us identify and focus on what we can actually influence, as opposed to factors outside our control. I have learned that leadership requires the capacity to work within my circle of influence and, in doing so, the sphere of influence broadens.

As my supervisor approached the situation from a standpoint of curiosity, analysis and reflection, she was ensuring that I continued to be engaged in the process and had some sense of having someone alongside me (partner) to support me to influence the situation (empower). This is reflected in the Victorian Best Interests Case Practice Model, which not only considers what we do (such as gathering information, analysis and planning, actions and review) but how we do it (such as relationships, engagement, partnering and empowerment) (Miller, 2012).

Implications for practice

Insights have been drawn from the lived experience of leadership as well as from theory and research. Many of us become leaders before receiving formal leadership training, bringing with it a personal and professional responsibility to engage in a steep learning curve. This transition may also involve transitions in relationships from colleague to supervisor to manager. We bring to leadership our earlier experiences of being led by others as well as other observations both personal and professional.

A leader and/or the staff group may inadvertently use fight, flight or freeze reactions in the face of stress and challenge. As discussed in Chapter 10, another common reaction to stress is to flock. Considering what such reactions look like for ourselves as leaders is illuminating. Reacting with aggression, yelling and perceiving everything as a battle are not uncommon signs of leadership in fight mode. Abdicating responsibility and leaving staff to fend for themselves can be leadership in flight. Being stuck, unable to make decisions and general inactivity can be indications of frozen leadership. As we are human, it is not avoiding stress and the accompanying reactions, but recognising them in ourselves and drawing on the support and energy of others that can turn these reactions into positive leadership. Being still is different to being stuck. Advocacy and 'taking a stand' is different to belligerence. Self-care and accepting help from others are different to going missing in action. Collaboration is different to collusion or group panic.

Creating a culture where mistakes and confusion can be reflected upon is crucial. To create a collaborative learning culture, leadership must establish and strengthen structures, processes and social norms to nurture thoughtful practice and embrace 'respectful uncertainty' and 'healthy scepticism.' For example, realising what is in our control and what is not, so as to appreciate what we can still influence, is more likely to occur in a learning culture. In each of our accounts, there was confusion, doubt and even fear. Whether or not mistakes were made, staff need a "positive work culture that values the place of thinking and the healthy expression of feelings such as not knowing, doubt and uncertainty about what to do" (Gibbs, Dwyer, & Vivekananda, 2014, p. 14).

The potential emotional toll of this work is evident. Our ability to recognise our own emotional state and how it impacts on our functioning is instrumental in our ability to recognise and co-regulate the emotional state of others. These stories illustrate the role of state-dependent functioning, including the way our state impacts on our ability to make decisions, reflect, learn, take risks and set the emotional tone of a group. Our state will be affected by the nature of the work as well as by the expectations of leadership.

The contagion of human interactions highlights the power a leader can have in setting the affective tone of the group. The more self-regulated the leader, the more likely the group will be able to self-regulate, even in times of stress and distress. The converse is also true. This also illustrates the use of the power differential between a leader and the group (see Chapter 10). Using the power implicit in leadership enables the leader to set the tone. It is not only through what is said, but also through our demeanour and actions. However the power differential can amplify messages beyond our intent. A mild critique or casual suggestion can be felt with exponential force depending on how we manage this power dynamic. It is not only the style of the leader but also the staff member's experiences of other leaders that can have unintended consequences if we are not mindful of the possibilities.

Recognising state-dependent functioning also means leaders taking into account what can be reasonably expected of workers when they are under duress. When Dr Perry's colleagues returned from Gilmer or Annette Jackson and her colleagues were dealing with the aftermath of a child's death or Sarah Waters was 'ranting' about the system, we could have gone to the best training ever and it would have been water poured on concrete. We would not have been in a state to take in new information or try new ideas. We were in a state to be supported, led and buffered so that later we were in a more conducive state to learn and reflect.

Recognising our state and adjusting expectations accordingly are imperative. We are not magic puddings, and cannot spontaneously regenerate and replenish our resources and defences ready for the next challenge. We need sustenance, energy and support.

Key messages from this chapter

- A biopsychosocial lens enables us to gain valuable insights about leadership from neuroscience, psychology and sociology.
- If our physical and emotional state impacts our capacity to think, learn and behave, it also impacts our ability to lead. Being self-aware of our state and what influences this state are skills that require practice, reflection and honesty.
- There is value in reflecting on our own experiences of being led and of leading. Learning from missteps, mistakes and times of confusion are as revealing, if not more so, as learning from success and achievement.
- We are contagious. We influence each other through word, action and state. Those in positions of leadership have explicit and implicit power that will impact on others. The question is how we use this power to positive effect.
- Leadership holds an imperative to build and maintain optimism and hope – with a mix of healthy scepticism – in ourselves and others.

Questions for further consideration

1. When reflecting on your experience of being led or of leading others, what stories come to mind?
2. During times of crisis or adversity, what did you learn at the time or with hindsight about yourself as a leader and leadership in general?

References

Covey, S.R. (1989). *The seven habits of highly effective people: Powerful lessons in personal change.* New York: Free Press.

Frederico, M., Jackson, A., & Dwyer, J. (2014). Child protection and cross-sector practice: An analysis of child death reviews to inform practice when multiple parental risk factors are present. *Child Abuse Review, 23,* 104–115.

Gaskill, R.L., & Perry, B.D. (2014). The neurobiological power of play: Using the Neurosequential Model of Therapeutics to guide play in the healing process. In C.A. Malchiodi & D.A. Crenshaw (Eds.), *Creative arts and play therapy for attachment problems* (pp. 178–194). New York: Guilford Press.

Gibbs, J., Dwyer, J., & Vivekananda, K. (2014). *Leading practice: A resource guide for child protection frontline and middle managers* (2nd ed.). Melbourne: Department of Human Services.

Lindsay, N. (1918). *The magic pudding: The adventures of Bunyip Bluegum.* Sydney: Angus & Robertson.

Miller, R. (2012). *Best Interests Case Practice Model: Summary Guide* (2nd ed.). Melbourne: State Government of Victoria.

Munro, E. (2008). *Effective child protection* (2nd ed.). London: Sage.

Perry, B.D., & Szalavitz, M. (2017). *The boy who was raised as a dog: And other stories from a child psychiatrist's notebook: What traumatized children can teach us about loss, love, and healing.* London: Hachette.

Reder, P., & Duncan, S. (1999). Auditing mental health aspects of child protection. *Child Abuse Review,* 8(3), 147–151.

Senge, P. (1990). *The fifth discipline: The art and practice of the learning organization.* New York: Doubleday/Currency.

7

CULTURALLY RESPECTFUL LEADERSHIP

Indigenous staff and clients

Muriel Bamblett, Cindy Blackstock, Carlina Black and Connie Salamone

Acknowledgements: The authors would like to thank Megan Van den Berg and Suzanne Cleary, whose reflections contributed to this chapter.

Introduction

The impact of invasion and subsequent racist legislation, policies and practices enacted on Indigenous peoples has led to intergenerational family breakdown, poverty, trauma and the over-representation of Indigenous children in out-of-home-care in both Australia and Canada. Similar patterns of inequality and disadvantage are evident in Indigenous communities in other invaded and colonised countries. A new approach is required that is holistic, addresses structural discrimination and racism and rights-based. This requires reconceptualising child welfare at a policy and practice level to reflect Indigenous ontology, culture and experience. This chapter explores the experiences of two Indigenous organisations working in Indigenous child welfare.

The Victoria Aboriginal Child Care Agency (VACCA) is internationally recognised for its innovative and culturally based child welfare services for Indigenous children and families in Victoria, Australia. Interviews with two VACCA leaders, one Indigenous and the other non-Indigenous, are included here to illuminate concepts of leadership and good child welfare practice in an Indigenous agency. The First Nations Child and Family Caring Society (the Caring Society) is a national organisation supporting over 100 First Nations child welfare agencies in Canada to provide culturally based and equitable services. It uses a reconciliation framework called the Touchstones of Hope (Blackstock, Cross, George, Brown & Formsma, 2006) and a combination of public education/engagement and litigation strategies to achieve its aims. Taken together, VACCA and the Caring Society provide insights into how leaders in Indigenous organisations are effectively addressing structural discrimination in ways that promote culturally based and equitable services for Indigenous families.

Despite the efforts of Indigenous peoples in Canada and Australia to affirm self-determination and ownership over their own knowledge systems, the reality is that Western child welfare continues to be applied to Indigenous children and families. There have been attempts within mainstream child welfare to develop culturally competent practice to facilitate effective intervention; however, this is often constrained by not adapting the fundamental ontological approaches of the system overall, meaning that Indigenous practice is often marginalised. Moreover, although government departments and mainstream organisations may recruit Indigenous staff to work in child welfare, as these organisations do not privilege Indigenous knowledge and practice approaches it is often difficult for Indigenous staff, including leaders, to make a difference in these organisations.

This chapter focuses on Indigenous peoples in Canada and Australia within the context of child welfare. It will first discuss the context of Indigenous child welfare, then the role of leadership in relation to Indigenous and non-Indigenous staff. This chapter presents Indigenous alternative approaches and unpacks what this means and how this can be put into practice.

Context: not properly cared for

Historically, the policies and practices of Western child welfare have led to devastating outcomes of disconnection, loss of identity and cultural genocide for Indigenous children, families and communities. In Australia, a report by the Human Rights and Equal Opportunity Commission (now the Australian Human Rights Commission – *Bringing them home: Report of the National Inquiry into the separation of Aboriginal and Torres Strait Islander children from their families* – details the experiences and impacts of the Stolen Generations, when many Indigenous children (predominately, but not exclusively, between 1910 and the 1970s) were forcibly removed from their families as part of the racist child welfare policies in place (HREOC, 1997). Meanwhile, the Truth and Reconciliation Commission of Canada (TRC, 2015) found the dramatic over-representation of Indigenous children in the child welfare system to be rooted in the country's residential school system (akin to the Stolen Generations in Australia), and the mass child welfare removals of Indigenous children and their placement with non-Indigenous families in what is known as the "Sixties Scoop". The TRC further linked this over-representation to Canada's failure to provide equitable child welfare services to First Nations children today.

Despite some progress, child welfare authorities in Canada and Australia continue to remove Indigenous children from their families at disproportionate rates. Equally concerning is the failure to ensure that these children remain connected with their families, community and culture when they are in out-of-home care. Children in care have already experienced disadvantages and traumas that leave them vulnerable (Commission for Children and Young People [CCYP], 2016;

Secretariat of National Aboriginal and Islander Child Care [SNAICC], 2017). Furthermore, Indigenous children in out-of-home care have poor outcomes and poor life trajectories once they leave care (Jackson et al., 2013).

Both countries have a plethora of credible research documenting the over-representation, the systemic and intergenerational causes and the solutions to address it, dating back decades. The ongoing problems are more apt to be rooted in an inability of child welfare and governments to implement promising solutions than because they do not know any better. This is due, in part, to the infusion of Western ontological preference for new knowledge into Western governments and child welfare. The reflex to wrongdoing is to search for new answers that are presumptively better than old answers. This approach is the antithesis of the Indigenous worldview that recognizes and validates ancestral knowledge. The current focus on evidence-based practice across Western countries has the capacity to further drive practice away from Indigenous practices. Promisingly in Victoria (Australia) there are recent examples of government supporting Indigenous-led solutions – including implementing Aboriginal Guardianship, an Australian first (see Box 7.1).

The child protection system viewed from a human rights perspective is damning. It has resulted in the loss of identity; disconnection from family, culture and community; and the loss of access to land rights for Indigenous children. With the social damage, intergenerational trauma and poverty of Indigenous communities resulting in high levels of reported abuse and neglect, the child welfare system responds by developing and providing services for disadvantaged Indigenous children and families using Western constructs designed and overseen by government departments, and delivered primarily by mainstream organisations. The current child protection systems in Australia and Canada focus on episodic approaches to risk, removal and narrowly defined safety – with too little focus on family, cultural and community strengths, family support and actively supported reunification provided within culturally grounded practice. The problem with child welfare for Indigenous children and families is that it is mainstreamed in its philosophy, policy, practice and funding.

Unpacking the problems and exploring solutions

The problems: lack of cultural vision

There is a fundamental need to affirm Indigenous child caring knowledge and to defend against colonial instincts to marginalise it. Native American legal scholar Robert Williams (2012) explains that colonialism embeds a knowledge dichotomy where Indigenous knowledge is assumed to be savage and Western knowledge is assumed to be civilised. More investment needs to be made in exploring and affirming Indigenous ontology and practices related to children, whilst taking a clear-eyed look at which Western approaches compliment, versus contradict or diminish, care for indigenous children. For example, engagement, assessment and interventions within Child and Family Practice are not always 'culturally neutral', and often rely on individual practice rather than a culturally grounded system. In addition, many Western child maltreatment risk assessment tools (structured decision-making) codify structural disadvantage as personal deficit. This means that workers are not called upon to consider what child risk factors the family can reasonably control versus those over which they have little influence. Moreover, there is no balancing between the risk the child is experiencing in their family and the risk posited by child welfare placement (Blackstock, 2009). This leads to multiple issues. First, it means engagement, assessments and interventions are based on mainstream values and standards which are inappropriate for Indigenous people as they are not culturally safe; and, second, there is no consideration as to whether child welfare has something better to offer.

Too many times child protection removes a child from a remote Indigenous community they deem is unsafe; apply their Western carer and family assessment lenses; decide that there is not one family in that child's community with the resources required to care for the child; and then place the child with a non-Aboriginal family in a distant rural town or city who do not know their language, culture or community. In doing so, it is implied that every family in that remote community is so impoverished that they cannot raise a child well, and the material well-being of the child is placed above their cultural well-being. Children are removed from material poverty and placed in cultural poverty (Bath, Bamblett, & Roseby, 2010; Pocock, 2003; TRC, 2015). The same thing happens in Aboriginal families in towns and cities. Children are removed for their safety and child protection is unwilling to find an aunt, uncle, cousin, brother, sister, grandmother, grandfather or any other kin to care for the child. It is much easier to find the non-Aboriginal stranger who, in their cultural habits and family background, better resembles the protective workers of the state than to place the child with what looks familiar to them (Sinclair, 2007). Given the distrust of child welfare by Indigenous families, protective workers are often unable to effectively engage in finding family within the Indigenous family. Furthermore, family is understood as meaning the nuclear family rather than the Indigenous understanding of family, which includes a wider kin system and sees raising children as a collective responsibility that a number of families can undertake.

Drs Marsiglia and Kulis, authors of *Diversity, Oppression and Change: Culturally Grounded Social Work*, contend that "when the desired results are not attained, there is a tendency to blame the client rather than to assess the cultural relevance of the service delivery system" (2009, p. 202). This is what plays out too often, and how the situation of punishing families and children but not the service systems occurs. This is the truth not just for Aboriginal children but for children of colour around the world. This is a system that sees difference as deficiency. Today, providing staff with cultural understanding training is the norm. However this is inadequate to the task of teaching at a profound level Indigenous knowledge and practice approaches. Assessment of Indigenous children and families is still done through a Western cultural lens. This lens requires the child or family to leave elements of their culture behind so they can satisfy a Western construct of family functioning. Furthermore, this lens places no weight on the impact of racism on individual functioning, so does not develop solutions to address system interface or seek community input to alleviate the issues.

The change we need to see

A new child welfare paradigm is required to engage families in a culturally embedded model of service. Research led by Professor Michael Chandler powerfully demonstrates what can be achieved: with more self-determination, community control and promotion of culture, communities have less incidence of youth suicide (Chandler & Proulx, 2006). There are six key areas Child and Family Practice needs to contribute to, to change, if better outcomes for Indigenous children, families and communities are to be realised. These are:

1. Self-determination and commitment to Indigenous human rights, including truth-telling about history.
2. Indigenous culture as central to Indigenous Child and Family Practice. Culturally grounded practice that amplifies the voice of community must be incorporated in all aspects of practice.
3. Prevention, holistic assessment and management of risk; this will maximize keeping children with their families when safe to do so, and assist in successful and timely reunifications.
4. Address structural inequalities, especially poverty within Indigenous communities.
5. Address systemic racism and discrimination, including the colonial diminishing of Indigenous knowledge and peoples.
6. Investment in workforce development and innovation.

Human rights interacting with practice

Indigenous Child and Family Practice needs to be based on the Indigenous status and rights of Indigenous children and the right of Indigenous people to self-determination. Indigenous children have rights under the United Nations Declaration of the Rights of Indigenous Peoples (UNDRIP) and the Convention of the Rights of the Child as interpreted pursuant to the United Nations Committee on the Rights of the Child (UNCRC) General Comment on 'Indigenous children and their rights under the Convention' (UNCRC, 2009). Classifying Indigenous people as disadvantaged and welfare dependent is to continue to colonise. Implementing self-determination restores power and agency, and places the onus for meaningful solutions where it belongs – with Indigenous people. This needs to occur within a framework that encompasses Indigenous people as culturally distinct with cultural and spiritual needs and an association with land as the original custodians. It requires non-Indigenous agencies to acknowledge that their current approach has not been effective.

Cultural healing

Much is written on Western approaches to trauma-informed therapeutic interventions. Less is written about Indigenous trauma-informed healing. Indigenous Australia and Indigenous Canada are in fact multicultural communities and consist of complex and diverse societies. Understanding and acknowledging these differences is required. However, there are common elements of Indigenous healing. Rather than focusing on ways of adapting Western models to an Indigenous context, it is vital to learn from more than 60,000 years of wisdom. According to the National Aboriginal Community Controlled Health Organisation, services from an Indigenous perspective do not just aim for an absence of the signs and symptoms of mental illness in an individual, but rather "strive to achieve the state where every individual is able to achieve their full potential as a human being of their community" (NACCHO, 2011, p. 5).

Cultural healing is integral to healing intergenerational trauma for Indigenous children. A trauma-informed approach is required which makes sense of children's presentations based on understanding intergenerational trauma – namely, the impacts of history on Indigenous people over the past centuries and the continuing traumatic effects on families today. Indigenous understanding of healing places the child or individual family within the context of their community and culture, and attempts to solely focus on an individual child or family without this will not succeed.

Prevention and management of risk

Numerous inquiries and policymakers have recommended earlier intervention and prevention support for Indigenous families. The strategies for prevention need to have community input into their design to be meaningful and ensure their effectiveness. They need to target areas of high concern such as maltreatment, family violence and substance misuse, and be cognisant of Indigenous understandings of their causes. For example, to adopt a structured, gendered, analysis understanding of family violence without understanding the impact of colonisation on the role of men, the separation of children from families and the importance of family-focused interventions will not be meaningful to Indigenous people, and thus will not be effective.

Indigenous children are removed from their families largely due to neglect and emotional harm. Risk needs to be understood in this context as not simply an event that occurred at a point in time. The capacity to tailor interventions on this understanding means having the capacity to manage risk whilst implementing long-term strategies. The risk-adverse nature of child protection systems results in the removal of Indigenous children without seeking to address ongoing issues that, if resolved, will ensure greater safety for children than being in out-of-home care and remove the risks posed by loss of culture and community to children's self-image and resilience. Furthermore, Indigenous agencies are more likely to actively engage the families, harness community assets and involve key family members in decision-making to address risks. Accordingly, Indigenous organisations are best placed to provide interventions that can both prevent and mitigate risks and promote safety and wellbeing through strong cultural and community connections. By their very nature mainstream services are unable to do this.

Structural inequalities

Child welfare interventions focus on the individual child or family and not on the causal factors that play a significant role in child maltreatment. Poverty is a common factor in the Indigenous child protection population, yet rarely does professional development deal with the impact of poverty on families and promote poverty-reducing strategies. Rather, the system blames the victim and their Indigenous status.

Systemic racism and discrimination

Good practice with Indigenous families factors into assessment and goal-setting the experience of racism. This is critical, for example to assess a child's poor educational outcomes: has the child been educationally disadvantaged by the school context where Indigenous styles of learning are not considered or the teachers' understanding of different cultures is limited? The family's inability to engage with local services may be due to a lack of cultural understanding by the agency rather than the client simply refusing to use support services. However, the impact of such factors does not appear in mainstream child welfare assessments.

Workforce development and innovation

A transformed system needs a capable and skilled workforce. What is needed is resource allocation that intentionally grows and restores the capacity of Indigenous communities, including their cultural regeneration. The education system has largely failed Indigenous people. A reconceptualisation of the tertiary system is required, especially in Australia. In Canada there are pockets of intentionally rethinking social work courses to be a better fit for Indigenous people (such as in Manitoba). Tertiary courses need to be designed to ensure methodologies used cater for Indigenous learning styles; and course contents need to reflect Indigenous understandings and show deep respect for Indigenous knowledge and knowledge makers. Education is a powerful enabler of change and a key facilitator in accessing leadership positions. More Indigenous people can then have an impact through leadership roles – in parliament, policy settings and creating change in service systems.

Box 7.1 provides two examples of cultural healing by VACCA (2015); both examples demonstrate how doing things differently can lead to positive outcomes for Indigenous children and their families.

BOX 7.1 CULTURAL HEALING EXAMPLES FROM VACCA

Healing through cultural strengthening: possum skin cloak-making

Like all cultural programs at VACCA, the Possum Skin Cloak Project was developed and implemented with community involvement, and guided by principles of empowerment and self-determination. The project involves Elders who teach the traditional skill of making a possum skin cloak to young people in out-of-home care. It is not only the action of making the traditional cloaks, but it is relational – a journey of people coming together and sharing knowledge. Traditional stories are told, and connection to community made. The young people listen to Elders speak about how the cloaks represent connection to country, language and clan. Parents and carers also attend; a collective healing and cultural strengthening practice that has impact beyond the workshops.

There have been significant transformations: young people have developed stronger relationships with each other and with Elders. They are using 'Aboriginal English' and show greater pride and confidence in themselves and their identity. The older youths appreciate that they will pass on these stories; they sense their role in passing on knowledge and take pride from this. Spending time with Elders, artists and community members helps young people understand who they are and where they come from, and helps their cultural connections develop (see also Bamblett, 2014).

Healing through self-determination in practice: Aboriginal guardianship

In Victoria, the legislation overseeing child welfare – the Children, Youth and Families Act 2005 – includes provisions on the protection of Aboriginal children. This allows the transfer of powers and functions from the Secretary of the Department of Health and Human Services to an Aboriginal organisation. In preparation for this section being enacted, VACCA operated a pilot project involving 13 children in out-of-home care on long-term court orders, taking on the primary role of case planner and decision-maker. The pilot outcomes were significant and positive. Families were actively involved in their children's lives, and culture was integrated into planning and decision-making. All children had cultural support plans and genograms (graphical representations family relationships and medical history). Children were engaged in cultural programs, and culturally based practices such as 'Return to Country' and children's involvement in 'Sorry business' (community loss and grief rituals) were attended to. Around 60 per cent of children returned to their parents' or families' care (some had been in out-of-home care since infancy; the majority for over five years).

> The most significant learning has been that, through the development of strong and positive relationships between a competent, professional, Aboriginal organisation and Aboriginal families who have previously been 'written off', children can be safely returned to their family's care. Self-determination in practice leads to powerful, positive outcomes (VACCA, 2015).

Reflections of leaders working within an Aboriginal Community Controlled child and family service

Child and Family Practice needs to be culturally grounded, trauma-informed, healing-driven and culturally safe in order to work respectfully and effectively with Indigenous children and families. The following section presents themes that arose from interviews with two leaders, one Aboriginal and one non-Aboriginal, with extensive experience working within Aboriginal Community Controlled Organisations (ACCOs) and currently in leadership positions at VACCA and leading large staff teams of majority Aboriginal staff. To effectively work with Aboriginal children, families and communities both leaders emphasised the need to understand and respect: history and its impacts today; the lived experience of Aboriginal people, including staff and clients; and Aboriginal culture and its healing force. Further themes essential to leadership that emerged were working differently, working together and organisational obligations. Each theme is discussed below and highlighted with a quote from the leaders.

Understand and respect history

"First and foremost is understanding of history and its impacts today."

Leaders need to have a deep knowledge of history and educate themselves about past governments' policies and practices of forced removal of children from their families and the continuing profound impact on Aboriginal children and families today resulting in both intergenerational trauma and community disadvantage. As leaders this means there is a responsibility to ensure that, through formal professional development, staff understand this history and how it impacts on families 'on the ground'.

Lived experience of Aboriginal people

"Let's listen."

Leaders must reflect on what they need to do to support staff and to fully appreciate the impact of the work on Aboriginal staff. Among Aboriginal staff it is about valuing life experience and not unduly privileging formal qualifications. Aboriginal people may be employed on the basis of their community knowledge.

This is seen as a key skill that needs to be respected. Some Aboriginal staff may not have formal qualifications and, although very good at the work with children and families, may struggle with reporting/compliance requirements. Taking on staff, leaders have the responsibility to ensure they have the opportunity to develop the full suite of skills that will ensure success. Coaching, mentoring and professional development need to be provided to ensure that Aboriginal people are not excluded from practising in child welfare as their lived experiences are invaluable in their personal understanding of families' experiences, the impact of the system on families and their capacity to engage isolated families.

Aboriginal staff members' experiences may not be that different to those of their clients. Leaders need to be mindful that this does not mean staff cannot do their job, just as it must never be assumed that clients cannot succeed. The majority of Aboriginal families are doing well, thriving and bringing up strong and proud children.

Aboriginal culture and its healing force

"It is much more about being than knowing."

Leaders need to ensure that their organisations – in their policies, systems and practices – embed the message that culture is healing and protective, and provides resilience and safety; it leads to identity and belonging.

Leaders need to ensure that governments' drive on compliance and reporting does not override the core purpose of the agency to promote healing and to ensure that there is capacity to do things differently to mainstream services. As leaders, it is critical that programs are designed and implemented that reflect Indigenous understandings and ways – such as narrative approaches, peer learning processes and community and Elder involvement in programs (see Box 7.1 for innovative culturally grounded programs).

Working differently and working together

"Throw out all that you know, and let go of your way being the way to get things done."

Working in Indigenous Child and Family Practice is different to the mainstream, and leaders need to be able to embrace rather than challenge this. Leaders need to be aware of the power of language. Aboriginal people have been *told, talked at* and *done for*. Leaders need to listen and be guided by what Aboriginal people tell them, and to embrace that there are usually many ways to achieve an outcome – not just the way things are done in mainstream agencies.

People who do well in leadership roles within Aboriginal Child and Family Practice are respectful of others and highly prize working together. It also requires accepting that a range of people are involved in decision-making. Being a leader in

Aboriginal child and family welfare is about galvanising others, encouraging them to come up with ideas and empowering Aboriginal staff to become leaders. In some instances lateral violence can result in staff not wanting to take up leadership roles. Leaders need to think creatively and flexibly to ensure that potential leaders feel safe and supported to explore leadership opportunities.

Developing an understanding of cultural protocols and cultural observance is required when working in Aboriginal communities. Spending time within an Aboriginal community, attending community events and understanding the importance of acknowledging Elders at these events are all important ways to develop understanding and show respect. Leaders need to appreciate the significance of men's and women's business and incorporate Sorry business, which may require staff to take additional leave. Working with Elders on the staff may need to be approached quite differently, and an additional level of respect must be demonstrated. As leaders, there will also be times when poor performance needs to be addressed, and this should not be avoided simply because a staff member is Indigenous. Ultimately, staff need to contribute to meeting the needs of the Aboriginal community.

Organisational obligations in employing Aboriginal staff

> "Staff wellbeing is not an add-on; it's the focus."

Leaders need to foster supportive and culturally safe workplaces. Policies and procedures play an important role in contributing to the culture of agencies. Racism is part of daily life for Aboriginal people and comes in many forms: casual, institutional, systemic. The increased exposure to trauma and discrimination for Aboriginal staff means organisations need to operate from a trauma-informed approach.

Organisations have an obligation to support the needs of Aboriginal staff, including through increased flexibility in recognition of the cultural load carried by Aboriginal staff. Figure 7.1 illustrates the cultural load as experienced by Aboriginal leaders working in their communities in Aboriginal Child and Family Practice. Recognition of this load highlights the importance of self-care for staff and leaders, and the need to ensure that regular supervision and mentoring is in place.

The role of advocacy in leadership

Leaders need to harness knowledge, creativity, faith (as in willingness to walk into the unknown), vision and passion. Leadership requires holistic and determined observation of the values of respect, moral courage, social justice and self-determination in action. Regardless of specific roles, all leaders in Indigenous Child and Family Practice need to act out these values by being advocates for Indigenous children, families and communities. Leaders must advocate for a system that ensures the rights of Indigenous children, families and communities are protected. Leaders need to believe in families and their ability to change; they need to empower families to change, and to be able to do so without having to deny or dismiss their Indigenous culture.

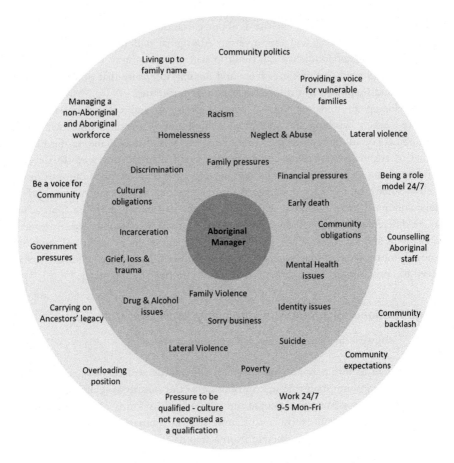

FIGURE 7.1 Cultural load, complexity and context for Aboriginal leaders

Deeply entrenched problems require a passing of the baton from one generation to another, rarely giving one generation the satisfaction of a job completed and done well. Leadership always looks more confident in the rear-view mirror. Leadership is messy, and leadership in social justice is even messier. So for leaders carrying the baton, there is a need to glance back and see our ancestors as confident and wise touchstones; they provide a steadying influence. Box 7.2 provides a powerful example of unrelenting advocacy in action from a leader past.

BOX 7.2 LEARNING FROM LEADERS PAST: UNRELENTING ADVOCACY

Dr Peter Henderson Bryce became Ontario's first Public Health Officer, and president of the American Public Health Association (Milloy, 1999). He was a staunch believer in science and government and a recognised expert on communicable diseases, and thus a natural choice when in 1904 the Canadian government commissioned a study on the health of First Nation children attending residential schools. In 1907, Bryce presented to Parliament a scathing report noting that 24 per cent of children died within a year of entering these schools due to abuse, fires and preventable disease, and that if children were followed over a three-year period, 48 per cent were dead. In one school for which there were complete records, 78 per cent of the children were dead before they reached 16 years. Child deaths were so prolific that graveyards became regular landmarks on residential school grounds.

Encouragingly, Bryce stated that 'medical science knows just what to do!' and all that remained was for the Canadian government to act with vigour on his recommendations (Milloy, 1999). The government did nothing to help the children, but it matched Bryce's unrelenting advocacy with an equally unrelenting campaign to discredit him (Bryce, 1922; Abley, 2013). Bryce's sense of personal betrayal by the government system he helped create ran deep; but his commitment to equality ran deeper, and thus he repeatedly subjugated his claims for personal justice beneath those for the children. In 1922, Bryce published 'A National Crime' setting out the preventable deaths in schools; what Justice Blake described as "bringing Canada into uncomfortable nearness with manslaughter". Commenting on Bryce's manuscript, *Saturday Night* magazine noted "children were dying like flies" in rates akin to soldiers dying in the First World War (Abley, 2013). But still Canada did nothing. Bryce continued to advocate for reforms until his death in 1932, and the Canadian government continued to resist his ideas. The last residential school closed in 1996. The Truth and Reconciliation Commission recently announced that at least 4,000 children died unnecessarily in the schools, and graveyards are still being discovered. Bryce reminds us – to be a leader is to be an advocate for change and to be unrelenting in the fight for social justice.

An impactful recent example of unrelenting advocacy comes from the Caring Society under the leadership of Dr Cindy Blackstock, who in 2007 and in partnership with the Assembly of First Nations brought a human rights case against the Canadian government to end its longstanding practice of providing First Nations children with significantly fewer child welfare services than other children in Canada receive. The Canadian Human Rights Tribunal (CHRT) released its landmark decision in 2016, substantiating the complaint and ordering the federal government to cease its discriminatory conduct toward over 165,000 First Nations children (*First Nations Child and Family Caring Society of Canada et al. v Attorney General of Canada*, 2016 CHRT 2). It was by all accounts a landmark win as it was the first time domestic human rights law was used to legally require the Canadian government to uphold the human rights of Indigenous children; and it was also the only human rights case to be nested in an on-line public education and engagement campaign, called 'I am a witness'.

Reflecting on the type of leadership necessary to successfully achieve justice for First Nations children, Dr Blackstock states:

1. Manage yourself. This means conducting yourself with the highest level of integrity and accountability to the best interests of children at all times, including in your personal life. This is not always easy so a good support system of Elders, family and friends who will support you and get you back on track when needed is essential.

2. Honour Indigenous values in all aspects of your advocacy. You cannot stand up for something unless you demonstrate it.

3. Lead with authority not with power. Authority is given and must be earned; power is asserted and often proclaimed by title alone. You must strive for the former and avoid the latter.

4. Be more interested in doing right than being right. Ensure you are advocating based on the self-defined interests of Indigenous peoples and that you are well prepared with facts, knowledge and ceremony. Be open to dissent and willing to adjust your thinking and actions when needed.

5. Be morally courageous, with honour. Moral courage is when you do or say something about an injustice which will result in some negative personal consequences. Indigenous social justice often means we must stand up and take a hit when needed but it must be done in ways that recognise the dignity of children and families we work with.

6. Love and light are more powerful than hate and darkness. Elders know that love and light are the only things that can defeat hate and darkness.

7. Welcome the participation of others and give thanks when they help. Thanksgiving is a cornerstone of Indigenous leadership often expressed through spirituality, ceremony and gift giving. It is recognition of the special gifts others bring and an encouragement for them to continue to give the best of who they are.

8. Keep focused and never give up until justice is done. It may take years or even decades but every child is worth standing up for and every child is worth the sacrifice.

9. Start anyway. When you are faced with a profound injustice that is deeply rooted in powerful organisations and governments some people say they cannot make a difference. You won't if you don't try.

Like Dr Bryce, Dr Blackstock experienced enduring attempts to stall her actions and discredit her personally, and she reflects; "I bask in the freedom of knowing that while all physical things and social relationships can be taken from me, only I can give away my values."

Conclusion

We conclude by talking about hope. We need sustained outrage, and we need this to be mixed with a healthy dose of hope. To sustain this hope a system is needed that recognises the strengths, protection and resilience that come from Indigenous culture. Culture provides healing. Culture is healing. We see it to be true, daily in our work.

We all need to hear, and respond to, the voice of Indigenous communities. As Professor Patrick Dodson (2009) stated: "a system that builds on the strength and resilience of Aboriginal people and recognises Indigenous knowledge systems can enable us to navigate our own path through modernity". Nothing should be too hard to contemplate if it could be part of the solution. The system includes different actors with varying degrees of power as well as resources. In this matrix the Indigenous community have the least control, power and resourcing. Nevertheless, Indigenous leaders have a key moral power and responsibility because it is about Indigenous children and families. The change needed cannot be achieved if it is only the Indigenous community that is mobilised. Non-Indigenous leadership and advocacy are also required.

It is our hope that this chapter encourages the reader to question their assumptions and inspires leaders to reflect on their practice. We hope we have made the reader feel somewhat uncomfortable because it means assumptions and views have been challenged in some way. Ultimately, we hope that by authoring this chapter we can inspire conversations and actions that can contribute to better outcomes for Indigenous children, families and communities in Australia, Canada and beyond.

Key messages from this chapter

- It is clear that the current approach to Indigenous child welfare, both in Australia, Canada and elsewhere, needs to be transformed. To achieve this requires a genuine commitment to further self-determination and address poverty and systemic racism.
- At a practice level what is required is a flexible, holistic approach that does not finish with the placement of children in out-of-home care, but instead focuses on children's cultural and trauma healing in the context of their families and communities.
- An alternative model will be best achieved by delegating the design, development and management of Indigenous child welfare from government child protection authorities to Indigenous community agencies.
- Communities must be empowered and supported to implement the solutions; solutions that will not only support the individual but that will also create stronger communities.

Questions for further consideration

1. What leadership elements struck you as the most important in this chapter, and what does mainstream child welfare have to learn from them?
2. What elements of leadership cut across organisations that provide direct services like VACCA and national organisations that focus on structural disadvantage and reconciliation like the Caring Society?
3. What do you do in your work to model the message that valuing difference is essential?

4.   What can you do – whether Indigenous or non-Indigenous, both individually and within your organisations and professions – to advocate for a child and family welfare system based on Indigenous rights and self-determination for Indigenous children and families?

References

Abley, M. (2013). *Conversations with a dead man: The legacy of Duncan Campbell Scott*. Madeira Park, BC: Douglas & McIntyre.

Bamblett, M. (2014). The Possum Skin Cloak: Being warmed by culture. *Children Australia*, 39, 134–136.

Bath, H., Bamblett, M., & Roseby, R. (2010). *Growing them strong, together: Promoting the safety and wellbeing of the Northern Territory's children*. Darwin: Board of Inquiry into the Child Protection System in the Northern Territory.

Blackstock, C. (2009). *When everything matters: Comparing the experiences of First Nations and non-Aboriginal children removed from their families in Nova Scotia from 2003–2005* (doctoral dissertation). University of Toronto, Canada.

Blackstock, C., Cross, T., George, J., Brown, I., & Formsma, J. (2006). *Reconciliation in child welfare: Touchstones of hope for Indigenous children, youth and families*. Ottawa: First Nations Child and Family Caring Society of Canada.

Bryce, J.H. (1922). *The story of a national crime: Being an appeal for justice to the Indians of Canada; the wards of the nation, our allies in the Revolutionary War, our brothers-in-arms in the Great War*. Ottawa: James Hope & Sons.

Chandler, M., & Proulx, T. (2006). Changing selves in changing worlds: youth suicide on the fault lines of colliding cultures. *Archives of Suicide Research*, 10, 125–140.

Commission for Children and Young People (CCYP). (2016). *Always was, always will be Koori children*. Melbourne: CCYP.

Dodson, P. (2009, February 17). Indigenous rights: Beyond symbolism. Invited lecture at the University of Notre Dame, Sydney.

Human Rights and Equal Opportunities Commission (HREOC). (1997). *Bringing them home: Report of the National Inquiry into the separation of Aboriginal and Torres Strait Islander children from their families*. Sydney: HREOC.

Jackson, A.L., Waters, S.E., Meehan, T.L., Hunter, S. , &Corlett, L.R. (2013). *Making tracks: A trauma-informed framework for supporting Aboriginal young people leaving care*. Melbourne: Berry Street.

Marsiglia, F., & Kulis, S. (2009). *Diversity, oppression and change: Culturally grounded social work*. Chicago: Lyceum.

Milloy, J. (1999). *A national crime: The Canadian government and the residential school system 1879 to 1986*. Winnipeg: University of Manitoba Press.

National Aboriginal Community Controlled Health Organisation. (NACCHO). (2011). *NACCHO Constitution*. Canberra: NACCHO.

Pocock, J. (2003). *State of denial: The neglect and abuse of Indigenous children in the Northern Territory*. Melbourne: Secretariat of National Aboriginal and Islander Child Care (SNAICC).

Secretariat of National Aboriginal and Islander Child Care. (SNAICC). (2017). *The Family Matters Report 2017*. Melbourne: SNAICC.

Sinclair, R. (2007). Identity lost and found: Lessons from the 60's scoop. *First Peoples Child and Family Review*, 3(1), 65–82.

Truth and Reconciliation Commission of Canada. (2015). *Final report of the Truth and Reconciliation Commission of Canada*. Toronto: James Lorimer & Company.

United Nations Committee on the Rights of the Child. (UNCRC) (2009). *Committee on the Rights of the Child General Comment No. 11: Indigenous children and their rights under the Convention.* Geneva: UNCRC.

Victorian Aboriginal Child Care Agency (VACCA). (2015). *Culture is healing: Evaluation of VACCA's cultural healing programs.* Melbourne: VACCA.

Williams, R. (2012). *Savage anxieties: The invention of western civilization.* New York: Palgrave Macmillan.

8

CULTURALLY COMPETENT LEADERSHIP

Culturally diverse clients and staff

Menka Tsantefski

Introduction

In recent years a shift in migration patterns in English-speaking countries has increased cultural diversity. Larger numbers of migrants now come from developing countries affected by war and political, social and economic turmoil, which reflects growing refugee movement on a global scale. These changing demographics require a culturally competent child protection response; one that is sensitive to differences between groups and is equally responsive to real or potential child maltreatment (Korbin, 2002). Delivery of a culturally competent service requires culturally competent leadership. This chapter commences with a broad definition of culture and considers its role in Child and Family Practice. The chapter addresses the implications for leadership in relation to direct practice with children and families and in supporting staff to provide culturally competent services.

What is culture?

To provide effective leadership in cross-cultural child protection practice it is first necessary to consider what culture is. Definition is elusive but tends to include ethnicity, practices, values and beliefs, or faith, shared among groups of people. Culture is regarded as a dynamic process in which populations continually adapt to changing circumstances (Johnson & Munch, 2009; Korbin, 2002; Mederos & Woldeguiorguis, 2003). Cultural differences are sometimes discussed in terms of dominant and minority groups. At the core of this difference is the power to determine a dominant discourse that defines social norms and rules, including appropriate parenting practices, which in turn shapes how child protection systems respond to families from minority or diverse backgrounds.

Cultural relativity or universal protection?

Indisputably, all children are equally entitled to protection. However, there is tension in child protection practice between cultural absolutism, which judges all parenting practices by the one standard, and cultural relativism, which questions a universal benchmark (Richards, 2016). Each approach has potential for harm. The absolutist approach fails to consider the influence of culture on parenting as well as differences in social, economic and political power between ethnic groups, while cultural relativism runs the risk of condoning harmful parenting practices if child protection workers consider them culturally appropriate and therefore acceptable (Sawrikar & Katz, 2014). By contrast, culturally competent practice does not accept all practices by all cultures and should not, therefore, be confused with cultural relativism (Johnson & Munch, 2009).

Ethnic minority families in child protection systems

Although they originally come from different countries, have migrated for different reasons and occupy different overall positions in society, all minority families face the challenge of migration and resettlement. While this may pose specific risks to children and increase the risk of maltreatment among some groups, it is difficult to reliably establish the number of children from immigrant or refugee backgrounds in child protection samples as many jurisdictions do not record these data. Le Brun and colleagues' (2015) systematic review of child maltreatment in immigrant and refugee families found that minority children are not at higher risk of maltreatment than their majority peers. The overall results of their study indicate that when children in immigrant and refugee families are notified to child protection authorities, the most likely reason for notification is physical abuse and, to a lesser extent, physical neglect, followed by emotional/educational neglect and sexual abuse, or emotional abuse. The latter sometimes arises from exposure to family violence. Importantly, analysis revealed a correlation between length of residence in the new homeland and severity of abuse, with recently arrived communities more likely to engage in harsher physical discipline of children, particularly adolescents.

There are similarities and differences in the characteristics and experiences of minority families compared to those from the 'majority culture' coming into contact with child protection services. Both groups tend to have experienced economic disadvantage, low educational attainment and high rates of unemployment. There are no significant differences between the groups, either, in relation to risk factors such as domestic violence, social or economic support or parenting stress (Dettlaff & Earner, 2010, as cited in Richards, 2016). However, some risk factors are unique to the migrant experience. These include: migration stress; loss of identity; the different level of acculturation of children versus parents; lack of awareness of child protection laws; fear of authority; racism and discrimination. Refugee families have the additional burden of legacies of trauma (Le Brun et al., 2015; Richards, 2016; Sawrikar & Katz, 2014). There have been few studies of protective factors in immigrant and refugee families. The evidence that does exist suggests that minority parents are less likely to use alcohol and other drugs, and that they are likely to have the support of extended family, when accessible (Richards, 2016). Having a mother born overseas has been found to lower the risk of maltreatment (Le Brun et al., 2015).

Reasons for minority families entering child protection systems

The reasons minority families enter child protection systems largely fall into three categories: factors within the family, such as parenting and cultural practices; discriminatory and inappropriate organisational responses; and factors beyond the child protection system, such as societal discrimination. Parenting practices may differ between minority families and the dominant culture, leading child protection workers to assume that actions by minority parents are harmful to children. Such parenting practices include differences in supervision when older children care for younger siblings (Sawrikar, 2014). Corporal punishment is another fraught area: while physical chastisement is legitimate in many jurisdictions, understanding of reasonable force can differ between families and authorities (Akilapa & Simkiss, 2012; Levi, 2014; Losoncz, 2016). The ensuing intervention by child protection services may be construed by parents as undermining their authority and status within the family (Levi, 2014; Losoncz, 2016). What parents consider reasonable chastisement of their children with the aim of protecting them from perceived dangers and risks in the new homeland – such as discrimination, violence, the influence of gang culture and drugs – may be physical in nature (Le Brun et al., 2015).

Parents can find the greater freedom experienced by young people in the host country threatening to family structure and balance. This is particularly problematic when young people are assisted by authorities to live independently from the family through financial and other support (Levi, 2014; Losoncz, 2016). Further, different acculturation rates between parents and children can shift power dynamics across generations as children become more proficient in acquisition of language and more rapidly develop understanding of systems and structures in the new community (Le Brun et al., 2015; Levi, 2014; Losoncz, 2016). This is particularly so for those migrants who are from non-Western cultural backgrounds and/or non-English speaking. In response, parents may attempt to reinforce cultural identity and accentuate traditional, more authoritarian parenting practices, sometimes resorting to corporal punishment, regarded by some minority groups as a responsibility of parenthood rather than abuse. While ideas and norms about child rearing vary among cultural groups, and both immigrant and refugee parents may not understand child protection laws in the new homeland, there is often shared perception of more extreme forms of abuse between the dominant group and minority families (Le Brun et al., 2015).

Specific cultural practices among some groups can predispose children to harm. Female genital cutting is one example. Although the effects vary widely depending on the type of procedure performed, consequences for girls can be severe and life-long (Akilapa & Simkiss, 2012). Children with disabilities are at greater risk of harm in the general population; however, disability is highly stigmatised and seen as a curse within some cultural groups. Children with disabilities, along with those with conditions such as epilepsy, learning difficulties and physical illness, can be per-ceived to be possessed by spirits and may be branded as witches. These children are at risk of being beaten to expel spirits or of being concealed, which has the con-sequence of denied access to valuable services. As Akilapa and Simkiss point out, while the number of children abused in this way is low, the effects can be sig-nificant. Traditional health practices such as coining and ritualistic cutting or pull-ing of teeth are defined as abusive in Western culture (Richards, 2016). Trafficked children are a highly vulnerable and largely invisible group at great risk of physical and mental harm (Akilapa & Simkiss, 2012). Honour killings are another example of unique risks for some minority children.

Factors related to resettlement among refugee families can intersect with cultural differences in the host community, leading to additional stressors for families and greater misunderstandings between family members and service providers (Losoncz, 2016; Richards, 2016). Insecure immigration status can increase levels of parental stress. Families with insecure residency are also more likely to be in insecure employment or to be unemployed. Additionally, immigrant and refugee families tend to be geographically located in socioeconomically disadvantaged neighbour-hoods, which suggests the influence of poverty and deprivation on family func-tioning rather than culture (Akilapa & Simkiss, 2012; Maiter & Stalker, 2011). Although the link is not significant, social isolation has, nevertheless, been found to contribute to maltreatment among immigrant and refugee families (Le Brun et al., 2015). Some refugee families, in particular, may no longer have the support of extended family to sanction traditional parenting practices; many of these families are headed by sole parent mothers in large family sizes, without the support of extended family members (Losoncz, 2016).

Discriminatory organisational responses include workers' lack of awareness of differences in parenting practices and racial stereotyping of families which can lead to erroneous assumptions about parenting practices. Cultures differ in their expec-tations of children, with some allowing children greater independence and responsibility at an earlier age. Some minority families have the support of exten-ded kinship networks, and the resulting caring arrangements for children may not be fully understood by child protection workers (Richards, 2016). Lack of cultural awareness, sensitivity or competence at the level of the worker and/or the orga-nisation can result in overly intrusive practice on the one hand or, on the other, inactivity with children in need of protection. Child protection workers may find it difficult to raise the topic of culturally appropriate parenting if they fear causing offence or if they mistakenly attribute harmful practices to issues of culture or faith. Organisational responses also fall short when the need for interpreter services is not adequately met, when culturally appropriate placements are not available and when the broader context of families' lives is not addressed (Earner, 2007; Maiter &

Stalker, 2011). Racial stereotyping and discrimination can lead to over-reporting of children from minority backgrounds, leading to greater scrutiny of families and increased likelihood of active involvement with child protection authorities (Richards, 2016). Once within the system, there is greater incidence of substantiation of concerns, leading to increased rates of child removal from parental care (Detlaff & Earner, 2010, as cited in Richards, 2016). The challenges of settlement in a new cultural environment, such as precarious employment and language barriers, make it more difficult for minority families to access services and support, including those needed for reunification with children removed from parental care (Earner, 2007; Le Brun et al., 2015; Maiter & Stalker, 2011).

Culture should always be considered when seeking to understand the context in which child maltreatment occurs; but it should not be regarded as the sole or even the most significant determinant. Cultural competence is needed to assess the role of familial, cultural, organisational and societal factors in reports of child maltreatment and for the provision of culturally appropriate service delivery.

Cultural competence and child protection

The term 'cultural competence' is variously interpreted, but generally refers to practice in which workers have the requisite knowledge and skills to effectively engage with different cultural groups (Johnson & Munch, 2009). Culturally competent child protection practice includes workers' awareness of, and sensitivity towards, their own values and biases and to difference in power between themselves and their clients. Workers also need to have knowledge of practice approaches that can be appropriately applied with families from a range of cultures, alongside skills in verbal and non-verbal communication (Yan & Wong, 2005). However, to be effective, cultural competence needs to operate beyond the level of the individual child protection worker who comes into contact with families and to include the child protection agency from which the worker operates and the wider child protection system (Sawrikar & Katz, 2014), as discussed below. The child protection manager has responsibility for practice in each of these areas.

Mederos and Woldeguiorguis (2003) propose three basic models of cultural competence: cultural sensitivity; self-reflective cultural sensitivity; and cultural collaboration. These are hierarchical, with each demanding different commitment and effort from the child protection manager and their organisation. The cultural sensitivity approach is largely concerned with the acquisition of knowledge about the target population and with using this knowledge to educate and inform staff. The process can be undertaken through focus groups, formation of collaborative relationships with individuals from the target population through engagement of consultants, or by partnering with communities to introduce knowledge into the organisation. In addition to training staff, recruitment might focus on hiring applicants from specific populations. The second approach, self-reflective cultural sensitivity, moves beyond knowing about others to reflection on the self and how the culture and values of the organisation can facilitate or impede work with minority groups. In this approach, managers reflect on personal and organisational values and promote a continuous process of group inquiry among staff, one that acknowledges that child protection work is value-laden rather than value-neutral.

The third approach, cultural collaboration, includes all of the elements of the first two approaches, and extends them by including a focus on institutional power and acknowledgement of the privilege vested in managers and institutions from the dominant culture. In order to engage with power, the cultural collaboration approach identifies that the organisation has acted oppressively towards certain groups and seeks to empower those same groups. At the same time, changes are made to understand and counteract organisational practices that negatively affect specific populations. The cultural collaboration approach is more inclusive of target communities and seeks to involve them as partners in the redesign of services, a process that is well organised, consistent and continuous. In this way, the manager works to counter personal and institutional privilege and to share power with the target community (Mederos & Woldeguiorguis, 2003).

The implications for practice

Managers aiming to provide culturally competent leadership need to consider issues in terms of: the individual workers who engage with and provide support to families; organisational factors that facilitate or impede good practice; and policy developments that perpetuate power relations or that promote continuous improvement through inclusive practice with families and communities.

Engagement with immigrant and refugee families

The involuntary nature of child protection intervention, which carries with it the very real risk of removal of children, understandably generates fear in parents. Depending on the family's history, a deep-seated fear of government organisations and authority may make engagement with immigrant and refugee families more challenging than working with families from the majority culture. Parents may also fear that child protection intervention could lead to deportation. These fears can contribute to a significant barrier in the establishment of rapport and in engagement, which makes good assessment and effective intervention more challenging (Slayter & Kriz, 2015). At the outset, the reasons for child protection involvement and the role of the worker need to be clarified. While this principle applies to all families coming into contact with child protection services, more care needs to be taken when working with minority families as they may not be familiar with the role of child protection services or understand the mandate to protect children (Maiter & Stalker, 2011).

Effective engagement with diverse families requires the creation of a culture of trust and respect, and the development of mutual understanding through open dialogue (Losoncz, 2016). Clearly, this is difficult when parents lack proficiency in the language of the host nation or where cultural differences in relations between men and women create obstacles to communication (Dufour, Lavergne, Gaudet, & Couture, 2016). Child protection leaders therefore need to take steps to ensure that communication barriers are overcome. This is usually achieved by matching the family with a caseworker from the same, or a similar, ethnic group or, at the least, one able to speak a language in common with the family. Matching of clients and workers is discussed in more length below in relation to allocation of cases.

When a matched worker is not available and language barriers remain, parents or carers may request that a child, friend or neighbour interpret for them (Earner, 2007; Maiter & Stalker, 2011; Sawrikar, 2015). Managers need to ensure that their staff not only understand the importance of explaining to families why this is not acceptable, but also that they have the requisite skills to clearly convey this information to the family. The family should be informed that although a trusted friend can be included in their interactions with the worker, a professional interpreter or translator will still be required to increase the likelihood of the parent receiving quality information. While interpreters can help facilitate a productive relationship with the worker, the solution brings its own set of challenges. To begin with, assumptions should not be made regarding the choice of interpreter. While families involved with child protection services have expressed preference for a worker able to converse in their language (Maiter & Stalker, 2011), the client family may hold concerns about confidentiality when the interpreter is from the same community, in which case an interpreter who speaks the same language but is from a different community could be employed. Child protection managers and managers also need to ensure that consideration is given to the gender of the interpreter, particularly when sensitive issues such as child sexual abuse are part of the reason the family is involved with services. In this instance, it may be important to match the gender of the parent with the interpreter, depending on the parent's preference.

Challenges in the use of interpreters also reside with the interpreter, the caseworker and the child protection agency. The quality of interpreting services and their sensitivity to child protection issues can vary significantly and result in inaccurate translations. While client family and interpreter may be matched to increase cultural awareness and empathy, differences between them can nevertheless result in biases and judgements on the part of interpreters. Sourcing an interpreter able to speak the required language or dialect can prove to be difficult, and availability for home visits and reliability may be problematic. On their part, workers may not be experienced in managing conversations mediated by an interpreter, which could compromise assessment and intervention. Using interpreters is also time-intensive and adds additional cost to casework. When factored in to case allocation, the implication for budgets is clear (Sawrikar, 2015). To adequately support staff and client families, the child protection manager needs to be aware of interpreting services in their area and to address shortfalls in availability and/or quality of services. This could involve arranging joint training between child protection staff and interpreter services to ensure sensitivity to child protection issues (Sawrikar & Katz, 2014) and advocating for funding to increase access, where required. The child protection manager may also need to advocate for additional resourcing from within their organisation when caseloads have larger numbers of families from minority backgrounds.

Supporting families

Appropriate support to immigrant and refugee families requires negotiation towards co-construction of meaning. While children are entitled to know their rights, child protection managers and their staff need to remain sensitive to how intervention in family life is perceived by minority parents. As previously mentioned, minority families have argued that child protection services empower adolescents to the extent that parental authority is undermined, thereby inadvertently increasing risk to the young person (Levi, 2014; Losoncz, 2016; Maiter & Stalker, 2011). Parents may not fully comprehend the gravity of concern expressed by child protection services in relation to inadequate supervision. In this instance, workers could convey that what is safe in one context may not be in another (Sawrikar, 2014). Parents may also need education and support to align cultural parenting practices with legal requirements in the host country, to learn new strategies for managing challenging behaviours and to assimilate new cultural norms (Levi, 2014). To achieve this, parents are often referred to parenting support services. However, ethno-specific services are sometimes not available, and parents can grapple with language barriers and cultural differences in parenting practices. When ethno-specific services are available, similar concerns about confidentiality mentioned above in relation to interpreter services apply and can form a significant barrier to service use. Minority families are also likely to require additional assistance in accessing services. The child protection manager needs to ensure that written information in the form of brochures in the family's language are available and provided to families (Earner, 2007). When they do access services, minority families can feel deceived into accepting intervention by child protection services if the monitoring role is not adequately explained, and the service is described as a support (Maiter & Stalker, 2011).

Training

Effective child protection services cannot rely upon a small number of nominated 'experts' among staff from minority groups (Sawrikar & Katz, 2014). It is the manager's role to ensure that staff members have the requisite training to deliver a culturally competent service which begins with self-awareness, with the under-standing of how one's own cultural identification influences the working relationship with families from different cultures. This is not about suspending one's own cultural influences and the inherent values and beliefs but, instead, about being aware of how the worker contributes to the interaction with the client and about seeking shared understanding as a basis for sound practice (Yan & Wong, 2005). Training needs to help workers identify barriers to communication and service use by specific groups and for individual families within groups. For example, a family may have heightened fears of involvement with child protection due to insecure immigration status (Earner, 2007). Training could help child protection workers understand and improve responses to the fear their presence may generate in parents (Slayter & Kriz, 2015). Much is known about risk factors for children in immigrant and refugee families, but there is little literature identifying strengths in minority families. Training on cultural and parenting practices of target groups could help workers identify strengths. There is an important role for managers and team leaders in child protection services in reviewing risk assessment instruments used in their agency and in providing quality supervision of staff to ensure comprehensive strength-based assessment.

Allocation of cases

There is very little literature on ethnically diverse workers and child protection outcomes. The literature that is available suggests increased cooperation by families and greater completion of treatment goals when clients and workers are matched (Ryan, Garnier, Zyphur, & Zhai, 2006). Matching the worker to the client family's ethnicity or language negates the need for interpreters and opens possibilities for easier, more nuanced communication and greater understanding of the family's needs and struggles (Maiter & Stalker, 2011). While there are distinct benefits, the child protection manager needs to consider the implications for confidentiality and the allocation of cases. A minority population can appear sizeable to those outside the group, but bonds of kith and kinship can be extensive, which has implications not only for the family but also for the worker appointed to a position of authority within their own community. Even when client family and worker share a common background, differences in education, socioeconomic status, gender, age or life experiences and acculturation can result in as wide a gulf as if the two were from different cultures; hence, differences in power and possible communication barriers remain (Korbin, 2002, p. 639). It is important that the child protection manager addresses these issues with their staff through regular supervision.

Despite the benefits for children and parents, it is not always possible to match the client family with a worker from the same ethnic group or one who speaks the family's language, and interpreters will sometimes need to be employed. This adds to the time needed for meeting with families. Further, services and support can be harder to find for minority families. To reflect additional complexity in practice, the child protection manager needs to consider if adjustments should be made to the caseloads of workers with high numbers of families from a minority background. As with the use of interpreters, managers need to guard against assumptions about client preferences. While some families will prefer an ethnically matched worker, others will not, and some may not have any preference. Ideally, the family's choice should be respected. Again, it may also be preferable to match the gender of the worker to the individual parent or family's preference, particularly when there are sensitive issues such as domestic violence or child sexual assault (Sawrikar, 2013).

Recruitment, supervision and professional development

Lack of staff diversity has been shown to lead to lengthy delays in court proceedings and in reunification of children to parental care in minority families (Earner, 2007). While it is clear that child protection managers need to build and maintain culturally diverse staff teams, this can be difficult to achieve and considerable time and effort may need to be allocated to reaching target groups through job advertisements. In addition, qualifications and experience may need to be evaluated to ensure that good applicants are not barred through rigid recruitment systems. Interview processes also need to be examined. For example, applicants from minority groups may be more reticent in interviews, which may be misconstrued. For majority applicants, the capacity to respond appropriately to the needs of minority groups is an important attribute for the manager to consider (Mederos & Woldeguiorguis, 2003).

Once employed within the organisation, it is likely that minority staff will encounter specific challenges in the workplace. In this under-researched area of child protection practice, it is reasonable to extrapolate that issues arising for parents and children in the majority culture will occur for minority workers. That is, the same power dynamics evident between minority families and workers from the majority culture are likely to characterise relations between workers from minority backgrounds and managers from the majority culture. Staff members from minority backgrounds may present differently in their teams and in supervision compared with other workers. If reflective practice skills are under-developed, there is a risk that workers from minority backgrounds could fail to challenge their own cultural values and biases, which could affect their practice, as has been argued above in relation to other workers. Supervision is an avenue for developing critical reflective practice, and is equally important when members of a minority group work with their own community. Group supervision within or, if numbers do not permit, beyond, the agency could help create a supportive environment for staff members from minority backgrounds.

As with client families and their workers, assumptions should not be made about the preferences of workers from minority backgrounds. Unless they are in a nominated specialist position, staff from minority backgrounds should be given a choice about the extent to which they work with their own community: some may prefer a mixed caseload; or they may prefer not to work with their own community, particularly if it is small and confidentiality is of concern. While staff members from minority backgrounds may welcome the opportunity to share their knowledge, care should be taken to not make generalisations which could risk individual staff members feeling like a 'token' member of a minority group being asked to speak on behalf of a larger, heterogeneous group. Nevertheless, the specialist knowledge of workers from minority backgrounds should be acknowledged and opportunities created for them to contribute to the improved cultural responses of their team and the wider organisation through consultations (Earner, 2007) and engagement with their community. In addition, staff members from minority groups may not readily gain higher qualifications and may be more likely to remain in direct practice (Palmer, Bexley, & James, 2011), in which case there is a very real risk that the benefits of their cultural sensitivity may not sufficiently permeate organisational knowledge and practice, or influence organisational culture. Managers therefore need to actively work towards ensuring that staff members from minority backgrounds have opportunities for professional development and leadership. They also need to examine staff turnover to see if staff from minority backgrounds are more likely to leave the organisation sooner than their counterparts as this could reflect lack of opportunity or higher burnout rates.

Service delivery including evaluation and community outreach

The child protection manager working towards culturally competent practice needs a strategic plan covering program development and service delivery, staffing and community engagement, with a well-defined vision supported by goal-setting and evaluation of progress. A good starting point is to examine the prevalence of families from specific ethnic minority or target groups in notifications to ensure that systemic bias is not inappropriately netting families. Consultation should take place with community groups in the local area to ascertain if assessment and intervention are appropriate to the community's understanding of parenting and childcare. This could include examination of risk-assessment instruments to ensure sensitivity to the strengths and needs of minority families (Mederos & Wolde-guiorguis, 2003; Sawrikar & Katz, 2014).

Conclusion

Connected to direct practice through their teams and in contact with higher levels of the organisation where decision-making power is greater, child protection managers and team leaders are well positioned to help pivot policies and practices beyond cultural sensitivity and towards cultural collaboration. This requires adherence to a few core principles. To begin with, there is a need to understand how power differences between members of minority and majority groups shape social norms and rules, and how these differences affect child protection practice with children and families. There is the onus not only to scrutinise one's own values and biases, but also to support critical self-reflective practice among staff through training and supervision. There must be commitment to inclusive practice that engages with immigrant and refugee communities and that includes them in decision-making. Finally, there is responsibility for ensuring that organisational policies and procedures do not result in discriminatory practices with minority families or staff from diverse backgrounds.

Key messages from this chapter

- Minority families may be brought to the attention of child protection services due to discrimination.

- Leadership in culturally appropriate child protection practice is premised upon an understanding of power differences that exist between minority families and the majority culture and the development of shared understanding of child maltreatment.
- Community engagement is essential in ensuring that responses to children and families are appropriate.
- The child protection manager needs to provide a supportive work environment for all staff working with minority families and staff from minority backgrounds.

Questions for further consideration

1. How can respectful conversations be supported when there are differences between the views of parents and communities and child protection managers regarding appropriate parenting?
2. How can child protection managers meaningfully engage with communities to improve responses to immigrant and refugee families?
3. What do child protection managers need to do to ensure that organisational policies and procedures are responsive to the needs of families from minority backgrounds?
4. How can staff from culturally diverse backgrounds be supported to maximise their contribution to effective cross-cultural child protection practice?

References

Akilapa, R., & Simkiss, D. (2012). Cultural influences and safeguarding children. *Paediatrics and Child Health*, 22(11), 490–495.

Dettlaff, A., & Earner, I. (2010). Children of immigrants in the child welfare system: Findings from the National Survey of Child and Adolescent Well-Being. Research brief, Migration and Child Welfare National Network (MCWNN).

Dufour, S., Lavergne, C., Gaudet, J., & Couture, D. (2016). Protecting visible minority children: Family–caseworker dynamics and protective authority intervention strategies. *Canadian Psychology/Psychologie Canadienne*, 57(4), 356–364.

Earner, I. (2007). Immigrant families and public child welfare: Barriers to services and approaches for change. *Child Welfare*, 86(4), 63–91.

Johnson, Y.M., & Munch, S. (2009). Fundamental contradictions in cultural competence. *Social Work*, 54(3), 220–231.

Korbin, J.E. (2002). Culture and child maltreatment: Cultural competence and beyond. *Child Abuse & Neglect*, 26(6–7), 637–644.

Le Brun, A., Hassan, G., Boivin, M., Fraser, S.L., Dufour, S., & Lavergne, C. (2015). Review of child maltreatment in immigrant and refugee families. *Canadian Journal of Public Health*, 106(7), Supplement 2, 45–56.

Levi, M. (2014). Mothering in transition: The experiences of Sudanese refugee women raising teenagers in Australia. *Transcultural Psychiatry*, 51(4), 479–498.

Losoncz, I. (2016). Building safety around children in families from refugee backgrounds. *Child Abuse & Neglect*, 51, 416–426.

Maiter, S., & Stalker, C. (2011). South Asian immigrants' experience of child protection services: Are we recognizing strengths and resilience? *Child and Family Social Work*, 16(2), 138–148.

Mederos, F., & Woldeguiorguis, I. (2003). Beyond cultural competence: What child protection managers need to know and do. *Child Welfare*, 82(2), 125–142.

Palmer, N., Bexley, E., & James, R. (2011). *Selection and participation in higher education: University selection in support of student success and diversity of participation*. Melbourne: Centre for the Study of Higher Education.

Richards, J. (2016). Refugee migration and the intersection with child protection services: A call for further policy discussion. *Social Development*, 38(2), 34–46.

Ryan, J.P., Garnier, P., Zyphur, M., & Zhai, F. (2006). Investigating the effects of caseworker characteristics in child welfare. *Children and Youth Services Review*, 28(9), 993–1006.

Sawrikar, P. (2013). A qualitative study on the pros and cons of ethnically matching culturally and linguistically diverse (CALD) client families and child protection workers. *Children and Youth Services Review*, 35(2), 321–331.

Sawrikar, P. (2014). Inadequate supervision or inadequate sensitivity to cultural differences in parenting? Exploring cross-cultural rates of neglect in an Australian sample. *Qualitative Social Work*, 13(5), 619–635.

Sawrikar, P. (2015). How effective do families of non-English speaking backgrounds (NESB) and child protection caseworkers in Australia see the use of interpreters? A qualitative study to help inform good practice principles. *Child and Family Social Work*, 20(4), 396–406.

Sawrikar, P., & Katz, I.B. (2014). Recommendations for improving cultural competency when working with ethnic minority families in child protection systems in Australia. *Child & Adolescent Social Work Journal*, 31(5), 393–417.

Slayter, E., & Kriz, K. (2015). Fear factors and their effects on child protection practice with undocumented immigrant families: 'A lot of my families are scared and won't reach out'. *Journal of Public Child Welfare*, 9(3), 299–321.

Yan, M.C., & Wong, Y.R. (2005). Rethinking self-awareness in cultural competence: Toward a dialogic self in cross-cultural social work. *Families in Society*, 86(1), 181–188.

9

LEADERSHIP PRACTICE IN DOMESTIC AND FAMILY VIOLENCE

Cathy Humphreys

Introduction

Leadership in the domestic and family violence (DFV) area will hold both similarities and differences with other practice domains. The areas of difference are potentially more interesting than the similarities. In this chapter, three specific points structure the chapter and respond to the question of 'what leaders need to know'. In each of the three sections, the practice implications will then form part of the discussion.

Firstly, strong leadership in the DFV area needs to support and connect with the social movement to end DFV and, more generally, violence against women and their children (Nixon and Humphreys, 2010). While the movement is diffuse, this is not an area where an individual acts alone. The quality of leadership is linked to the extent to which collaboration and strategic alliances are built to progress a broad social agenda connected to practice. Secondly, the context for DFV is constantly changing. Embracing and indeed leading in new areas for policy and practice change while remaining committed to core principles which hold the safety and well-being of women and children and accountability for perpetrators of violence and abuse are determining characteristics of leadership in this area. The dynamic nature of the knowledge base requires leaders in the field to be aware of and responsive to the changing nature of the field. Intersectionality (McKibbin, Duncan, Hamilton, Humphreys, & Kellett, 2015) and attention to diversity (disability, poverty, ethnicity, LGBTI issues) – alongside the service system developments in relationship to child protection, drug and alcohol services, and health and mental services – exemplify the changing nature of the sector. Thirdly, the domestic and family violence system is complex and requires leadership that can grasp the multiple layers of primary, secondary and tertiary intervention and the interactions between these different levels for effective engagement (Desmond, 2011).

The chapter works from an inclusive definition of domestic and family violence drawn from the Australian National Plan to reduce violence against women and their children 2010–2022 (Council of Australian Governments, 2009). It defines domestic and family violence as:

> acts of violence that occur between people who have, or have had, an intimate relationship. While there is no single definition, the central element of domestic violence is an ongoing pattern of behaviour aimed at controlling a partner through fear, for example by using behaviour which is violent and threatening. In most cases, the violent behaviour is part of a range of tactics to exercise power and control over women and their children, and can be both criminal, and non-criminal. Domestic violence includes physical, sexual, emotional and psychological abuse … Family violence is a broader term that refers to violence between family members, as well as violence between intimate partners … the term family violence is the most widely used term to identify the experiences of Indigenous people, because it includes the broad range of marital and kinship relationships in which violence may occur. (p. 2)

In keeping with the dominant patterns of domestic and family violence, throughout this chapter we refer to 'victim survivors' as women and men are referred to as perpetrators (Cox, 2015; Walby & Allen, 2004). We recognise that this is the dominant but not the only pattern of DFV. Women can be perpetrators and men may be victims. However, these are minority patterns and the language reflects the majority pattern.

Understanding leadership in context

> To hold traumatic reality in consciousness requires a social context that affirms and protects the victim and that joins victim and witness in common alliance. For the individual victim, this social context is created by relationships with friends, lovers and family. For the larger society, the social context is created by political movements that give voice to the disempowered.
>
> *(Herman, 1992, p. 9)*

This profound statement by Judith Herman – an early advocate, writer and practitioner in the area of trauma and violence – situates leadership in the domestic and family violence (DV) area within its wider context. Domestic violence thrives in secrecy and is diminished when brought into the open. In this context, a stance against violence requires not only a response to an individual 'client' but also recognition of the role the organisation needs to play in 'standing up to violence', or a 'whole of organisation' response (Victorian Royal Commission, 2016).

Implications for practice

The issues for leadership in this area differ depending on whether the role is within a specialist domestic violence organisation or a 'mainstream' organisation. In the former, those accessing the organisation, whether women, children or men, will have domestic violence already identified as an issue in their lives. In mainstream services, DFV will be present as an issue for those accessing services, but it is not named as the primary business of the organisation: for example, statutory child protection; a children's hospital; a family support service for vulnerable families.

Within the broader context of Child and Family Practice organisations, there has been a strong tendency to allow domestic violence to 'disappear' (Murray & Powell, 2011). Mental health issues, gambling, drug and alcohol issues, the neglect of children can all assist in moving domestic violence to the background. Unless the DFV is blatantly physical, it is often easier to name and confront other issues in the lives of children and their families. The fear for workers of being a target of violence or of escalating the violence towards women and children markedly constrains the work in this area and contributes to its invisibility in an intervention with a vulnerable family (Baynes & Holland, 2012). It is work where an effective response requires a level of specialist training, ongoing support through supervision and procedures which create a context for worker safety to make domestic violence 'visible'. These are key leadership issues for supervisors and managers to create the context for responding to DFV. The Judith Herman quote reminds us that the ethics of responding to DFV are central to the efficacy of the response – creating an alliance between 'victim survivor' and worker to: assist in naming the range of behaviours that constitute DFV (physical, psychological, sexual and financial abuse, and the impact of fear on the cognitive, behavioural and emotional development of children); understand and expand the attention to protective actions which have been taken and assess their continued effectiveness in the face of violence and abuse; and to help her assess the risks and safety issues for herself and her children, and to access appropriate support. The service system has also been replete with mother-blaming, holding victim survivors responsible for protecting children rather than responding effectively to curtail the abusive actions of fathers who use violence (Galvani, 2006). Clear and principled leadership is required to provide an affirming and ethical response which holds safety for adult victim survivors and children and accountability for perpetrators as foundations for practice.

The notion of an alliance between a worker (or witness) to the victim's account of violence and abuse is assisted by the recognition by supervisors and managers that within their own workforce are many victim survivors of DFV. The evidence in this area indicates that within the health and human services arena the workforce experiences violence and abuse at the same rate as the community as a whole (McLindon, Humphreys & Hegarty, forthcoming). A 'whole of organisation' response acknowledges the need to address the needs of the organisation's own workforce in this area if they are to respond effectively. The provision of domestic violence leave for those experiencing current abuse; the responsiveness of managers to staff who require support with their experience of DFV; proactively responding to bullying and harassment; training in responding to DFV which recognises the ways in which it touches their own workforce are examples of responding as a 'whole of organisation'. In effect, the organisation models and responds to the ubiquitous nature of DFV, providing the foundation for responding to those employed and those accessing the service (Powell, Sandy, & Findling, 2015).

In modelling the practice at an organisational level that is expected of frontline workers, the significance of strategic alliances across the service system and with 'victim survivor' representatives cannot be underestimated. Assisting children, women and men to navigate the service and justice system is particularly difficult if there are no strategic partnerships between organisations in which agreements about intervention in DFV have paved the way for action. No organisation alone responds effectively to DFV. Effective action requires close and tight collaboration between services and high levels of trust about the need for safety, confidentiality and accountability (Ross, Healey, Diemer, & Humphreys, 2016). Assertive advocacy and leadership are required to affect a change response. At the heart of advocacy lies the respect for 'victim survivors' to be given a voice and a platform from which they can be heard (Hague & Mullender, 2006). In Australia, Rosie Batty became the Australian of the Year and exemplified the leadership that 'victim survivors' can provide (Australian Broadcasting Corporation, 2015). She supported other men and women to speak out with passion and commitment; she was tireless in her speaking engagements across the year; and she strategically used her role for policy advocacy with senior public servants and politicians. She and others with the lived experience of DFV help attract public attention to the private pain of violence and abuse in the home. There is a role for all those in senior roles in organisations to ensure the legitimacy of the 'victim survivor' in naming DFV. Without such advocacy, victims lose their voice and the ability to name the violence they are experiencing.

Embracing the context for change

The prevention of and response to DFV has undergone seismic changes since the late 1990s (Murray & Powell, 2011; Stanley & Humphreys, 2015). Four areas that have been chosen for discussion epitomise the change process and configure the discussion of requirements for effective leadership. They include: 'mainstreaming' the DFV response; engaging with the issues of diversity and intersectionality; tilting the work to hold a stronger focus on men, and particularly fathers who use violence; and addressing the changing nature of DFV.

The establishment of the first women's refuges in the 1970s responded to the issues emerging in the second wave of feminism. For many years, responding to DFV became part of a specialist, largely women-only response (Hanmer & Itzin, 2000). The work was expanded when the Duluth Model developed by Ellen Pence and colleagues provided credible interventions for men who use violence. This extended the response to interventions that targeted the perpetrator of violence and the need for integrated community responses that tightened the accountability of the system to respond to violence (Pence & McDonnell, 1999). In this process, it became clear that police, courts, housing services, health services and children's services needed to develop a specialised response to DFV within their mainstream service system. This major shift in the service system response has significantly broadened the range of services available to children, women and men. However, it has brought with it further challenges when these systems are not designed to respond to DFV.

Linked to the shift from a specialist women's response has been the acknowledgement of a wider range of issues beyond gender which affect the lives of those subjected to violence and abuse. In Australia, the response to family violence in Aboriginal communities has brought particular challenges to feminist perspectives on DFV, demanding a more complex approach which takes greater account of community connection and potentially restorative justice for those who perpetrate violence (Nancarrow, 2010). An understanding of intersectionality initially brought into focus the particular issues affecting black and minority ethnic women. The work of a range of other diverse groups who experience marginalisation and oppression quickly gathered momentum to highlight the issues for women with disabilities; lesbian, gay, bisexual, transgender and intersex (LGBTI) communities; men as victims of DFV; women living in poverty, and older women. Intersectionality provided a common feminist voice which could claim to simultaneously acknowledge diversity and recognise that gender was not the only dimension critical to identity and oppression. It enabled policymakers and practitioners interested in feminism to speak about the way in which various groups of women (as well as men and children) experience difference and disadvantage (McKibbin et al., 2015, p. 101; Crenshaw, 1991).

The work which came to light through the Duluth Model of focusing on creating system accountability for men who use violence has continued to develop. For instance, the work of the Safe and Together group (Mandel, 2014), with its focus on DFV responses in the child protection system, has coined the phrase 'pivot to the perpetrator'. The historically poor attention to men in child protection work is countered through this emerging focus on fathers who use violence. The point is made that without a perpetrator of violence there are no victims to attend to. While a blatantly obvious statement, it is needed to counter what has been the primary focus by child protection workers on women and the assessment of their role in protecting their children in spite of being victims themselves.

The concerted attention to men who use violence and the demands to look beyond gender to other sources of vulnerability have brought to attention the need for a more diverse understanding of DFV. A wider range of offenders are coming to notice. In particular, adolescent violence in the home is now becoming recognised as a significant problem as mothers, but also fathers, siblings and grandparents, are subjected to violence by young adolescents (Wilcox & Pooley, 2015). To date, the service system response is undeveloped and inconsistent for both the adults and the young people involved. A similar statement could be made about the abuse of older people. Again, the patterns of abuse and violence show similarities (DFV perpetrators continue their controlling behaviours as they age), but also differences as the children of older people abuse and control their more vulnerable parents (Brandl, Hebert, Rozwadowski, & Spangler, 2003).

While the knowledge of the diversity of groups impacted by DFV increases, the range of strategies used to control abuse is also increasing. The use of new technologies to cyber-stalk or abuse sexting communications has gained momentum. The ubiquitous nature of violent pornography is normalising the humiliation of women as a source of sexual stimulation for men and boys. Such imaging is reported to be framing the expectations of sexual relations among some young men, and constitutes new vulnerabilities for the exploitation of and violence against women and girls (Owens, Behun, Manning, & Reid, 2012).

Practice implications

Each area of change provides a reminder of the need for dynamic leadership. The second wave feminists and early activists developed important principles which remain pertinent to current practice. The priority on safety, the respect for survivor perspectives, the push to recognise the need for justice, the recognition that acts of gendered violence are set within a wider social context of inequality and violence-supportive attitudes are all hallmarks of the earliest developments that remain relevant for current practice (Laing, Humphreys, & Cavanagh, 2013). Leadership in this area will ensure that these important principles are not lost.

However, the decades have witnessed a more complex understanding of DFV. The need for a response within the mainstream of the service system presents particular leadership challenges. Mainstreaming not only holds a tendency for DFV to 'disappear', but also lack of specialist training and attention to the foundational principles identified above can lead to poor practice which colludes with the perpetrator of violence and provides blame rather than a supportive alliance with 'victim survivors'. In the process the voice of children may also be lost (Kimball, 2016).

The difficulties of mainstreaming children living with DFV into the statutory child protection response exemplifies the problems which practitioners struggle with and which DFV leaders need to negotiate. The issues for the organisation include: the problems of dealing with both an adult and a child victim (given the adult victim is usually the child's mother); the requirement to work with fathers who use violence; the problem of post-separation violence which means that child protection in many cases should remain involved in spite of there being a protective parent; and understanding and responding to the connections between DFV, drug and alcohol problems and mental health issues (Humphreys & Absler, 2011). Overcoming these structural organisational barriers provides key challenges for DFV leaders to create a response which is fit for purpose.

Responding to diversity also provides an arena where energetic engagement with particular communities and their organisations is required. For example, in Australia working with and through Aboriginal organisations does not occur without building extensive relationships based on trust and respect. A sensitive response cannot be imposed by government departments or predominantly white women's organisations (Nancarrow & Viljoen, 2011). Strong DFV leadership recognises and values the time required to build these relationships, including allowing staff the time to meet with Aboriginal leaders to customise and support their response to DFV. Each area of intersectionality will provide its own challenges and requirements which recognise that a 'one size fits all' response to DFV will never be effective.

The need to adapt to diversity is writ large in the renewed focus on working with perpetrators of violence. Perpetrators of DFV vary greatly in their use of drugs and alcohol, their mental health problems, their socio-economic status and the cultural communities through which they rationalise their abusive behaviours. Their status as fathers (either biological or social) may provide a significant point of difference which widens the reach of their abusive behaviours, but also may positively affect their motivation to change (Stanley, Graham-Kevan, & Borthwick, 2012). However, the commonalities between perpetrators of violence may be much greater than their differences. The desire to control others and to use violence and abusive tactics to realise this aim is common across perpetrators of violence. For men who use violence, deprecating attitudes towards women can fuel their sense of entitlement to use violence. Most important for DFV leaders is the recognition that it may not be the level of severity of violence that points to the greatest risk, but the lack of consequences for violence and abuse which influences decisions to continue the use of violence: the system matters (Gondolf, 2002). It is here that DFV leaders, with their oversight of the system, have a role to play in noticing where the vulnerabilities to poor practice lie.

An area of increased vulnerability in the system's response to violence and abuse lies in the lack of preparedness to intervene effectively to counter the use of new technologies available to perpetrators of violence to control their victims. Working closely with police to curtail cyber-stalking and supporting legislative and policy developments to provide appropriate consequences are examples of where flexible and informed leadership is required. Other areas would include attending to the ways in which young adolescent men are accessing online pornography (Owens et al., 2012). This latter issue draws us to the next aspect of leadership, namely under-standing the complex and multi-layered requirements for intervening in DFV.

The complexity of the public health response

Leadership in DFV requires an understanding of and engagement with the multiple levels at which intervention is required. An ecological approach has informed the development of a public health model of prevention (Heise, 1998). This model recognises that primary prevention (prevention of the problem developing in the first instance), secondary prevention (directing resources to vulnerable groups) and tertiary prevention (preventing further development of the problem once it is occurring) provide useful framing of the service system. However, adaptations have also been made to address some specific issues in the DFV sector: in particular the need to disaggregate the crisis response from the healing and recovery issues when addressing the tertiary prevention agenda (Figure 9.1).

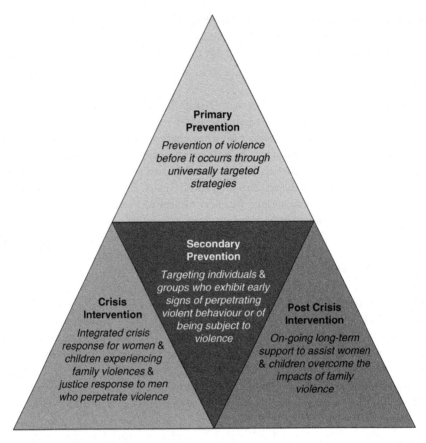

FIGURE 9.1 Family violence intervention pyramid
Source: Desmond (2011, p. 7)

Currently, most of the DFV resources are directed to crisis intervention at the tertiary end of the system. While important, the long-term answers to the 'wicked problem' of DFV lie in the primary prevention area (Ellis & Thiara, 2014). We will not treat our way out of this major social problem. Resourcing child care centres, youth clubs, and primary and secondary schools to develop and implement respectful relationship programs which counter violence-supportive attitudes that children may experience in their homes, communities and the wider culture are critical responses to DFV. At the secondary school level they also need to address issues of managing pornography, sexting and internet bullying (Walsh, Zwi, Woolfenden, & Shlonsky, 2015). Social marketing campaigns also have a role to play in providing messaging about the unacceptable nature of DFV.

In relation to secondary prevention, many groups within the community have been identified as more vulnerable than others, and hence could be the subject of targeted resourcing and earlier intervention. The attention to intersectionality highlights the wide variety of ways in which particular individuals and communities may be more exposed to DFV (Hague, Thiara, & Mullender, 2011). Importantly, their diversity also shapes the need for a customised response. For example, the accessing of organisations and women with disabilities will not involve the same strategies as those used to engage young mothers who have recently left state care. Both are vulnerable to DFV; there will be some overlap in these two populations, but the differences in approach would be greater than the similarities.

The tertiary prevention arena has been divided conceptually into crisis and post-crisis or healing as the service system is organised differently around each of these responses (Desmond, 2011). In general, the healing and recovery services for women and children, and the longer-term interventions for men who use violence, are thinly resourced compared to the crisis response. The crisis response will usually involve helpline services, access to refuges, outreach support following an incident of violence and assistance with accessing the justice system. For children, child protection has often been the frontline response following serious incidents of violence. Services and resources that address the long-term issues of recovery for both women and children are often to be found in mainstream mental health, substance use, parenting centres and counselling services. With some exceptions, there is a general lack of a specialist response (Laing, Irwin, & Toivonen, 2012).

Practice implications

A number of implications flow from understanding the multiple layering within the DFV prevention and response system. Importantly, leaders in the DFV area need a conceptual map through which to understand the service system and where they might most effectively intervene. Strong leaders hold an understanding of complexity which can take account of unintended consequences that may flow from policy and practices changes. They also have a profound grasp of the broader arena in which they are intervening, understanding where the strengths and vulnerabilities in the system lie (Ison & Blackmore, 2014).

Communicating insights about the conceptual map of the system is valuable for both those workers whom DFV leaders report to and those whom they supervise. Much of the frustration of working in this field can be sourced to the lack of services. Understanding the differentiation between crisis and recovery services, including not expecting the former to do the latter, is helpful knowledge for frontline workers in managing their collaborative relationships. However, it is equally important to be advocating 'upwards' for resourcing and policy reform which expands the service provision in the underfunded areas. It is much more efficient, effective and ethical to intervene early (Humphreys, 2008).

Key messages from this chapter

In conclusion, this chapter has paid attention to the context in which DFV leadership operates. It argues that there are three key elements which distinguish strong DFV leadership: attention to the historical, socio-cultural aspects of DFV; recognition of the need to remain inclusive and attend to emerging issues such as adolescent violence in the home; and recognition that DFV requires intervening at primary, secondary and tertiary levels in a public health approach.

The historical as well as the changing and complex nature of the current context configure the leadership challenges in this area, creating both similarities and differences with other practice settings. This context lends itself to a distributed form of leadership. It is generally not characterised by charismatic 'stars'; but rather leadership involves promoting a wider agenda to connect to others concerned to prevent, respond to and publicly identify violence against women and their children as a destructive social problem.

In this process, researchers and professionals have an important role to play to ensure that the voices of survivors are respected and foregrounded wherever possible. This alliance with DFV survivors is both an historical and a current characteristic of the social movement to end DFV. It is one which emerging leaders should continue to nurture if the professionalisation and mainstreaming of DFV prevention and response are to be enhancements for survivors and children, and not a shift that diminishes the passion and commitment to make a difference in this destructive social problem.

Finally, embracing the changing nature of the sector requires leaders who respect the notion of 'live knowledge'. This requires constant openness to the relationship between researcher and practitioners collaborating in their response to the changing face of DFV. In the DFV arena, this responsiveness recognises that many practitioners and researchers are also those with 'lived experience'. This rich respect for different forms of knowledge is one that can infuse the sector to create the change we wish to see.

Questions to configure DFV leadership in practice

1. What are the elements of management or senior leadership which would distinguish a worker in providing effective DFV leadership in their current workplace?
2. In what ways could the leadership in your workplace do more to tackle the issues of diversity in relation to DFV intervention?
3. Are there opportunities in your workplace to engage at different levels and with different clients in forging a more comprehensive approach to DFV?

References

Australian Broadcasting Corporation. (2015, 26 January). Australian of the Year: Rosie Batty awarded top honour for efforts to stop family violence. *ABC News*. Retrieved from www.abc.net.au/news/2015-01-25/rosie-batty-named-australian-of-the-year-2015/6045290
Baynes, P., & Holland, S. (2012). Social work with violent men: A child protection file study in an English Local Authority. *Child Abuse Review*, 21(1), 53–65.

Brandl, B., Hebert, M., Rozwadowski, J., & Spangler, D. (2003). Feeling safe, feeling strong: Support groups for older abused women. *Violence Against Women*, 9(12), 1490–1503.

Council of Australian Governments. (2009). *National Plan to reduce violence against women and their children, 2010–2022.* Canberra: Commonwealth of Australia. Retrieved from www. dss.gov.au/sites/default/files/documents/08_2014/national_plan1.pdf

Cox, P. (2015). Violence against women: Additional analysis of the Australian Bureau of Statistics' Personal Safety Survey. Horizons Research Paper No. 1. Retrieved from http://anrows.org.au/publications/horizons/PSS

Crenshaw, K. (1991). Mapping the margins: intersectionality, identity politics and violence against women of color. *Stanford Law Review*, 43(6), 1241–1299.

Desmond, K. (2011). *Filling the Gap service model: Integrated post crisis response for women and children who have experienced family violence.* Melbourne: Good Shepherd Youth and Family Services and McAuley Community Services Women.

Ellis, J., & Thiara, R.K. (Eds.). (2014). *Preventing violence against women and girls: Education work with children and young people.* Bristol: Policy Press.

Galvani, S. (2006). Alcohol and domestic violence: women's views. *Violence Against Women*, 12(7), 641–662.

Gondolf, E. (2002). *Batterer intervention systems: Issues, outcomes, and recommendations.* Thousand Oaks, CA: Sage.

Hague, G., & Mullender, A. (2006). Who listens? The voices of domestic violence survivors in service provision in the United Kingdom. *Violence Against Women*, 12(6), 568–587.

Hague, G., Thiara, R., & Mullender, A. (2011). Disabled women, domestic violence and social care: the risk of isolation, vulnerability and neglect. *British Journal of Social Work*, 41(1), 148–165.

Hanmer, J., & Itzin, C. (Eds.). (2000). *Home truths about domestic violence: Feminist influences on policy and practice: A reader.* London: Routledge.

Heise, L. (1998). Violence against women: An integrated, ecological framework. *Violence Against Women*, 4(3), 262–290.

Herman, J. (1992). *Trauma and recovery.* New York: Basic Books.

Humphreys, C. (2008). Problems in the system of mandatory reporting of children living with domestic violence. *Journal of Family Studies*, 14(2), 228–239.

Humphreys, C., & Absler, D. (2011). History repeating: Child protection responses to domestic violence. *Child and Family Social Work*, 16, 369–489.

Ison, R., & Blackmore, C. (2014). Designing and developing a reflexive learning system for managing systemic change. *Systems*, 2(2), 119–136.

Kimball, E. (2016). Edleson revisited: Reviewing children's witnessing of domestic violence 15 years later. *Journal of Family Violence*, 31(5), 625–637.

Laing, L., Humphreys, C., & Cavanagh, K. (2013). *Social work and domestic violence: Critical and reflective practice.* London: Sage.

Laing, L., Irwin, J., & Toivonen, C. (2012). Across the divide: using research to enhance collaboration between mental health and domestic violence services. *Australian Social Work*, 65(1), 120–135.

Mandel, D. (2014). Beyond domestic violence perpetrator accountability in child welfare systems. *Ending Men's Violence Against Women and Children: The No to Violence Journal*, Spring, 50–85.

McKibbin, G., Duncan, R., Hamilton, B., Humphreys, C., & Kellett, C. (2015). The intersectional turn in feminist theory: A response to Carbin and Edenheim (2013). *European Journal of Women's Studies*, 22(1), 99–103.

McLindon, E., Humphreys, C., & Hegarty, K. (forthcoming). 'It happens to clinicians too': Intimate partner, family and sexual violence against health professionals. *Medical Journal of Australia*.

Murray, S., & Powell, A. (2011). *Domestic violence: Australian public policy*. Melbourne: Australian Scholarly Publishing.

Nancarrow, H. (2010). Restorative justice for domestic and family violence: Hopes and fear for Indigenous and non-Indigenous women. In J. Ptacek (Ed.), *Restorative justice and violence against women* (pp. 123–149). New York: Oxford University Press.

Nancarrow, H., & Viljoen, R. (2011). *Breaking the cycle: Trial integrated response to domestic and family violence. Client experiences and outcomes*. Mackay: Queensland Centre for Domestic and Family Violence Research.

Nixon, J., & Humphreys, C. (2010). Marshalling the evidence to inform an intersectorial framing of domestic violence. *Social Politics*, 17(2), 137–158.

Owens, E., Behun, R., Manning, J., & Reid, R. (2012). The impact of internet pornography on adolescents: A review of the research. *Sexual Addiction & Compulsivity*, 19(1–2), 99–122.

Pence, E.L., & McDonnell, C. (1999). Developing policies and protocols. In M.F. Shepard and E.L. Pence (Eds.), *Coordinating community responses to domestic violence: Lessons from Duluth and beyond* (pp. 41–64). Thousand Oaks, CA: Sage.

Powell, A., Sandy, L., & Findling, J. (2015). *Promising practices in workplace and organisational approaches for the prevention of violence against women*. Melbourne: Our Watch and RMIT.

Ross, S., Healey, L., Diemer, K., & Humphreys, C. (2016). Providing an integrated response to family violence: Governance attributes of local networks in Victoria. *Australian Journal of Public Administration*, 75(2), 127–136. doi:10.1111/1467-8500.12162

Stanley, N., & Humphreys, C. (2015). *Domestic violence and child protection: New challenges and developments*. London: Jessica Kingsley.

Stanley, N., Graham-Kevan, N., & Borthwick, R. (2012). Fathers and domestic violence: Building motivation for change through perpetrator programmes. *Child Abuse Review*, 21(4), 264–274.

Victorian Royal Commission. (2016). *State of Victoria, Royal Commission into Family Violence: Report and Recommendations, Vol. VI*. Melbourne: Royal Commission into Family Violence.

Walby, S., and Allen, J. (2004). *Domestic violence, sexual assault and stalking: Findings from the British Crime Survey*. London: Home Office.

Walsh, K., Zwi, K., Woolfenden, S., & Shlonsky, A. (2015). School-based programmes for prevention of child sexual abuse (review). *Cochrane Database of Systematic Reviews*, 4, Art. No.: CD004380.

Wilcox, P., & Pooley, L. (2015). Children who are violent to their parents need protection too. In N. Stanley and C. Humphreys (Eds.), *Domestic violence and child protection: New challenges and developments* (pp. 81–96). London: Jessica Kingsley.

10

TRAUMA-INFORMED LEADERSHIP

Bruce D. Perry and Annette L. Jackson

Introduction

This chapter explores trauma-informed leadership in the context of child and family services. A discussion of the types and prevalence of trauma and its many consequences on the day-to-day functioning of the workforce and its leaders is presented. Concepts of vicarious trauma, state-dependent functioning, and power differential and relational contagion are discussed. They are considered against a backdrop of a range of trauma-informed principles and the margins and limitations of trauma-informed practice.

What do leaders need to know about trauma-informed leadership?

1. Types and prevalence of trauma

A trauma-informed leader should be aware of the prevalence of both developmental adversity and traumatic experiences that can impact the lives of anyone in an organisation.

Our world has been shaped and shaken by traumatic events. Every day we read stories of violent conflicts between and within nations, in communities, in the streets and in homes. It is not a rarity that makes traumatic events noteworthy: "Traumatic events are extraordinary, not because they occur rarely, but rather because they overwhelm the ordinary adaptations to life" (Herman, 1997, p. 33).

The Adverse Childhood Experiences studies (ACEs) demonstrate both the prevalence and consequences of childhood trauma and other adversities. These landmark studies sought information from over 18,000 adults about their childhood experiences and compared this with other available health information. The ACEs found very high 'dose-dependent' correlations between adversity in childhood and a range of physical health, psychological and social problems in adulthood. The adversities included physical, sexual or emotional abuse, neglect, family violence and growing up in a household with mental illness, incarceration or separation (Dube et al., 2003).

Numerous health problems in adulthood associated with childhood adversity included increased likelihood of autoimmune diseases (Dube et al., 2009), heart disease (Anda et al., 2008), liver disease (Dong, Anda, Dube, Felitti, & Giles, 2003) and cancer (Brown et al., 2010). Moreover, adverse childhood events were associated with a range of other problems, including substance abuse, mental health problems, suicide and perpetrating violence on an intimate partner (Whitfield, Anda, Dube, & Felitti, 2003).

Trauma does not only impact on children and families; it often also has consequences for workers and leaders. These can be both direct and indirect, such as through witnessing trauma, known as 'vicarious trauma' (Fallot & Harris, 2009). One such example was Wade Noonan, the Victorian Minister of Police who took a leave of absence after he announced publicly:

> It has been difficult to cope with the constant exposure to details of unspeakable crimes and traumatic events that are an everyday part of my role and the accumulation of these experiences has taken an unexpected toll ... I need time to receive further support and assistance including professional counselling.
>
> *(Noonan, 2016)*

This example of courageous leadership was generally understood as such. Noonan later returned to a different cabinet position.

Despite the pervasive nature of trauma in our world, a major challenge with any systematic study of trauma has been defining what is 'traumatic'. One hears 'trauma' used as a noun, 'traumatise' as a verb and 'traumatic' as an adjective. Even within professional circles the meaning of the term 'trauma' can vary tremendously from case worker to case worker, clinician to clinician, and even from study to study. The *Diagnostic and Statistical Manual* (DSM) has changed the definition and criteria for trauma several times over the decades (Perry, 2017). Recently, many laypeople and some professionals have come to use 'ACEs' as interchangeable with 'trauma', even to the point of some organisations claiming to have 'ACE-informed' programs. This sloppiness in language contributes to the current confusion about the actual elements of 'trauma-responsive' versus 'trauma-aware' versus 'trauma-specific' versus 'trauma-informed' practice, program and policy (Bloom, 2016).

One of the most useful conceptualisations of trauma comes from the Substance Abuse and Mental Health Services Administration in the United States of America (SAMHSA). Its 'Three E's' framework recognises that: 1) the event(s); 2) the experience of the individual; and 3) the enduring effects are all important components of 'trauma'. According to SAMHSHA (2014):

> Individual trauma results from an event, series of events, or set of circumstances that is experienced by an individual as physically or emotionally

harmful or life threatening and that has lasting adverse effects on the individual's functioning and mental, physical, social, emotional, or spiritual well-being. (p. 6)

An earlier framework for thinking about trauma helped distinguish exposure to a single traumatic experience from more complex and repetitive or ongoing trauma. Terr's (1991) descriptions of trauma had two categories: Type I trauma following a one-off or time-limited incident; and Type II trauma resulting from long-standing or repeated ordeals, usually in the context of a relationship and often beginning in childhood. Both types of trauma can be interpersonal, although the nature of the relationship influences the type and impact of the trauma.

Type I traumas include exposure to natural disaster, assault by a stranger and a car accident leading to a near-death experience. Type I traumatic events are usually sudden and shocking, causing chaos, havoc and devastation to individuals, communities and nations.

Type II traumas include physical abuse, sexual abuse, emotional abuse, neglect and family violence. These are inherently relational and rarely a single event. Not only is the source of danger the supposed source of support, but there also is an absence or inadequacy of protection. The severity of trauma cannot be measured on any single dimension: "simplistic efforts to quantify trauma ultimately lead to meaningless comparisons of horror ... the salient characteristic of the traumatic event is its power to inspire helplessness and terror" (Herman, 1997, p. 34).

Interpersonal traumatic experiences, especially those categorised as Type II trauma, make up much of a society's police, child protection and health statistics. Another marker of the prevalence and impact of trauma is to consider the associated economic costs. In Australia, governments spend almost $4 billion (AUD) a year on protecting children from their own families (Australian Institute of Health and Welfare, 2017). This is a conservative estimate of the economic cost as it does not count the health cost burden and is only a fraction of the social burden (Moore et al., 2015). In estimating the total lifetime economic burden from new cases of child maltreatment in the United States in 2008, costs were calculated as approximately $124 billion (USD) (Fang, Brown, Florence, & Mercy, 2012).

The realities and implications of trauma have been subject to various public, legal and government inquiries. For example, in Australia there has recently been a Victorian Royal Commission into Family Violence and a South Australian Child Protection Systems Royal Commission; and there is currently a national Royal Commission into Institutional Responses to Child Sexual Abuse and a Royal Commission into the Protection and Detention of Children in the Northern Territory. This is not an Australian phenomenon, as indicated by a number of public inquiries into institutional sexual abuse in England and Wales, Ireland, Scotland and Jersey. In the United States, these issues are sometimes the subject of White House Summits, but are commonly contested through civil courts and settlements which in turn have implications for policy.

Considering the pervasive nature of both developmental adversity and exposure to other trauma, it is inconceivable that the workplace would not have a significant number of individuals with histories of trauma. The trauma-informed leader must consider what the impact of these experiences may be.

2. Ways in which trauma can impact our functioning

A trauma-informed leader knows how developmental adversity and traumatic experiences can impact the bodies and brains of anyone in the organisation – including the leader. Emerging research on the neurobiological impact of trauma points to multiple ways that psychological trauma can have physiological impacts on the brain and body, which in turn have psychological and social implications. The human brain is organised to respond efficiently to stress, distress and threat in various ways, such as through hyperarousal and/or dissociation. These heterogeneous stress responses involve multiple neural networks across many areas of the brain, including the hypothalamic-pituitary-adrenal (HPA) axis, the amygdala, the hippo-campus, the prefrontal cortex, the vagal nerve and the locus coeruleus (see, e.g., Bogdan, Williamson, & Hariri, 2012; Chugani et al., 2001; Crozier, Van Voorhees, Hooper, & De Bellis, 2011; De Bellis, Baum, et al., 1999; De Bellis, Keshavan, et al., 1999; De Bellis, 2005; Hull, 2002; Perry, 2002; Perry, Pollard, Blakely, Baker, & Vigilante, 1995; Porges, 2004; Twardosz & Lutzker, 2010; van der Kolk, 1996a).

A major consequence of exposure to trauma is its capacity to alter the reactivity of these important neural stress-response systems; the effect is to then alter a cascade of functions in the body and brain. Primary among these effects is the shift in 'state dependence'. All brain-mediated functions are 'state-dependent' (Perry et al., 1995). In addition to whatever gifts and challenges we have genetically, developmentally and relationally, some days are better or worse than others. When under threat, tired or ill we will not think, feel or behave as effectively and efficiently in our interactions, let alone when dealing with major change or challenges. This is true throughout the lifespan; we are all impacted by our internal states. And, these effects are complex and interactive. Cognition, emotions and social and motor functioning can shift our internal state, which in turn impacts on these functions. In addition to being affected by exposure to trauma, our state is affected by the extraordinary and the mundane. It is influenced by surprise and novelty; by fatigue, alcohol, drugs, threat, pain and pleasure; and by being in the presence of others with whom we feel safe or unsafe.

When exposed to threat there is a shift in a person's state from calm through to alert, alarm, fear or terror. Children who have been abused or neglected often have a persisting baseline state of alarm or higher, and are sensitised to any potential threat. As this shift in state takes place and they move up the stress continuum, the part of the brain that 'orchestrates' functioning shifts as well. Table 10.1 outlines this continuum and how different mental states and stress responses are activated. A common description of a typical stress response is fight, flight or freeze. However, the human ability to flock towards others is a less recognised but important aspect of our stress system.

TABLE 10.1 State-dependent functioning and stress-response continuum

"Classic" Adaptive Response	Rest (M > F)	Flock	Freeze	Flight	Fight
Arousal Continuum	Rest (M > F: A > C)	Vigilance	Resistance	Defiance	Aggression
Dissociative Continuum	Rest (F > M: C > A)	Avoidance	Compliance	Dissociation	Fainting
Primary secondary Brain Areas	NEOCORTEX *Subcortex*	SUBCORTEX *Limbic*	LIMBIC *Midbrain*	MIDBRAIN *Brainstem*	BRAINSTEM *Autonomic*
Cognition	Abstract	Concrete	Emotional	Reactive	Reflexive
Mental State	CALM	ALERT	ALARM	FEAR	TERROR

Not everyone who experiences a traumatic event will be traumatised. They will certainly not all have symptoms consistent with a diagnosis of post-traumatic stress disorder (PTSD) (Perry et al. 1995). Stress is not inherently harmful. Dealing with tolerable, predictable and moderate stress builds capacity to adapt and survive and to develop resilience (Perry & Szalavitz, 2017). "The ability to cope with novel and/or potentially threatening situations, such as an unfamiliar environment or physical danger is essential to survival" (National Scientific Council on the Developing Child, 2005/2014, p. 1).

Resilience refers to a person's ability to withstand the consequences of adversity. The person may be more resilient to one type of experience than another. The concept of resilience can also be applied to families, organisations and communities. Resilience is influenced by a variety of factors, including early in life experiences, attachment relationships, social support and genetics. In contrast, overwhelming, unpredictable and intense stress can be traumatic, leading to increased vulnerability (Perry & Szalavitz, 2017). This is also influenced by the context, timing and responses of others. Intolerably stressful situations can lead to neurobiological systems remaining dysregulated and less able to achieve a new equilibrium. Trauma overwhelms the person's internal and external resources, and if it continues can deplete future capacity to cope (van der Kolk, 1996b).

Trauma has implications for many biopsychosocial functions mediated by the brain. These include physical regulation, affect regulation, capacity for communication, capacity to experience and express pleasure, information processing, executive functioning and memory (Cook et al., 2005; De Bellis, 2005; Nikulina & Widom, 2013, Perry, 2002; van der Kolk, 1996a). These fundamental difficulties have wide-ranging implications for people's functioning. Such problems include violence, alcohol and other drug abuse, relationship breakdowns, education problems, developmental delays, insecure attachment and mental health problems (e.g. Cook et al., 2005; van der Kolk, 1996b).

Considering this array of potential effects, the trauma-informed leader must understand how to lead so as to minimise the negative impacts of trauma and optimise opportunities for potential growth and healing, both of which will improve the organisational climate and lead to increased creativity and productivity from the full workforce.

3. Implications for trauma-informed leadership

A trauma-informed leader recognises the potential role s/he plays in determining the characteristics of the workplace that can lead to optimal performance. Fortunately, these same qualities create a regulating and resilience-building climate that help individuals impacted by trauma to grow and heal and others to build resilience.

Sustained implementation of the trauma-informed principles described later is predicated on strong leadership. Not only the most senior people but also people with personal authority, role authority and/or professional authority (Obholzer, 1994) play powerful leadership roles in building and sustaining (or undermining) a trauma-informed organisational culture and championing positive organisational change.

An example of leadership-driven trauma-informed practice is the principle of safety. Safety for all begins with an unequivocal leadership stance including how this is modelled by leaders. Developing policies, responding to incidents of concern, and offering personal and systemic support and analysis to prevent unsafe situations are examples of leadership. Leaders have responsibilities to ensure workers that are supported to prevent or reduce vicarious trauma and burnout and to prevent re-traumatisation wherever possible.

Some but not all trauma-informed models are overt about the role of leadership. A highly regarded evidence-informed example is the Sanctuary Model (Bloom, 2005). This is an organisation-wide, leadership-led model aimed at ensuring a sustained, trauma-informed – not trauma-saturated – organisational and practice culture.

A number of useful constructs emerging from neuroscience and trauma theory have relevance for trauma-informed leadership in the context of child and family services.

State-dependent functioning at individual and organisational levels

State-dependent functioning is a highly useful construct for leadership anywhere in any field of endeavour. Whether CEO of a mining company or a hospital, principal of a school, leader of a church or mosque, board director, or manager of child protection, community service or Indigenous organisation there is high value in recognising our own and others' state and how that affects our functioning. When leading an organisation in a field characterised by frequent crises, high risk, adversity and trauma (and usually resource-depleted), state-dependent functioning has particular resonance.

As shown in Table 10.1, our mental state impacts on our cognition. When calm we are more likely to be creative, think in abstract concepts and explore new ideas. When alert we are less creative but more concrete. This is useful when learning new content and focusing on a specific event, but not as useful when trying to solve a complex problem, to think 'outside the box'. When in an alarm state or higher up the stress continuum we are unlikely to think in more concrete terms, but be more reactive. Establishing a workplace environment and culture that encourages the leadership team and workforce to think in abstract and creative ways goes alongside understanding that external and internal pressures will elicit more concrete thinking.

Another implication of state-dependent functioning is recognising when a worker is in a heightened state and needs a particular response from management. Being effective is not just about skills, knowledge, capability and attitude. It is also about state-dependent functioning. A worker may have more capacity than suggested by his/her presentation on a given day. Workers can feel under threat for a variety of reasons, not only work-related. They may have experienced or witnessed a violent incident or threat; they may be new in their role; they may have had a fight with someone before leaving home; they may feel disempowered and invisible; they may be tired and overworked; they may lack confidence, and so on. We do not need to be traumatised to be in a heightened state. In an alarm or fear state we are less likely to take in new information, trust others, have a clear sense of time, to think of anything other than the here and now, and to be able to cope with change. We are less able to calm ourselves and self-regulate, or help others be calm.

Realisation that a worker's state impacts his or her usual capacity and competence offers ways to assist performance and sense of meaning, and can contribute to building resilience. If a worker is not in a state to take in necessary information, such as for their own or others' safety, we build scaffolds until they are once again in the state to do so. For example, if a supervisor is trying to support a worker who has been assaulted, offering suggestions and phone numbers to call for assistance is unlikely to register. Immediately after such an incident, ensuring the worker is not on their own, being alongside them and keeping conversation to a minimum are more useful. Later on, concrete advice may be helpful, but one suggestion at a time. Not taking away power whilst not bombarding the worker with decisions to be made is a balancing act which requires knowledge of the impact of trauma.

Leaders need to be aware of their own state-dependent functioning. Leaders are not immune to pressure and stress. When we are not in a calm or alert state, we need to be more cautious regarding decision-making (as discussed in Chapter 6). Of course it is in these times of high stress that the leader is required to make quick and important decisions. It can be useful for the leader to practise possible scenarios prior to real threats occurring as this can help identify personal and organisational resources available. Leaders need access to support the same as anyone else. Isolation increases a sense of threat and reduces the capacity to think and problem solve.

A leader's state-dependent functioning is another reason to review decisions and actions after a crisis event has been resolved. Table 10.2 presents this state-dependent concept from an organisational perspective. The organisational state is represented as the prevailing affective tone; in other words, what is the predominant state of

TABLE 10.2 State dependence in organisations (groups)

	Resource-surplus Predictable Stable/Safe	Resource-limited Unpredictable Novel	Resource-poor Threatening Inconsistent
	Abstract Creative (IQ = 120)	Concrete Superstitious/Defensive (IQ = 100)	Reactive Regressive (IQ = 80)
	CALM	ANXIETY	FEAR
	Reflective INNOVATIVE	Concrete SIMPLISTIC	Fear-based REACTIONARY
	FUTURE Intentional Inflection	SHORT-TERM SerendipitousInflection	PRESENT Forced Inflection
	Abstract Conceptual	Concrete Superstitious Intrusive	Restrictive Punitive
	Nurturing Flexible Enriching	Ambivalent Obsessive Controlling	Apathetic Oppressive Harsh

the organisation? A resource-surplus, predictable and safe organisation provides the climate for creative thinking, innovation, future orientation and nurturing and enriching of staff practices. This is in contrast to a resource-limited, unpredictable organisational climate – which is more likely to entail concrete and defensive thinking, have an anxious affective tone and be less future-oriented.

Most effective child and family services do not have a resource surplus but are working to enable a predictable and safe organisation. However some organisations are in a more precarious position, with reduced or lost funding and a chaotic culture.

Seeking resource certainty in an uncertain funding world has led to many not-for-profit organisations seeking funding independent of government. Given the typical constraints facing the child and family services sector, leaders need to focus on how to build and sustain a safe, predictable organisation with coherent policies and practices for service delivery and workforce management. The individual's capacity for self-reflection, planning and intentional behaviour requires a relatively organised and regulated cortex (Gaskill & Perry, 2014). Metaphorically, we can surmise that for an organisation to have the capacity for reflection, planning and intentional behaviour requires relatively organised and regulated leadership. Although such leadership can be provided by an individual, it may be most effective as a leadership team.

The power differential

"Trauma robs the victim of a sense of power and control; the guiding principle of recovery is to restore power and control to the survivor" (Herman, 1997, p. 159).

Power and powerlessness are pervasive elements of trauma and traumatised systems. Leadership represents power and can inadvertently add to the sense of being disempowered. Alternatively, leadership can use the position of power to create a positive culture.

Understanding power and powerlessness is crucial when working with people who already feel robbed of power and have reason to mistrust authority. Children and families involved with child and family services often have particular experiences of disempowerment. This can also be the experience of foster parents, residential care workers, case workers and the overall workforce. It is not uncommon for everyone involved in these systems, including leaders, to feel powerless.

We are organised to quickly perceive threat and act accordingly. For example, we are less likely to feel calm when interacting with someone we believe has power over us. This power differential is not about an individual but the degree of perceived difference between one and the other. It is context specific. For example, a judge holds great power in the court room, but in the doctor's surgery is reliant on the care of the physician; the physician is in charge of the clinical setting, but in a court room is subject to the judge's decisions.

Our perception of power and who wields such power is culturally laden and often implicit. An elderly person may have little power in one culture but in another culture be honoured as an elder. Power differentials can be experienced through gender, age, job title, height, wealth, unfamiliarity and interpersonal history.

The greater the perception of power difference, the more it is likely to impact on our state and therefore our functioning. This offers clues to how to assist someone who is dysregulated and perceives us as having formal or informal power. Increasing familiarity, being at a similar height, considering personal space and being side by side rather than face to face can help reduce associated fears that come with power. Meanwhile, using the dominant (not dominating) position to help co-regulate can be crucial to help someone return to a state of calm. For example, using slow, regulated, rhythmic breathing when sitting beside a distressed worker can help co-regulate and calm someone without a word being uttered. There is a fine balance between recognising that perceived power as a leader may increase someone's dysregulation compared to using that perception to help them be more regulated.

A hallmark of trauma-informed practice is avoiding re-traumatisation. The power differential can mean the manager's actions or inactions following a major adverse event have an exponential impact. Whilst there is debate about the efficacy of psychological debriefing (e.g. Hawker et al., 2011), it is clear that offering debriefing does not fulfil the obligations of leadership, and that there is an undeniable need for strong leadership of organisational culture at times of ordinary and extraordinary stress.

Relational contagion and the importance of self-care

A core concept informing a trauma-informed leader is recognition of the remarkable social contagion of humans. Humans are a social species; we have an array of complex neurophysiological mechanisms that are continually monitoring the social milieu helping us connect and communicate with others. Being part of a group becomes an important and powerful pull for the majority of us; and the leader of a group – for a variety of reasons – can set, and influence, the prevailing emotional tone of that group. Calm, clear communication from a regulated leader can regulate and calm an anxious team. Over-anxious, frustrated or angry communication can dysregulate the group. Combined with the concepts of 'state dependence' and the power differential, it becomes clear that if the group is to be most productive, the leader has to understand and value self-regulation. The importance of self-care for trauma-informed leaders – and their teams – becomes obvious. A regulated leader can create a positive, healing and productive organisational climate; a dysregulated leader can literally make people develop stress-related emotional and physical health problems.

4. Broader context of trauma-informed practice

It is not enough to know trauma theory for a person or organisation to be 'trauma-informed'. A trauma-informed program, organisation or system

> realizes the widespread impact of trauma and understands potential paths for recovery; recognizes the signs and symptoms of trauma in clients, families, staff, and others involved with the system; and responds by fully integrating knowledge about trauma into policies, procedures, and practices, and seeks to actively resist re-traumatization.
>
> *(SAMHSA, 2014, p. 9)*

There is a plethora of programs and systems with documented trauma-informed frameworks. These include child protection, out-of-home care, education, youth justice, adult corrections, disability, family violence, general health, mental health, substance abuse, Indigenous services, refugees and migrants, education, homelessness and gender-specific services (see also Kezelman & Stavropoulos, 2012; Atkinson, 2013; Bloom, 2005; Canadian Centre on Substance Abuse, 2014; Chadwick Trauma-Informed Systems Project, 2013; Elliott, Bjelajac, Fallot, Markoff, & Glover Reed, 2005; Fallot & Harris, 2006, 2009; Guarino, Soares, Konnath, Clervil, & Bassuk, 2009; Harner & Burgess, 2011; Jackson & Waters, 2015; Jennings, 2008; Kaplan, 1998; Kramer, Sigel, Conners-Burrow, Savary, & Tempel, 2013; Mental Health Coordinating Council (MHCC), 2013; Sweeney, Clement, Filson, & Kennedy, 2016; Bouverie Centre, 2013; Wilson, Fauci, & Goodman, 2015; Wisconsin's Violence Against Women with Disabilities and Deaf Women Project, 2011).

Trauma-informed practice is sometimes relegated to a three-word slogan. This poses a genuine risk to it being dismissed as a fad, or watered down to a set of vague principles that cannot realistically impact on practice. When accompanied by high expectations that being trauma-informed is the answer to all complex problems, it is set up to fail. Alternatively, trauma-informed can be misinterpreted to mean 'soft on crime', with no limits, routines or consequences. When misconstrued, being trauma-informed can be epitomised paradoxically as both 'Pollyanna' and 'Moaning Myrtle'.

Trauma-informed principles

There are numerous trauma-informed frameworks, each with their own emphasis; however many share key principles following the seminal work by Fallot and Harris (2006). Table 10.3 summarises guiding principles for trauma-informed practice.

Implications for leadership: the margins of trauma-informed practice

There are common misunderstandings about what trauma-informed practice is and is not. Trauma-informed practice is not the answer to every problem. To treat it as such poses the risk of it being the 'emperor's new clothes'. In the context of services working with children and families at-risk, in addition to being trauma-informed we also need to be developmentally informed and attachment-informed, and to ensure a human rights and social justice perspective. We also need to continuously strive towards cultural competence.

Trauma does not describe all adversity. To suggest something is not traumatic can be mistaken as suggesting it is not devastating, distressing or wrong. For example, neglect can have disastrous consequences on a child's developing brain and body and thus their overall development, and yet not activate the stress response. A three-year-old suffering malnutrition due to neglect is likely to have an activated stress response that is usefully explained through trauma theory. A three-year-old who has not experienced play and fun will not necessarily have an activated stress system. A neurodevelopmental perspective is more useful. Whether or not adversity is traumatic, trauma-informed principles can be of assistance as long as we do not reduce every experience to a single phenomenon.

If trauma-informed practice is confused with trauma-specific practice too much will be asked of it. This can set up services and workers aiming to be trauma-informed to fail, or potentially do harm. Not every child or adult is ready for psychotherapy, let alone tackling trauma memories. We need to be careful we are not implying that every worker is a therapist or that every child who has suffered trauma needs therapy. They are likely, however, to benefit from a therapeutic, trauma-informed response. Someone once asked if teaching trauma-informed practice meant training everyone to talk to children about their trauma. It does not! Indeed, that could lead to the child being triggered or re-traumatised every time a worker felt pressure to ask certain questions.

Trauma-informed practice is not and cannot be the solution to complexity. We are extraordinary and unfathomable creatures, yet we strive to discover, explore and question ourselves and our environment to try to understand our own and others' complexity. Complexity is not a vice; but it is a challenge, and one that leadership grapples with constantly.

TABLE 10.3 Trauma-informed principles

Trauma lens	Trauma is not everywhere but it can be anywhere. Understanding prevalence, signs and impacts of trauma, not just focused on at-risk behaviours.
View of person's uniqueness and strength	Acknowledging the person who has experienced trauma is more than a victim. Each is unique in abilities and vulnerabilities, personality, history and potential.
Safety for all	An emphasis on safety for all, including physical, emotional, social, moral and cultural safety. This is true for clients, workers, carers, volunteers and community.
Re-traumatisation	Proactive attention to reducing or avoiding re-traumatisation. People exposed to trauma are at increased risk of re-exposure. This can be influenced by their adaptations to the initial trauma, placing them in more high-risk situations. However, it can also be due to the way systems respond after a trauma. Overt and covert operational practices and power differentials can exacerbate already precarious client–worker relationships. Sometimes we cannot avoid a potentially re-traumatising experience such as a medical examination or inpatient treatment, police interview or court appearance. We can work to minimise or eliminate the negative implications of these and other experiences.
Recovery is possible	Acknowledging that recovery is possible and that it looks different from one person to another. Recovery does not equate to the trauma never having occurred or the person not being changed by the experience. We are not born resilient. Resilience is developed in the context of individual growth and relationships. It can be strengthened through exposure to adversity, but only when the person is not isolated in the face of overwhelming threat. Therapy is not the only path to recovery, although it can be vital for some. Recovery signals the importance of hope, fun, joy and support.
Access to trauma-specific services	Ensuring accessible pathways to trauma-specific services delivered by appropriately trained professionals. Trauma-specific services directly provide therapeutic interventions to help people recover from the impact of trauma.
Attention to culture and community	Being culturally respectful and ensuring we are culturally informed are cornerstones of best practice, with particular resonance when acknowledging community- and cultural-specific trauma. Recognising cultural ways of healing is pivotal to trauma-informed practice.
Gender respect	Whether or not the service is gender-specific, the service must be gender-appropriate and gender-respectful. This includes acknowledging structural and historical power issues and different ways trauma and healing can be expressed.
Attention to workers	Workers and carers need to be and feel safe. This acknowledges the potential for vicarious trauma as well as more direct exposure to trauma, and emphasises the need for self-care and organisational care.

Trustworthiness	Ensuring decisions are transparent and inclusive, with the aim of building trust. This includes not promising the impossible and following through on commitments; and being honest when we don't know something or don't know what to do next.
Relationships	Healing occurs through relationships. Ensuring respect and facilitating connections are key to safe and genuine relationships. This is not just between the worker and client but also involves supporting safe and strong relationships for the person with his or her family and friendships.
Empowerment, choice and voice	Supporting the person's control, choice and voice to have or work towards genuine autonomy, self-determination, participation and respect for human rights. This includes sharing power in a genuinely inclusive way. Even when the client or staff member does not have the final say over an issue their voice must be heard.
Processes and systems	Building and reviewing transparent and trauma-informed policies, processes and systems within each organisation for clients and staff.
Trauma-informed leadership	A trauma-informed organisation needs trauma-informed leadership. This involves ensuring a healthy and transparent organisational culture and processes and a positive, strong and collaborative leadership approach.

Kezelman & Stavropoulos (2012), Atkinson (2013), Bloom (2005), Chadwick Trauma-Informed Systems Project (2013), Fallot & Harris (2009), Guarino et al. (2009), Hummer (2010), Jackson & Waters (2015), MHCC (2013), Sweeney et al. (2016), Bouverie Centre (2013)

Key messages from this chapter

- Trauma-informed leadership means knowing what is meant by trauma and how it can impact on the functioning of our workforce and ourselves.
- Recognising that our functioning is state-dependent and that there are numerous factors that can influence our state is a key aspect of trauma-informed leadership.
- With increasing knowledge about what children need, particularly those who have experienced trauma, we have a commensurate responsibility to meet those needs. Part of our problem is language. Being trauma-informed does not go far enough, and yet sometimes it is stretched so far it becomes thin. We need to go beyond trauma-informed!

Questions for further consideration

1. What are the possible implications of having a workforce where many will have experienced adversity and trauma in their personal and/or professional lives?
2. What are the signs that, as a leader, your state is heightened and so your state-dependent functioning is affected?
3. How can you influence the 'affective' or emotional tone of your team or organisation through overt strategies and through your demeanour and state?

4. What strategies can be used to mitigate the sense of powerlessness or threat due to power differential?
5. What do these trauma-informed principles look like in your organisation, or how would you build them into the culture?

References

Anda, R.F., Brown, D.W., Dube, S.R., Bremner, J.D., Felitti, V.J., & Giles, W.H. (2008). Adverse childhood experiences and chronic obstructive pulmonary disease in adults. *American Journal of Preventive Medicine*, 34(5), 396–403. doi:10.1016/j.amepre.2008.02.002

Atkinson, J. (2013). Trauma-informed services and trauma-specific care for Indigenous Australian children. Resource sheet no. 21 produced for the Closing the Gap Clearinghouse. Retrieved from www.aihw.gov.au/uploadedFiles/ClosingTheGap/Content/Publications/2013/ctg-rs21.pdf

Australian Institute of Health and Welfare. (2017). *Child Protection Australia 2015–2016*. Canberra: AIHW.

Bloom, S.L. (2005). The Sanctuary model of organizational change for children's residential treatment. *Therapeutic Community: The International Journal for Therapeutic and Supportive Organizations*, 26(1), 65–81

Bloom, S.L. (2016). Advancing a national cradle-to-grave-to-cradle public health agenda. *Journal of Trauma & Dissociation*, 17(4), 383–396.

Bogdan, R., Williamson, D., & Hariri, A. (2012). Mineralocorticoid receptor Iso/Val (rs5522) genotype moderates the association between previous childhood emotional neglect and amygdala reactivity. *American Journal of Psychiatry*, 169, 515–522.

Bouverie Centre. (2013). *Guidelines for trauma-informed family sensitive practice in adult health services*. Retrieved from www.childaware.org.au/images/the_bouverie_centre_la_trobe_university-web.pdf

Brown, D., Anda, R., Felitti, V., Edwards, V., Malarcher, A., Croft, J., & Giles, W. (2010). Adverse childhood experiences are associated with the risk of lung cancer: A prospective cohort study. *BMC Public Health, 10*(311), 1–12. doi:10.1186/1471-2458-10-311

Canadian Centre on Substance Abuse. (2014). Trauma-informed care. Ottawa: CCSA. Retrieved from www.ccsa.ca/Resource%20Library/CCSA-Trauma-informed-Care-Toolkit-2014-en.pdf

Chadwick Trauma-Informed Systems Project. (2013). *Guidelines for applying a trauma lens to a child welfare practice model*. San Diego: Chadwick Center for Children and Families.

Chugani, H., Behen, M., Muzik, O., Juhasz, C., Nagy, F., & Chugani, D. (2001). Local brain functional activity following early deprivation: A study of post-institutionalized Romanian orphans. *NeuroImage*, 14, 1290–1301.

Cook, A., Spinazzola, J., Ford, J., Lanktree, C., Blaustein, M., Cloitre, M., … van der Kolk, B. (2005). Complex trauma in children and adolescents. *Psychiatric Annals*, 35(5), 390–398.

Crozier, J.C., Van Voorhees, E.E., Hooper, S.R., & De Bellis, M.D. (2011). Effects of abuse and neglect on brain development. In C. Jenny (Ed.), *Child abuse and neglect: Diagnosis, treatment and evidence* (pp. 516–525). St. Louis: Elsevier Saunders.

De Bellis, M.D. (2005). The psychobiology of neglect. *Child Maltreatment*, 10(2), 150–172. doi:10.1177/1077559505275116

De Bellis, M.D., Baum, A.S., Birmaher, B., Keshavan, M.S., Eccard, C.H., Boring, A.M., … Ryan, N.D. (1999). Developmental traumatology part I: biological stress systems. *Biological Psychiatry*, 45(10), 1259–1270. doi:10.1016/S0006-3223(99)00044-X

De Bellis, M.D., Keshavan, M.S., Clark, D.B., Casey, B.J., Giedd, J.N., Boring, A.M., … Ryan, N.D. (1999). Developmental traumatology part II: brain development. *Biological Psychiatry*, 45(10), 1271–1284. doi:10.1016/S0006-3223(99)00045-1

Dong, M., Dube, S.R., Felitti, V.J., Giles, W.H., & Anda, R.F. (2003). Adverse childhood experiences and self-reported liver disease: New insights into the causal pathway. *Archives of Internal Medicine*, 163(16), 1949–1956. doi:10.1001/archinte.163. 16. 19doi:49

Dube, S.R., Fairweather, D., Pearson, W.S., Felitti, V.J., Anda, R.F., & Croft, J.B. (2009). Cumulative childhood stress and autoimmune disease. *Psychosomatic Medicine*, 71(2), 243–250.

Dube, S.R., Felitti, V.J., Dong, M., Chapman, D.P., Giles, W.H., & Anda, R.F. (2003). Childhood abuse, neglect, and household dysfunction, and the risk of illicit drug use: The Adverse Childhood Experiences Study. *Pediatrics*, 3(3), 564–572.

Elliott, D.E., Bjelajac, P., Fallot, R.D., Markoff, L.S., & Glover Reed, B. (2005). Trauma-informed or trauma-denied: Principles and implementation of trauma-informed services for women. *Journal of Community Psychology*, 33(4), 461–477. doi:10.1002/jcop.20063

Fallot, R.D., & Harris, M. (2006). Trauma-informed services: A self-assessment and planning protocol. Retrieved from http://smchealth.org/sites/default/files/docs/tisapprotocol.pdf

Fallot, R.D., & Harris, M. (2009). Creating cultures of trauma-informed care (CCTIC): A self-assessment and planning protocol. Retrieved from http://sfbhn.org/misc%20pdf/Fa llot%20Tool%20Explanation%20TIC.pdf

Fang, X., Brown, D.S., Florence, C.S., & Mercy, J.A. (2012). The economic burden of child maltreatment in the United States and implications for prevention. *Child Abuse & Neglect*, 36, 156–165. doi:10.1016/j.chiabu.2011.10.006

Gaskill, R.L., & Perry, B.D. (2014). The neurobiological power of play: Using the neuro-sequential model of therapeutics to guide play in the healing process. In C.A. Malchiodi & D.A. Crenshaw (Eds.), *Creative arts and play therapy for attachment problems* (pp. 178–194). New York: Guilford Press.

Guarino, K., Soares, P., Konnath, K., Clervil, R., & Bassuk, E. (2009). *Trauma-informed organizational toolkit for homeless services*. Rockville, MD: Center for Mental Health Services.

Harner, H., & Burgess, A.W. (2011). Using a trauma-informed framework to care for incarcerated women. *Journal of Obstetric, Gynecologic, and Neonatal Nursing*, 40(4), 469–476. doi:10.1111/j.1552–6909.2011.01259.x

Hawker, D.M., Durkin, J., & Hawker, D.S.J. (2011). To debrief or not to debrief our heroes: That is the question. *Clinical Psychology and Psychotherapy*, 18, 453–463.

Herman, J.L. (1997). *Trauma and recovery: The aftermath of violence – from domestic abuse to political terror*. New York: Basic Books.

Hull, A.M. (2002). Neuroimaging findings in post-traumatic stress disorder: Systematic review. *British Journal of Psychiatry*, 81, 102–110.

Jackson, A.L., & Waters, S.E. (2015). *Taking time: A trauma-informed practice framework for supporting people with intellectual disability*. Melbourne: Berry Street.

Jennings, A. (2008). *Models for developing trauma-informed behavioral health systems and trauma-specific services*. Alexandria, VA: National Center for Trauma Informed Care (NCTIC). Retrieved from www.ct.gov/dmhas/lib/dmhas/trauma/TraumaModels.pdf

Kaplan, I. (1998). *Rebuilding shattered lives*. Parkville, VIC: Victorian Foundation for Survivors of Torture. Retrieved from www.foundationhouse.org.au/wp-content/uploads/2014/08/Rebuilding_Shatterd_Lives_Complete.pdf

Kezelman, C., & Stavropoulos, P. (2012). 'The last frontier': Practice guidelines for treatment of complex trauma and trauma informed care and service delivery. Kirribilli, NSW: Adults Surviving Child Abuse (ASCA). Retrieved from www.recoveryonpurpose.com/upload/ASCA_Pra ctice%20Guidelines%20for%20the%20Treatment%20of%20Complex%20Trauma.pdf

Kramer, T.L., Sigel, B.A., Conners-Burrow, N.A., Savary, P.E., & Tempel, A. (2013). A statewide introduction of trauma-informed care in a child welfare system. *Children and Youth Services Review*, 35(1), 19–24. doi:10.1016/j.childyouth.2012.10.014

Mental Health Coordinating Council (MHCC). (2013). *Trauma-informed care and practice: Towards a cultural shift in policy reform across mental health and human services in Australia. A national strategic direction.* Position paper and recommendations of the National Trauma-Informed Care and Practice Advisory Working Group. Lilyfield, NSW: MHCC.

Moore, S.E., Scott, J.G., Ferrari, A.J., Mills, R., Dunneh, M.P., Erskinea, H.E., ... Norman, R.E. (2015). Burden attributable to child maltreatment in Australia. *Child Abuse & Neglect*, 48, 208–220. doi:10.1016/j.chiabu.2015.05.006

National Scientific Council on the Developing Child. (2005/2014). Excessive stress disrupts the architecture of the developing brain. Working paper 3, Center on the Developing Child, Harvard University. Retrieved from www.developingchild.harvard.edu

Nikulina, V., & Widom, C. (2013). Child maltreatment and executive functioning in middle adulthood: A prospective examination. *Neuropsychology*, 27(4), 417–427.

Noonan, W. (2016, 8 February). Victorian Police Minister Wade Noonan steps down due to 'unexpected toll' of job. *ABC News*. Retrieved from www.abc.net.au/news/2016-02-08/police-minister-wade-noonan-steps-down-trauma-of-job/7149332

Obholzer, A. (1994). Authority, power, and leadership. In A. Obholzer & V. Zanier (Eds.), *The unconscious at work: Individual and organization stress in the human services* (pp. 39–47). New York: Routledge.

Perry, B.D. (2002). Childhood experience and the expression of genetic potential: What childhood neglect tells us about nature and nurture. *Brain and Mind*, 3(1), 79–100. doi:10.1023/A:1016557824657

Perry, B.D. (2017). Trauma- and stress-related disorders. In T.P. Beauchaine & S.P. Hinshaw (Eds.), *Textbook of child and adolescent psychopathology* (3rd ed.) (pp. 683–705). New York: Wiley.

Perry, B.D., Pollard, R., Blakely, T., Baker, W., & Vigilante, D. (1995). Childhood trauma, the neurobiology of adaptation and 'use-dependent' development of the brain: How 'states' become 'traits'. *Infant Mental Health Journal*, 16(4), 271–291.

Perry, B.D., & Szalavitz, M. (2017). *The boy who was raised as a dog: And other stories from a child psychiatrist's notebook. What traumatized children can teach us about life, loss and healing.* New York: Basic Books.

Porges, S.W. (2004). Neuroception: A subconscious system for detecting threats and safety. *Zero to Three*, 24(5), 19–24.

Substance Abuse and Mental Health Services Administration (SAMHSA). (2014). *SAMHSA's concept of trauma and guidance for a trauma-informed approach.* Rockville, MD: SAMHSA. Retrieved from http://store.samhsa.gov/shin/content/SMA14-4884/SMA14-4884.pdf

Sweeney, A., Clement, S., Filson, B., & Kennedy, A. (2016). Trauma-informed mental healthcare in the UK: What is it and how can we further its development? *Mental Health Review Journal*, 21(3), 174–192. doi:10.1108/MHRJ-01-2015-0006

Terr, L.C. (1991). Childhood traumas: An outline and overview. *American Journal of Psychiatry*, 148(1), 10–20.

Twardosz, S., & Lutzker, J.R. (2010). Child maltreatment and the developing brain: A review of neuroscience perspectives. *Aggression and Violent Behavior*, 15, 59–68.

van der Kolk, B.A. (1996a). The body keeps the score: Approaches to the psychobiology of posttraumatic stress disorder. In B.A. van der Kolk, A.C. McFarlane, & L. Weisaeth (Eds.), *Traumatic stress: The effects of overwhelming experience on mind, body, and society* (pp. 214–241). New York: Guilford Press.

van der Kolk, B.A. (1996b). The complexity of adaptation to trauma: Self-regulation, sti-
mulus discrimination, and characterological development. In B.A. van der Kolk, A.C.
McFarlane, & L. Weisaeth (Eds.), *Traumatic stress: The effects of overwhelming experience on
mind, body, and society* (pp. 182–213). New York: Guilford Press.

Whitfield, C.L., Anda, R.F., Dube, S.R., & Felitti, V.J. (2003). Violent childhood experiences and the risk of intimate partner violence in adults: Assessment in a large health
maintenance organization. *Journal of Interpersonal Violence*, 18(2), 166–185. doi:10.1177/
0886260502238733

Wilson, J.M., Fauci, J.E., & Goodman, L.A. (2015). Bringing trauma-informed practice to
domestic violence programs: A qualitative analysis of current approaches. *American Journal
of Orthopsychiatry*, 85(6), 586–599. doi:10.1037/ort0000098

Wisconsin's Violence Against Women with Disabilities and Deaf Women Project. (2011). *A
practical guide for creating trauma-informed disability, domestic violence and sexual assault organizations*. Madison, WI: Disability Rights Wisconsin, Wisconsin Coalition Against Domestic
Violence andWisconsin Coalition Against Sexual Assault. Retrieved from www.disabili
tyrightswi.org/wp-content/uploads/2012/05/Trauma-Informed-Guide.pdf

11

LEADING FOR THE FUTURE

Margarita Frederico, Maureen Long and Annette L. Jackson

Introduction

Leading for the future is about ensuring the best outcomes for vulnerable children and families through quality practice developed and supported by strong leadership. The task of delivering high-quality Child and Family Practice is challenging and complex. This book has provided different insights about a range of aspects of Child and Family Practice, including child protection, out-of-home care and family services. As such, there is not only reference to children and families, but also to the workforce and carers. This is in keeping with findings that the best outcomes for children and families occur when the workforce and carers are supported (Munro 2011; Ofsted, 2012).

Promoting good practice and supporting staff to develop and achieve positive outcomes for children and families requires substantive knowledge and skills in leadership, substantive knowledge of children and families at risk, and an ability to self-reflect and engage in continuous learning. This may seem a Herculean task. It can also seem obvious and ordinary. Creating a caring culture in which workers feel safe and trust each other and their managers whilst holding the vulnerable child at the centre is core to good practice, yet difficult to achieve and sustain. In Chapter 6, Perry, Jackson and Waters provide examples of the importance of creating a culture wherein workers are supported during intensely challenging times – potential lack of trust and its devastating consequences are made explicit. Maintaining the flexibility to manage constant change, which is the reality of child and family work, is pivotal. All the chapters in this book offer guidance and many examples of leadership that can guide emerging and experienced leaders to achieve their tasks.

The challenges for leadership in this area will not diminish over time. Globally, societies are facing a growing gap between rich and poor and causing significant negative consequences for the well-being of vulnerable populations (Pickett & Wilkinson, 2010). The impacts of climate change and the increase in natural disasters (Dominey-Howes, 2015) have profound consequences for the most vulnerable families and communities who have the least economic and social resources to call upon. The influence of the neo-liberal agenda has impacted welfare expenditure since the late 1990s, promoting principles of individualism and individual responsibility and tightening eligibility for services. Armed conflicts continue to disrupt children and families in many countries, leading to high numbers of internally displaced people and huge flights of refugees.

These factors are outside the realm and control of child and family practitioners. Nonetheless, local implications of global pressures can exacerbate the risks for children and families already vulnerable, and leaders in the sector should be aware of their impact as this will assist their understanding of the pressures on practice in this area. For example, there may be increasing competition for resources and, moreover, increasing compassion fatigue for families and children at risk as many in the broader community grapple with frequently evolving challenges associated with living in the new 'ordinary' times.

The work of Child and Family Practice leaders across all settings requires them to build and sustain strong, child-safe organisations which in turn support staff to provide quality practice. Such organisations also enable continuous education and supervision for workers, which promotes critical reflection and in-place learning of knowledge and skills whilst at the same time engaging with, critiquing and implementing cutting-edge research and theory development.

This final chapter of the book considers seven areas that leaders in Child and Family Practice should focus on by building on the knowledge and insights from the previous chapters, and presents the information within seven categories. The purpose of this chapter is to facilitate experienced and emerging leaders to reflect on their own leadership style and approach in relation to each of these areas. This is not an exhaustive list; rather, it provides guidance in areas for reflection. The areas are:

- modelling leadership in a complex environment
- leadership in organisations
- leading in communities
- leading through education
- building and leading trauma-informed organisations
- leading through supervision
- leading through evidence-based and evidence-informed reflective practice.

Modelling leadership in a complex environment

One of the messages not sufficiently emphasised about leadership is that in order to be a leader, the leader requires substantive personal and professional knowledge of leadership (see Chapter 4). However, leading is in the doing. It is in the listening, in knowing when to be still and when to be active; when to coach and when to delegate; when to dot the 'i's and when 'good enough' is best; when to let individuals learn by their mistakes and when failure is not an option; when to lead from the front and when to support from the back; when to work alongside someone and when to let them move on by themselves. Leadership implies there are people to lead, but it may relate to leading an individual, a team, an organisation or a system. It may be formal leadership roles associated with particular positions or informal roles associated with personal and/or professional authority.

Leadership is always complex. Leading in a complex environment magnifies this complexity. A complex environment is one in which unknown factors are substantial and the environment is in a constant state of change. The black swan effect (Taleb, 2007) is a construct which describes one aspect of complexity with relevance for Child and Family Practice. It has three attributes: namely, when the event or phenomenon (i) is considered highly improbable, an outlier lying outside reasonable expectations (as happens every day in Child and Family Practice); (ii) has potential for extreme impact (such as the impact of child abuse); and (iii) in spite of it not being foreseen, in retrospect it can be explained and even identified as predictable. The findings of the Australian Royal Commission into Institutional Responses to Child Sexual Abuse (2017) points to such a black swan effect, as do many child death inquiries. Complex environments carry uncertainty. Rigid risk-avoidance practices cannot be relied upon to foresee all events that impact negatively on the child. Nonetheless, such adverse events must be prevented where possible, and responded to and understood when they occur in the continuous efforts to inform the future. In Chapter 6, Perry et al. explore some of the ramifications for leadership.

Effective leadership requires commitment and continuous study, and understanding that in this field of practice there will be constant change, be it in knowledge development (e.g. neuroscience) or policies or shifting causes of vulnerability. At its foundation, however, leadership requires an understanding of oneself and an ability to reflect on one's own values, motivations, ideas, strengths, weaknesses, biases and knowledge, including recognition that such self-study is an ongoing task. Effective leadership requires strong communication skills. In Chapter 2 Long discusses the skills required in Child and Family Practice, and in Chapter 5 McPherson summarises key attributes of supervisors that promote worker competence: warmth, humour, integrity and loyalty, and the ability to communicate complex ideas. However, whilst essential, communication skills are not enough to make an effective leader.

In Chapter 9 Humphreys explores family violence and leadership, highlighting the importance of an in-depth understanding of the phenomenon to deliver quality practice. Particular focus is given to the understanding of working with different cultures (Tsantefski in Chapter 8) and the importance of recognising potential bias of the worker's cultural approach. Chapter 7 (Bamblett, Blackstock, Black and Salomone) addresses the special issues for Indigenous families and communities in child and family work. As highlighted in Chapter 6, whilst applying this knowledge to guide leadership, leaders need to develop their own leadership style and approach. Leadership is personal as much as it is externally driven. Practitioners respond to the person the leader is and the values they model as well as to the competence and knowledge they display. The leader responds to the nature of the situation, which includes having their own vision whilst leading individuals and organisations. Child and Family Practice leaders need to have a clear vision of what is best practice and influence practitioners to commit to achieving this vision so that vulnerable children and families remain the focus of all decisions.

Leadership in organisations

Strong, child-safe organisations structured to keep children safe and to empower them and their families are essential for organisations that engage in Child and Family Practice. The Royal Commission into Institutional Responses to Child Sexual Abuse confronted the community with the reality that organisations had allowed, and in some cases facilitated, abuse of children. Moreover, when abuse occurred these organisations did not protect children from ongoing harm. Leadership in these organisations failed vulnerable children time and again by not having structures in place which would promote safety for children as well as provide effective oversight and supervision of staff. The consequences for the children and the community are profound. The Commission's findings led to the introduction of Child Safe legislation for all organisations that come into contact with children in the State of Victoria. Key elements of this policy are that organisations must have leadership and governance that ensure children are protected. The task of leadership is to promote a strong culture of safety for children and to ensure that organisational policies promoting child safety are in place. This includes the importance of having oversight procedures and systems in place that do not just rely on good will. Attention to recruitment of staff, supervision and training is essential (Royal Commission into Institutional Responses to Child Sexual Abuse, 2017).

An organisation is more than a sum of its parts. Part of the role of leadership within an organisation is usually to work within a leadership team. How we conduct ourselves as part of this team is also a testament to our leadership style. Looking for opportunities to build collaborations within and external to the organisation, resolving conflicts in respectful and clear ways, strategic planning, integrated practice across silos and shared problem solving are just some examples of this aspect of organisational leadership.

One of the interesting facets of La Trobe University's Graduate Diploma in Child and Family Practice Leadership which provided impetus for this book was bringing together emerging and established leaders to work on shared projects as well as on individual assignments (see Preface). This enabled a cross-fertilisation and genuine opportunity to try out new ways of thinking and working as leaders in a semi-protected space.

Leading in communities

Children and families need strong communities if they are to flourish. Strong communities are characterised by high social inclusion and partnerships between

government, business, schools and community organisations that promote economic and social advantages for all members (Frederico & Whiteside, 2015). If a
child requires out-of-home care, the immediate community will be that of the
family or residential setting where they are placed at the time. These communities
need to be safe and nurturing, and a leader in Child and Family Practice will have a
direct influence on these environments. However, the aim for most children is a
return to their own family or a permanent placement in the broader community.
Chapter 7 on leadership in Indigenous communities highlights the role of community for Indigenous children. Without engagement with their native culture and
community, Aboriginal children cannot thrive. This has implications for all children.
For all children and families to thrive, they need access to well-resourced
community support, including quality child care, pre-school education, general
schools, health services and social and cultural recreational opportunities that
promote participation, economic opportunities and social inclusion.

In contemporary and future complex organisations it is, and will continue to be,
increasingly important that leaders in Child and Family Practice assist staff to
engage effectively with the communities in which they operate to work in partnership. If interventions for vulnerable children are to be successful, there needs to
be a holistic approach which works seamlessly with all stakeholders. Moreover, it is
important that services are integrated across all systems.

Leading through education

It is essential that a leader in Child and Family Practice creates opportunities for
continuous learning for staff as well as for self. However, often the experience of
many managers has been that practitioners in the field do not find that additional
professional education enhances their work with children, hence the value of the
concept of 'live knowledge' (Cameron and Frederico, Chapter 3). Live knowledge
engages the learner in exploration of theory and evidence-based practice whilst
drawing upon practitioners' own experiences and knowledge to facilitate further
development of theory and the building of new skills. The complex nature of
Child and Family Practice and the continuous changing of the environment within
which practitioners work require an active learning environment. Many years ago,
a social work educator, Mary Louise Sommers (1971), stated that:

> Learning is essentially personal and individual, even though it is often socially
> invited, derived, induced and supported. Since it involves modification of
> thinking, feeling and doing, learning can be accomplished only by the learner,
> and not by transmission by the teacher of what he (she) has learned. (p. 51)

Too often education in Child and Family Practice has focused on transmitting to
the learner the knowledge and skills it is considered he or she should possess. The
model developed in the Graduate Certificate and Graduate Diploma in Child and
Family Practice Leadership has been more successful, as was evident in the program

evaluation (Frederico et al., 2016). As elaborated upon in Chapter 3, the model highlights that practitioner contributions to the development of theory are equally as important as those of academics. The role ascribed to participants in the model is supported by Sommers (1971), whose view is that "problem solving learning must lead to problem finding or the envisioning of further problems to be discovered, formulated and solved if the learner is to sustain their learning process throughout their life" (p. 51). In other words, knowledge cannot be treated as static. Knowledge is a process, and in the field of Child and Family Practice it is practitioners as well as researchers who continuously develop knowledge.

The Graduate Certificate and Graduate Diploma in Child and Family Practice Leadership are examples of a curriculum which utilised the live knowledge model. Evaluation of the program by all stakeholders highlighted the success of the curriculum and learning/teaching model in improving participants' quality of practice and facilitating their use of evidence-based and critical-reflection approaches to their work. Whilst it is not expected that the individual leader will conduct programs such as those described, the leader needs to ensure that there are learning opportunities through formal courses and that these recognise the active role of the participant. One way the leader can do this is to work within the organisation's governance to build a leadership strategy which encompasses all levels of leadership and promotes leadership skills in all staff; and the strategy should include an education pathway. Similarly, leaders can incorporate a number of the lessons from this educational approach into professional development opportunities within the organisation.

Building and leading trauma-informed organisations

Trauma, resilience and attachment are key concepts that drive and support interventions in Child and Family Practice. The trauma experienced by vulnerable children impacts their social and emotional development, but it can also impact the systems around the child. Moreover, consequences of trauma can be manifested in challenging behaviour which requires interventions that are trauma-informed and recognise the depth of the impact of trauma on the child. Practitioners and carers can experience direct and vicarious trauma as they work with children and families who have been traumatised. Organisations need to operate in a manner which is trauma-informed. Perry and Jackson highlight this in Chapter 10 whilst also recognising that being trauma-informed is not enough on its own. Indeed, leading a trauma-informed organisation is as much about understanding the limitations of trauma theory as it is about understanding its importance.

The creation of a trauma-informed organisation can strengthen safety for children, their families, carers and workers. The leader needs to recognise that there must be fluidity in the trauma-informed structures developed so that they can be responsive to the changing demographics of children and families, and practitioners. At the heart of a trauma-informed organisation is a caring organisation. If practitioners feel supported they will be better able to support their families, carers and the children with whom they work. A trauma-informed organisation ensures that it engages in evidence-based and evidence-informed practices at the same time as promoting critical reflection. The leader also needs to model collaborative relationships within the organisation and with other service providers and the community.

Leading through supervision

A trauma-informed and child-safe organisation has structures which promote and support effective supervision. In the future, leaders will best lead through a network of leaders and leadership teams placed strategically throughout the organisation (Bower, 1997). Leadership occurs at all levels of the organisation. It is the organisation's leadership team who develop a leadership strategy and identify the points within the organisation where a network of leaders will be best placed to guide these strategic areas. From this network, supervisors will be identified and implement leadership through supervision of practitioners.

Just as the concept of live knowledge in education builds on the expectation that the practitioner is a partner in the development of knowledge and skills, effective supervision also requires the supervisee to be an active participant in solution finding.

In addition to supervising direct practice with children and their families, the role of supervision also requires assisting the supervisee to manoeuvre around the managerialist agenda which is not always supportive of complex practice. As McPherson points out in Chapter 5, it is supervisors who have the responsibility for navigating the inevitable tensions that confront practitioners and are expected to support them to maintain an ultimate focus on vulnerable children. Organisational structures need to be in place for supervisors and supervisees to work effectively together. Inadequate time for supervision, a negative or blaming culture, lack of resources to support the work and poor recruitment of workers all impact on the capacity of workers to deliver high-quality, effective practice. All these elements can be influenced by the leader.

Leading through evidence-based and evidence-informed reflective practice

Chapters 1–3 in this book discuss the need for both evidence-based and evidence-informed practice. In addition, they highlighted the role of critical reflection in Child and Family Practice. In Chapter 1 Miller and Frederico highlighted that practitioners perceive a disconnect or gap between research and practice. However, the application of substantive knowledge is essential in child protection, family violence, family services, out-of-home care, trauma, Indigenous trauma and cultural work. Leadership needs to promote ways to bridge this perceived gap between evidence and practice. As discussed, this can be done through education as in La Trobe University's Graduate Certificate and Graduate Diploma Leadership model. It can also be addressed in supervision. Moreover, the perceived disconnect can be addressed directly by organisational leadership through the establishment of structures and policies that support inclusion of evidence-based knowledge, balanced with the support and time for reflective practice and ongoing learning. For this to occur there needs to be attention to workload management to ensure that workers have adequate time for learning and reflection. This also should include ongoing attempts to simplify and make systems and processes more efficient. Scrutiny regarding possible duplication and unnecessary requirements needs to occur regularly as expectations grow and change over time. There also needs to be attention to recruitment to ensure that staff have adequate initial training and a commitment to continual learning for the purpose of improving outcomes for vulnerable children and families.

Conclusion

This chapter has identified seven elements which are part of effective leadership in Child and Family Practice, each of which has been discussed in the foregoing chapters. It has also aimed to synthesise the lessons from these chapters in thinking about leadership in the future. As noted in the Preface, these areas were identified from the experience of La Trobe University's Graduate Certificate and Graduate Diploma in Child and Family Practice Leadership. The aim of each chapter and the book as a whole has been to advance an understanding of the elements of leadership in each of the areas and to contribute to further discussion.

Key messages from this chapter

- Effective leadership is essential in Child and Family Practice to facilitate good outcomes for children and families.
- There are many components that influence the implementation of leadership, and these are developed in the chapters in this book.
- Leadership education in Child and Family Practice needs to include practitioners, leaders and researchers in the building of a curriculum.

Questions for further consideration

1. As a leader, how do you influence effectiveness in Child and Family Practice?
2. What is your plan for further education in leadership for Child and Family Practice?

References

Bower, M. (1997). *Will to lead: Running a business with a network of leadership*. Boston, MA: Harvard Business Review Press.

Dominey-Howes, D. (2015, 25 March). Explainer: Are natural disasters on the rise? *The Conversation*. Retrieved from http://theconversation.com/explainer-are-natural-disasters-on-the-rise-39232

Frederico, M., & Whiteside, M. (2015). Building school, family, and community partnerships: Developing a theoretical framework. *Australian Social Work*, 69(1), 1–16. doi:10.1080/0312407X.2015.1042488

Frederico, M., Long, M., McPherson, L., McNamara, P., & Cameron, N. (2016). A consortium approach for child and family practice education. *Social Work Education*, 35(7), 780–793. doi:10.1080/02615479.2016.1206520

Munro, E. (2011). *The Munro review of child protection: Final report. A child-centred system.* London: Department for Education.

Office for Standards in Education, Children's Services and Skills (Ofsted). (2012). *High expectations, high support and high challenge; Protecting children more effectively through better support for front-line social work practice.* Manchester: Ofsted.

Pickett, K. & Wilkinson, R. (2010). *The spirit level: Why equality is better for everyone.* London: Penguin.

Royal Commission into Institutional Responses to Child Sexual Abuse (2017). *Final Report.* Canberra: Commonwealth of Australia.

Sommers, M. (1971). Dimensions and dynamics of engaging the learner. *Journal of Education for Social Work*, 7(3), 51–53.

Taleb, N. (2007). *The black swan: The impact of the highly improbable.* New York: Random House.

INDEX

Note: page citations in **bold** indicate text contained within tables, and page citations in *italics* indicate text contained within figures.